The
EVERYTHING®
Tween Book

Dear Reader:

Every stage of childhood is special in its own way, but tweens are my hands-down favorite. While working with youngsters in my psychology practice, teaching in the United States and abroad, and foster-mothering, tweens shared their personal joys, secret sorrows, and favorite knock-knock jokes. I learned about their fears of the dark and family breakups, their victories over spelling tests and bullies, and their delight over Valentines, video games, and summer vacations. Mostly, they taught me that while it is often fun being a tween, it is not always easy.

It's not always easy parenting a tween, either. It can be hard to remember that beneath the know-it-all attitude, despite the grown-up clothes, and under the pink-and-blue hair your child simply wishes to be successful in school, liked on the playground, and affirmed by you.

Although it is very hard to limit your child's exposure to the images and ideas streaming into your living room from the larger society, it is important to contain destructive electronic influences with the same zeal that you approach destructive human ones. Given the stress and pressure of modern life, it can be especially hard to refrain from nagging and criticizing to keep your tween on track, but it is imperative to avoid negative methods of disciplining. The memories your child gleans from these special years will last a lifetime. Do what you can to make them good ones!

Dr. Ly Thomas

Welcome to the EVERYTHING® Series!

These handy, accessible books give you all you need to tackle a difficult project, gain a new hobby, comprehend a fascinating topic, prepare for an exam, or even brush up on something you learned back in school but have since forgotten.

You can choose to read an *Everything*® book from cover to cover or just pick out the information you want from our four useful boxes: e-questions, e-facts, e-alerts, and e-ssentials.

We give you everything you need to know on the subject, but throw in a lot of fun stuff along the way, too.

We now have more than 400 *Everything*® books in print, spanning such wide-ranging categories as weddings, pregnancy, cooking, music instruction, foreign language, crafts, pets, New Age, and so much more. When you're done reading them all, you can finally say you know *Everything*®!

QUESTIONS?
Answers to
common questions

FACTS
Important snippets
of information

ALERTS!
Urgent
warnings

ESSENTIALS
Quick
handy tips

PUBLISHER Karen Cooper

DIRECTOR OF ACQUISITIONS AND INNOVATION Paula Munier

MANAGING EDITOR, EVERYTHING SERIES Lisa Laing

COPY CHIEF Casey Ebert

ACQUISITIONS EDITOR Lisa Laing

DEVELOPMENT EDITOR Elizabeth Kassab

EDITORIAL ASSISTANT Hillary Thompson

THE
EVERYTHING®
TWEEN
BOOK

A parent's guide to surviving the turbulent preteen years

Linda Sonna, Ph.D.

Adams Media Corporation
Avon, Massachusetts

An Everything® Series Book.
Everything® and everything.com® are registered trademarks of F+W Media, Inc.

Published by Adams Media, a division of F+W Media, Inc.
57 Littlefield Street, Avon, MA 02322 U.S.A.
www.adamsmedia.com
ISBN 10: 1-58062-870-2
ISBN 13: 978-1-58062-870-9
Printed in the United States of America.

J I H

Library of Congress Cataloging-in-Publication Data
Sonna, Linda.
The everything tween book / Linda Sonna.
p.   cm.   – (An everything series book)
ISBN 1-58062-870-2
1. Preteens. 2. Child rearing. 3. Parenting. 4. Parent and child.
I. Title. II. Series: Everything series.
HQ777.15 .S66   2003
649'.124–dc21   2002015050

This publication is designed to provide accurate and authoritative information with regard to
the subject matter covered. It is sold with the understanding that the publisher is not engaged
in rendering legal, accounting, or other professional advice. If legal advice or other expert
assistance is required, the services of a competent professional person should be sought.
—From a *Declaration of Principles* jointly adopted by a Committee of the
American Bar Association and a Committee of Publishers and Associations

Many of the designations used by manufacturers and sellers to distinguish their products are
claimed as trademarks. Where those designations appear in this book and Adams Media was
aware of a trademark claim, the designations have been printed with initial capital letters.

The information contained in this book is designed for educational purposes only and is not
intended to provide medical advice or other professional services. The information should
not be used for diagnosis, treatment, or as a substitute for professional care. If your child
has a medical or behavioral problem or you suspect such a possibility, consult your health
care provider. All case studies are composites designed to reflect common behaviors and
situations. Information has been changed to protect parents' and children's identities.

This book is available at quantity discounts for bulk purchases.
For information, call 1-800-289-0963.

Contents

Sports and Recreation / 139

Scores of Chores / 149

Fun and Games / 163

Food for Life / 177

Sleep Easy / 191

Tween Health and Safety / 203

Acknowledgments

Debi Gutierrez, Lois Mark, Michele Potter, Nathan LaZar, Joan Kirk, Michael Dudelczyk, Tobin Herold, David Valerio, Helen Dixon, Sean Richardson, Connor Chinn, Zachary Ashton, Mary Gugino, Christina Archuleta, Mauna Richardson, Monica Melk, Emma Meaker, Nicole LaValley, Michael Kittredge, Christopher Gonzales, Margie Henzel, and Andrea, Xavier, Ana-Alycia, and Jessica Quintana.

Top Ten Tips to Help You
Understand Your Tween

1. Tweens truly appreciate all-or-nothing logic; they see the world in black and white and have great difficulty discerning shades of gray.

2. Tweens don't always like to talk and may express themselves more readily via actions.

3. Peer pressure is real. To help your tween, keep reminding her that when her peers mature, they'll be more tolerant of differences, but don't dismiss her efforts to fit in.

4. It's normal for tween boys to be rowdy and aggressive; you need to provide them with physical activities that can serve as an outlet for their energy.

5. Even though your tween may post a "Keep Out" sign on her door, she still needs your love and guidance; the sign is her way of trying to establish boundaries between herself and the outside world.

6. Tweens do need rules and discipline, but make sure you are fair and consistent. Allowing your tween to break the rules will send him a message that rules are meant to be broken.

7. To remain close with your tween, you need to spend time together. Take her with you to the grocery store, ask her to help you make dinner, or watch a movie together and then talk about it.

8. If your tween is suddenly not doing well in school, don't assume he's slow. He may be having problems with his teacher or classmates, or he may simply be uninterested, and he needs your help in resolving these issues.

9. If your tween never cleans up her room, no matter how many times you remind her, it may be that she doesn't know where to start or how to go about it. To teach her, break down the process into small steps and check her progress along the way.

10. The best guide to how much your child needs to eat is his appetite, but boredom, anxiety, stress, and depression can trigger or suppress it. Help him sort out the differences and learn how to avoid unhealthy eating habits.

Introduction

▶PSYCHOLOGISTS AND CHILD DEVELOPMENT EXPERTS have traditionally viewed the tween stage (from age eight to thirteen) as hardly worthy of consideration. In fact, they haven't even bothered to name it. Since this "in-between" time occurs after the early childhood developmental whirlwind and before the maelstrom of adolescence, it is perhaps understandable that this period is so easy for professionals to overlook. Despite the dramatic physical changes that transform tweens into biological adults in a few short years, experts have maintained that development in other areas slows to a snail's pace. Parents know that nothing could be further from the truth, and professionals are beginning to agree.

Tweens' intellectual and academic development is central in determining whether they will eventually drop out of high school at age sixteen or graduate from an Ivy League college. The kind of social savvy youngsters develop during this stage will affect how well they function in one-on-one relationships and in groups for many years to come. Moreover, the values they acquire during these five short years will go a long way toward defining the kinds of struggles they will endure during adolescence, and how they resolve them. Change is always possible, but the fundamental character children develop during this critical period is likely to last a lifetime.

Now especially, it is imperative for adults to consider how to usher this historically neglected group through the difficult period of being a tween. Although some modern tweens enjoy the protected, carefree childhoods that generations past remember with such fondness, most youngsters now face the same thorny issues once reserved for older adolescents. The schoolyard bully who once attacked victims with flailing fists may now be toting a gun. Family battles over makeup and clothing that used to begin as the tween years drew to a close now may become a source of family friction shortly after age eight. Worries about stranger danger cause many parents to confine their tweens to the safety of the house, depriving them of the exercise and unstructured social contact they need for optimal health and happiness.

Not only do modern tweens have to face more difficult issues and cope with more complex situations than youngsters from generations past, they receive a lot less help and guidance. Increasing numbers of households lack a stay-at-home parent and a network of extended family members living nearby; teachers are overburdened, and most neighbors are strangers. As a result, tweens receive far less adult supervision, nurturing, and support than in days gone by.

While working parents make great sacrifices to locate quality care for their toddlers, and while they exercise care in structuring teenagers' spare hours to minimize the time they spend unsupervised, millions of latchkey tweens return to an empty house three or more days per week. Too many wander aimlessly through the empty rooms until someone comes home, tells them what to do, and walks them through the initial steps to help them get started.

Parents are increasingly aware of the pressures tweens face and are trying harder to understand their personal struggles, but advice about how to help them through the challenges they encounter can be hard to come by. Most parenting books focus on ways to strengthen youngsters for the difficult teenage years ahead, but the best way to prepare children for adolescence is to help them to flourish as tweens. If youngsters enter the teenage years with a solid set of values, good social skills, a love of learning, healthy self-esteem, and warm family relationships, they are in a better position to get through their teenage years without falling victim to the serious problems that undermine the happiness and well-being of so many young people.

This book guides parents through the interior landscape of the tween mind. It reveals what tweens are doing and learning in the classrooms, playgrounds, and soccer fields where they spend their days, and provides the tools for guiding these special little people through a highly complex stage of life. (E)

Chapter 1

Meet the Tweens

Tweens are a mass of contradictions. Even as their bodies are maturing in preparation to create other human beings, they can have temper tantrums worthy of a two-year-old, sleep with stuffed animals, and need Mom to remind them to wash their ears when they take a bath. It's a hard age to comprehend—but it's also a wonderful one.

Inside the Mind of a Tween

Tweens see the world in black and white and have great difficulty discerning shades of gray. Accordingly, they consider people nice or mean, situations fair or not, and can easily categorize almost everything else in the world under the headings of "good" and "bad." They are not rigid, however, because they change their minds at the drop of a hat and have no problem deciding that someone they previously regarded as nice is really mean, or that something that they thought was terribly unfair is really just, after all.

Accordingly, their opinions can change dramatically from moment to moment and day to day. Parents are often mystified by what they see as their child's wild mood changes, but often the changes have little to do with emotion and everything to do with calm, rational tween logic. When the "bad" kid who has been a long-term enemy does something nice, he can instantly become a "great" person, while the long-term best friend can just as suddenly be consigned to the category of a complete "loser."

Your child may no longer scream, "I hate you!" during a fit of temper as she did during the toddler years, but as the parent of a tween, you are likely to notice that you can be transformed from the greatest mom or dad in the world to the meanest ogre on the planet in the blink of an eye.

All-or-Nothing Logic

Only with great difficulty do tweens grasp that an idea can be partially true and partially false at the same time. Holding the tension of opposites is a painful endeavor, and if a contradiction is pointed out to them, they literally wiggle with discomfort before shrugging the problem off. For instance, ask your tween how a teacher can be a total creep given that he did something very nice, and you're likely to get a vague "He's okay, I guess" answer. Tweens can verbally acknowledge the existence of "sort of," "somewhat," and "sometimes," but what they really mean is, "I don't know, but I'll agree with anything so we can get onto a subject I can make sense of." The notion that people can be nice in some ways and mean in others, or that fairness and goodness depend on the situation, seems constantly to slip from their mental grasp.

The Black Cat Phenomenon

Tweens have a strong superstitious streak. They may conceal it from adults and peers if they sense disapproval, but it colors their thinking. Young tweens may laugh to think that little kids actually believe all that foolishness about the tooth fairy and the Easter bunny, while remaining convinced that St. Nicholas and Rudolph, in fact, have a workshop at the North Pole. A nine-year-old's proof positive was, "He brought me a pogo stick for Christmas. My mom never could have afforded that."

At age eight, tweens may be afraid to go home after stepping on a crack for fear they will indeed find that their mother has been carted off to the hospital. At age twelve, girls recite incantations to conjure Mad Mary at slumber parties and are terrified for weeks afterward because they glimpsed the bloody murderess herself in a friend's bedroom mirror. Meanwhile, boys spout facts about aliens and life on other planets. Both boys and girls worry about walking under a ladder, allowing a black cat to cross their path, and having to endure seven years of bad luck after breaking a mirror.

ALERT!

Part of the magic of childhood is the belief in magic itself. If you feel compelled to get your tween to stick to hard facts and cold logic, buy her a magic kit. That way, she can at least trade the fun of believing in magic for being a magic maker.

Thoughts Set in Stone

By teen and adult standards, even the brightest tweens are extremely concrete in their thinking. They have a marked tendency to be very literal, which may partly explain why puns so delight them. The idea that the same word can have two meanings that have nothing to do with each other fascinates them, so the joke, "What's black and white and red all over? A newspaper!" strikes them as hilarious.

The fact that tweens are so literal and concrete creates endless conflicts with parents who have a hard time comprehending that a child who is sprouting hair on his legs can't readily generalize and think abstractly. When you find the floor of your child's closet strewn with moldy banana peels and pluck stinky socks from under his bed two seconds after he swore he cleaned his room, don't assume he was trying to put something over you. Out of sight is out of mind for this age group. Plus, the big unanswered question that lurks in every tween's mind is, "What's a few old banana peels and stinky socks under the bed got to do with clean?"

Do your duty and explain it because your tween needs to know about cleanliness and hygiene. But don't be upset the next time you find apple cores in his desk drawer and underwear stuffed under the bed. During your last discussion you said *bananas* and *socks*, not *apple cores* and *underwear*. You should have said *fruit* and *clothing* if that's what you meant! Because you feel frustrated and angry, don't assume your tween was trying to make you feel that way! He is still young, doesn't think like you do, and has lots to learn.

The Silent Years

Tweens tend not to reveal much about themselves in conversation, and their standard replies to questions are often shrugs, vague nods, and uncertain shakes of the head, interspersed with withering glances and sassy retorts or the ever-mystifying "Whatever." The latter basically means they don't like the direction the discussion has taken and want it to end ASAP.

Women are particularly likely to use words to pull people closer, and the lack of meaningful conversation can make a mother feel that her child doesn't like her. If tweens could be moved to give an opinion on the subject, the vast majority would say, "Not!" In fact, while they may occasionally confide in a friend that they dislike being subjected to certain rules, most tweens are extremely protective of their parents. Like Americans who complain about the U.S. government but become defensive if a foreigner points out a single minor flaw, tweens feel defensive if anyone dares to imply anything negative about their family.

Although little chatterboxes typically grow silent during the tween years, tweens do express themselves as much as they did during early childhood and will undoubtedly do so as teenagers. The difference is that tweens more readily express themselves via actions rather than words.

Interacting with Tweens

The lack of words may make you feel as though you are losing touch with your child, but the truth is more likely to be that your child has lost touch with herself. Most tweens are too busy looking outward and experiencing the moment to ponder what is happening inside of them and assess their reactions. They are too busy living life to think too much about it. Hence, when you ask your tween how she feels about something, don't assume she's holding out on you when she gives you the standard "I dunno" response. She probably doesn't know. Moreover, she probably doesn't care to know. Most tweens work very hard to avoid feelings.

FACT

It's good to keep asking tweens how they feel about things and suggest some possibilities, such as "maybe that hurt your feelings" or "I bet that made you mad," but don't expect a quick response, and don't feel rejected if none is forthcoming. It's hard for tweens, especially boys, to identify and express their emotions.

When adults confront tweens with their misdeeds or omissions and seek to convince them of the error of their ways, conversations usually follow a predictable course. While upset parents and teachers deliver long-winded lectures, plead, and interrogate young criminals to get them to "fess up, shape up, and fly right," the tween side of the conversation is likely to go like this: "No, I didn't do it. Okay, yeah, I did. Yeah—I mean no—I don't know why I did it. Yeah—I mean, um, no, I didn't mean to. I dunno—I guess I just forgot. I dunno. I dunno. I dunno. Okay, yeah, I promise. Okay: I promise that from now on I will. . . . Could you say it again 'cause I forgot? Well, you could maybe ground me/take away the TV/take away my allowance/spank me? No—I dunno/sure/maybe that would help."

It's no wonder tweens find confrontations with peers far easier to manage. When an outraged peer points out a faux pas and yells, "You idiot!" or whatever put-down is in vogue, the tween who has been accused can simply roll his eyes at the accuser and exclaim, "Whatever!" before walking on. Yet the peer has driven home the very same message the parent spent an hour trying to get across: The tween has committed some sort of no-no, and somebody is mad about it.

Exactly what the crime of the moment consists of doesn't much matter; tweens cannot in good conscience promise to mend their ways, because they may well commit the very same crime in the future. They may feel horrendously guilty, but guilt may not stop them from making the same mistake again. When adults force promises that the same problem will never again occur, tweens will, of course, agree. And when they break that promise, it doesn't mean they told a lie! At the moment they gave their word, they meant it. They are sorry for messing up again, and they will be sorry the next time, too.

Of course you should talk to your tween, discuss problems, and you certainly should *not* resort to childish behavior by name-calling or using derogatory labels. Being called an idiot by an adult has terrible implications, since adults are thought to know the truth about who the idiots of the world really are. Be aware that raising your voice and demanding answers aren't effective ways to get your tween to open up and explain herself. In fact, many of your questions may remain unanswered for years. The challenge is to keep the lines of communication open so that your tween will talk when he needs to.

Looking for Authority

Tweens separate truth from fiction by analyzing the source of information, and in the process they may end up crediting particular people, books, or movies with truth, knowledge, and wisdom that are as vast as they are undeserved. They have a propensity to accept everything they hear and read as God's own truth. Early in the tween years, most youngsters assume their parents to be the experts on every subject. Next, they believe their teachers to possess all wisdom and knowledge. Later, admired peers become the fountains of perfect truth.

ALERT!

Don't denigrate the outlandish "facts" your tween reports or disparage his ideas or sources of information. That will erode his trust in his teachers and eventually his trust in you. Share your own views and sources without criticizing your child's ideas or where they came from.

For instance, a third grader can easily decide that his arithmetic teacher knows all about long division and that his parent isn't doing the problems correctly, despite the fact that the parent holds a Ph.D. in math and teaches it at a university. A fourth grader can believe that her soccer coach knows the one correct way to fry hamburgers and that an admired peer has all the facts about God and dinosaurs. The book or movie that reports sightings of alien spaceships in New Mexico, of course, gives the straight scoop about life on Mars. By junior high, if a friend does something a certain way, that is the one right way to do it.

The parent who questions such esteemed sources of information is likely to be met with disbelief or hostility. However, after giving the matter some thought, a tween may decide her parent is the expert on this or that particular subject after all and the other person knows nothing. In truth, mothers remain heroines for girls and fathers retain their heroic status for boys throughout the tween years.

The Emotional Years

Tweens' sudden bouts of intense emotion can make them seem unpredictable, and many parents insist that their tween is moodier than a teenager. Despite the widespread belief that hormones drive the drama, a relationship between testosterone and behavior has not been established for this age group.

When typically placid youngsters become emotional and chronically edgy ones explode, they are as likely to be reacting to an offense or injustice from long ago that flitted across their minds and has made them cranky as to something that is happening now. Parents may think that an issue must be of earth-shattering importance to have triggered such a dramatic reaction, and many lose sleep worrying about how to help. Yet if they broach the subject an hour, a day, or a week later, they are likely to learn that their tween now considers it inconsequential and is actually put out that a parent wants to revisit territory that no longer concerns her.

The Testosterone Myth

Although toddler boys are more aggressive than toddler girls, the testosterone levels of the two groups are indistinguishable. At age eight, boys' testosterone levels are approximately five times that of boys entering puberty. Studies comparing extremely aggressive institutionalized boys with normal ones have failed to detect significant differences in their testosterone levels.

Actually, an increase in a boy's testosterone level is the *result* of certain intense emotions, not the cause. Boys' testosterone levels increase after they have a "successful dominance experience," which can include winning a game or having the team they were rooting for emerge victorious. It can also include conquering something difficult, such as doing well on a task or bullying other children. Being dominated by someone else causes testosterone to decrease.

ESSENTIAL

Rather than assuming your tween's anger will diminish and he will return to an even keel when he gets through puberty, you need to help him learn to manage his negative emotions productively. Your child must be taught how to control his temper and manage his anger to succeed at school, a job, and life.

The combination of immaturity and social pressures are probably more important than hormones in explaining why older tweens are so emotional. The age at which the roller coaster begins seems to parallel the age at which young people become seriously interested in members of the opposite sex—which, surprisingly, is driven by convention, not pubescence. The age for escalating mood swings and interest in dating has dropped farther over the last century than the average age for entering puberty. In cultures where love liaisons don't begin until late adolescence, tweens are far more staid than their American counterparts.

Overdramatizing?

Some parents become jaded about their youngster's tendency to overdramatize, while others worry about the wellspring of unhappiness that gives rise to such emotional intensity and so many outbursts. Bouts of crying and abject despair do not necessarily signal that a tween is struggling under a lingering cloud of misery. Often by the time tweens can talk about a problem, they have processed it to the point that it is no longer an issue for them. You may not hear about the difficulties your tween is dealing with until they are basically resolved.

Chapter 2
Girl Tweens

Girls have a reputation for becoming emotional basket cases halfway through the tween years, traveling from giggles to rage to despair and back at warp speed. Don't write off your daughter's careening emotions to hormones. The social pressures with which girls must cope are enough to make the sanest among them act a bit crazy.

Growing Up and Falling Apart

Katlin had been an outspoken, self-confident, somewhat feisty child with a ready smile and some special athletic abilities. Up until seventh grade she had been an outstanding student, active in the church choir and youth group in addition to playing soccer and swimming. Two months into seventh grade, Katlin dropped out of her church activities. A few months later she wanted to drop out of the swim team, too. Since her grades had declined, her mother agreed. Katlin's grades didn't improve, however, and she started getting in trouble for being late to school and talking to her friends in class.

At home Katlin began sniping at her mother, declaring her "uncool." From Katlin's many derogatory comments about herself, it was apparent that she didn't consider herself to be cool, either. Her parents, who had divorced when she was eight, agreed to put their personal differences on hold and meet to discuss how to help their daughter.

Her father had read that a good father-daughter relationship was critical for girls' self-esteem, and believed that Katlin should resume weekend visits at his house. He understood that she disliked her stepmother and didn't want to be separated from her friends, but he felt that spending more time with him would be helpful to her at this critical stage. Her parents agreed that Katlin needed to be involved in an activity she really cared about, but she had lost interest in her old ones and her mother feared that Katlin would rebel if forced.

Finding a Niche

What Katlin needed, they decided, was to try something new. Having an activity to look forward to might make her less resistant to spending time at her father's house. Since Katlin had always been passionately interested in horses and said she wanted to be a veterinarian when she grew up, her father offered to arrange for her to take a riding lesson during her every-other-weekend visits. To encourage Katlin to broaden her horizons beyond the middle-school social scene, her parents decided to see if she could do some volunteer work at the Humane Society or for a local vet.

It was hard to tell exactly what made such a difference, but a few months later pictures of horses lined Katlin's bedroom walls and she was intent on bringing up her grades in math and science so she could go to college to study veterinary medicine. She invited some of her friends to her dad's house to spend the weekend so that they could take riding lessons, too. Her mother laughed to see Katlin acting like a haughty super sophisticate one minute and cantering through the yard playing "horses" with her girlfriends the next. The only thing that worried her parents was that Katlin was saving up to buy a horse. They didn't aspire to keeping that kind of pet in their backyard.

From Girls to Women

Between the ages of eight and thirteen, girls undergo a mysterious transformation that has long been the source of concern to parents, educators, and psychologists. Even very saucy, self-confident, outspoken second-grade gals are apt to shrivel into shy, insecure shadows of their former selves before they become teenagers.

ESSENTIAL

No one has as yet found the keys to reviving Ophelia, but perhaps by understanding the forces that conspire to undermine tween girls' feisty, self-confident selves, you can find ways to help your daughter continue to appreciate those aspects of herself that don't fit the supermodel and rock star ideal.

Preadolescent girls have a disturbingly predictable pattern of scaling back their far-flung aspirations. They soon convince themselves and everyone else they are not as bright or capable as everyone previously assumed. The downward spiral in grades, especially in math and science, does not seem to be for want of trying or intelligence. No one has found a way to reverse girls' flagging grades, self-esteem, and goals, but extra doses of encouragement might help support them.

Forming Friendships

Girls' fascination with relationships infuses almost all of their activities. Their favorite books are stories about people, and young tweens are often more concerned with how everybody is getting along than with what they are doing. This is in marked contrast to boys, who can argue endlessly and call it fun. Older tween girls work hard to understand their friends' feelings, actions, and motivations. Still, turning the mirrors on themselves to ponder the whys and wherefores of their own behavior requires complex mental gymnastics they aren't very adept at performing.

Young Tween Friendships

Young tweens like to have someone special to serve in the role of best friend, although the person who fills that lofty role may change from day to day. The glue that holds young tween girlfriends together is equal parts shared interests and compatible personalities.

Although your young tween can probably identify which girls in her class are the popular ones, and while she might like to have the top-dog status of an "alpha girl," she is probably content to belong to the crowd of "gamma girls." These girls have a number of friends, or perhaps just one or two like-minded friends with whom they are particularly close, and some interests or activities they are quite passionate about. At ages eight and nine, those could be anything from collecting stuffed animals to dancing lessons.

ALERT!

No youngster is impervious to the attitudes of other children. Continued emotional battering from a sibling or being regularly scapegoated at school can undermine self-esteem. But in general, peer approval for girls age eight to ten is the icing on the cake, not the bread that sustains them.

Although young tweens get their feelings hurt if they are left out at recess or teased on the playground, their main concern is about pleasing their parents and teachers. If a child worries a lot about not making the grade academically or dislikes her looks, personality, or social status, she is likely to be reacting to the disapproval from the adults who matter most to her. Whether parents' disapproval is overt or covert, real or imagined, their opinions will loom large in how a girl views herself.

Young girls differ in their attitudes toward boys. Little "tomboys" have more athletic interests and prefer boys as companions and playmates. Although such girls may be teased for their boyish ways, they tend to remain more assertive during the older tween years and are less likely to suffer the crisis of confidence that besets girls whose interests are more stereotypically feminine.

However, many young tweens make it clear that they dislike all boys. They don't take kindly to having their hair pulled or being chased and want nothing whatsoever to do with them. Tween girls may need help to understand that these small torments are how young boys flirt. They benefit from being taught how to protect themselves from unwanted advances by being encouraged to say, "No, don't do that! I don't like it!" "If you want to be my friend, you've got to stop doing that." "If you want to play, you must ask me nicely." Many young tweens have a secret crush on one or more boys, and many have someone they refer to as their boyfriend. Being part of a tween "couple" means they greet each other in the halls and talk during recess. Some more sophisticated couples may hold hands or even see a movie together.

Older Tween Friendships

Girls become extremely self-conscious during the latter tween years, and most women are emphatic that this constituted the most difficult and unhappy period of their lives. Girls feel as if they are always on stage and the curtain is always up; they find it impossible to believe that others aren't scrutinizing them as intensely as they scrutinize themselves. They become sensitive to interpersonal criticism to the point that a raised eyebrow from a friend or an unkind word from a peer carrying the coveted title of "popular" can engender tremendous misery. Not being invited to a party or being ignored in the hall can precipitate an agony of self-doubt or even despair.

Many parents, and even some professionals, attribute preadolescent girls' intense mood swings and emotional fragility to hormones. Since the untoward emotional reactions typically intensify at about age twelve, which is also the average age for entering puberty, it seems reasonable to assume that hormonal changes are indeed responsible. However, at other times in U.S. history, the increased emotionality, self-consciousness, moodiness, and boy craziness didn't start until long after puberty. Further, not all girls go through a period of instability. In cultures where they do, the timing coincides with the onset of the dating game.

The intense social pressures girls experience are probably largely responsible for their crisis of confidence. Having other interests and receiving consistent infusions of emotional support from their families can help them remember that there is more to life than being part of the in-crowd and being liked by boys. However, girls tend to withdraw from activities and easily alienate their parents with their moodiness and irritability, which can make it hard for them to find positive outlets and receive the positive affirmations they need at the time they most need them.

FACT

Concerns with clothes, makeup, and looking sexy are at an all-time high as tweens strive to imitate the teen models and rock stars they so admire. This is no easy task during the time of braces, glasses, awkward conversation, and gangly bodies that tower over the boys.

During the second half of the tween years, fitting in and conforming become all-consuming goals for most youngsters. Being liked by the right boy can assume life-and-death proportions. Even girls who are not yet particularly interested in boys or clothes or makeup may act as though they are. They may feign interest in having a boyfriend while secretly worrying about their failure to develop at the same rate as their friends. If they aren't as physically developed as their peers, girls are likely to feel as if they are being left behind.

Meanwhile, girls who develop early endure so much teasing and harassment from boys that they suffer, too. It is important to let your daughter know that tween boys become so nervous around a girl who is turning into a woman that they just "lose it." They focus all of their fears and worries about growing up and becoming men on the girl who is the first to start to look like a woman. Although she probably dislikes her tormentors so much she wouldn't want to step out of her way to help them, she might consider that by starting to teach them how to treat a woman properly, she'd be doing them and the other girls a service. Assertive comments like "You may think that's funny, but women take offense at those kinds of comments. The sooner you learn that, the better off you're going to be" can help drive the message home.

The most important thing is to emphasize that the maltreatment doesn't signify that something is wrong with her. Reassure her that as the boys mature, they'll be less threatened by female sexuality. Then they'll be able to relate to her as a person and appreciate her beautiful body instead of feeling overwhelmed.

Separating girls and boys for some of their academic subjects results in better class participation and improved grades for both groups. A return to sex-based segregation is politically abhorrent to many adults, but some educators insist that the educational benefits to girls as well as boys are too valuable to dismiss out of hand.

Dating can have more serious implications in the later tween years. Although "going with" someone for three days still qualifies as a long-term relationship in most junior high schools and many first kisses happen during a game of spin the bottle, some couples advance to serious petting. In urban junior high schools, couples may conduct more intense sexual liaisons. It is no longer such a rarity for a twelve-year-old to get pregnant.

Understanding Peer Pressure

Pressures once reserved for the teenage crowd have also filtered all the way down to some primary-school classrooms. If the trend continues, girls age eight to ten may show the same symptoms of stress and poor self-esteem that older tweens have manifested in recent years. In general, there is still a big difference between the psychology of girls in the eight-to-ten and eleven-to-thirteen groups, but the gap is narrowing.

Younger Tweens: It's Probably Not Peer Pressure

When your eight-to-ten-year-old wants you to let her do or have something, she may well toss in some statements about what other kids get to do and what other parents give their children in hopes of convincing you. This may be a good moment to stop and reflect on your rules and limits, but if you feel pressured to give in so that your child can go along with the crowd, or if you deliver lectures about the evils of conformity, you have probably misunderstood the issue. Tweens don't typically become obsessed with fitting in until they are older.

Seeing what peers are getting or doing may well have implanted the seed of desire that has blossomed into longing, but peer pressure doesn't usually become an issue until later in the tween years. An eight-, nine-, or ten-year-old usually wants to have what her friends have and wants to do what they do because *she* thinks it would be fun, not because she is trying to fit in. If a school dance is being held and you don't believe in dances for young tweens on principle, your daughter's upset probably isn't from fear that missing out will destroy her socially, although if she's already a social outcast she might hope to make some friends by attending. Rather, she probably wants to go because a dance sounds like great fun to *her*. If so, scheduling another activity she considers great fun might overcome her disappointment.

The same principle applies to clothing. Young tweens have difficulty comprehending the subtle differences that make things look too babyish or too old for them. They tend to have more general reactions: A particular outfit is either "pretty" or "yucky." Of course, fashion taste is dictated by what children are exposed to, so from that standpoint seeing what other tweens and teens wear does have an influence. If your young tween wants an outfit that you consider unfit for someone her age, her statement that "everybody else" gets to wear such clothes is probably an attempt to figure out why *you* think these particular clothes aren't appropriate.

This is the time to explain that some people think it's fine for anyone to wear anything at any age, but you think it would look silly for a three-year-old to wear stiletto heels, even if the shoes were very pretty, just as it would look silly to see a woman wearing baby clothes! Similarly, although some parents might think this outfit looks fine on anyone because it's so pretty, to you it looks like it is for older girls and will be appropriate for her in a few years.

Conformity among Older Tweens

As the tween years progress, peers' opinions become ever more important. By age twelve, too many girls define their self-worth almost exclusively in terms of what their peers think of them—or in terms of what they *think* their peers think of them. No matter how much emotional support and reassurance you try to give your daughter at home, you may feel impotent to combat a peer group that seems to be catching her more tightly in its grip with each passing day.

Your daughter may now write off her special talents and strengths as unimportant or even try to hide them unless she is sure of peer approval. If she feels certain that her peers would *not* approve, she may try to hide differences that have long been a source of pride. Just to fit in, she may forgo loved activities for pastimes she doesn't like or even believe in. It is common for older tweens to become obsessed with wearing clothes they think would get peer approval.

E ALERT!

Don't write off your daughter's emotional swings to puberty. Whether or not hormones are a factor, failing to take her seriously will erode your relationship and cause her to look for support elsewhere. Even if you are certain that hormones are involved, she needs to learn to ride the emotional waves without damaging her relationships by upsetting and alienating others.

It is easy to lecture tweens about the importance of individuality, but only a very exceptional youngster can remain centered in the face of blatant peer cruelty. Students at middle and junior high schools can be vicious. School cultures vary, but in some of the more emotionally taxing ones, many youngsters have proudly walked onto the stage for a talent show and lived to regret it. While doing an admirable job of twirling a baton, dancing a ballet, playing the piano, singing a song, or reciting a poem, they are assaulted by hoots, catcalls, and spit wads. If such mortification isn't bad enough, the mocking jeers that assail many tweens in the halls at school the next week may convince them that their faux pas was horrendous and will never be forgotten. Close friends may keep their distance for fear that association will sully their own reputations.

At a stage of life when a day seems like a year, a tween may be convinced that she has alienated everyone forever. The fact that she never fathomed such an outcome can make her fearful of committing some other accidental social blunder. Girls don't even have to undergo such a public humiliation to be traumatized. Seeing others being victimized is enough to drive home the message that they simply must fit in.

Don't shame your tween for wanting to fit in. Just keep reminding her that when her peers mature, their values will change and they'll be more tolerant of differences. Offer hope that by continuing to develop her talents and intelligence, others will come to see her for the wonderful woman she is becoming.

Tweens and Their Mothers

Mothers serve as powerful role models for their daughters. Even if girls become hostile and rebel, they are likely to form adult love relationships that are similar to the ones their mothers had and to struggle with similar life dilemmas.

Most girls start the tween years as mamas' girls. Even if a young girl regularly back-talks, drops hints about wanting to be adopted out, and seems much more amenable to taking direction from her father, her mother is likely to be featured in her essay entitled "The Person I Most Admire." As your tween grows older, she will probably begin pulling away from physical contact, which may reflect her growing awkwardness with her rapidly developing body and her desire to have more control over physical contact, as well as to establish herself as a separate person.

ESSENTIAL

You are bound to make some mistakes as you respond to the push/pull of "You don't love me/you never hug me any more" and "Don't touch me/get away." If your daughter reacts negatively to a hug, do what you would want someone outside of the family to do if they physically overwhelmed her: back off and apologize!

American customs dictate that physical displays of affection in public are only acceptable between adults and young children on the one hand, and between love-smitten couples on the other. If your daughter doesn't learn this social rule on her own, her friends will teach her by teasing her mightily if they see her being openly affectionate toward you. She may resist when you try to pull her onto your lap, not take kindly to having you tousle her hair, and be quite indignant if you reach over to wipe a mustard smear from her chin. She may be especially adamant about not wanting kisses or hugs when you drop her off at school for fear her friends might see.

Loving Touches

Nevertheless, if your relationship is healthy, your young tween will still cuddle up for a story, leap onto your lap at unexpected moments, and exchange back rubs. She will undoubtedly be grateful to have you put your arm around her when she is crying and may let you wipe away her tears, too, when she is in need of comfort.

Hugs can comfort and communicate "I love you" better than words, and even though your daughter is withdrawing from physical expressions of affection, no one ever outgrows the need to be touched. Withholding physical affection can cause her to doubt the attractiveness of her changing body. Squelch your urge to tell the seventy-five-pound daughter who has leaped into your lap that she's too big to do that; don't tell her to grow up and act her age.

As with every other point of discipline, telling your child what *not* to do doesn't teach her what she *should* do. Before your legs go numb, compliment her on the fact that she is getting so big, note that she's outgrowing your lap, and tell her that you and she need to find another, more comfortable position. Find a way she can be physically close, perhaps by cuddling up next to you with your arm around her shoulder. If she's squeezed you into an overbearing hug, tell her to be gentle with her old mother, but make sure she knows you are receptive to being physically close to her by adding, "Now that's the kind of hug I like" when she eases up.

Respect Her Wishes

Expect your daughter to become more protective of her personal space as she begins claiming her body as her own. It is important that she understand that she has the right to say "no" to touches from anyone at any time, so honor her wishes not to be touched. You can tell her that boys who truly care about her will respect her and not try to push her into having more physical contact than she is comfortable with. But if *you* become angry, indignant, hurt, disappointed, or feel rejected and pressure her when she says "no" to *you,* you are teaching her to put other people's feelings first and that it is wrong to try to protect herself from unwanted physical advances.

Her Father's Daughter

Lots of girls begin relating to their mothers as rivals. They may escalate conflicts so that Dad will step in and side with them against their mother, or at least offer some sympathetic solace. This can drive mothers up the wall, and many are upset because they believe that their husbands are allowing themselves to be manipulated by a demon child who turns into sweetness and light when he appears.

While fathers need to insist their daughters remain respectful toward their mothers, the chance to confide in and be comforted by a male is important for girls. By consoling their daughters without denigrating their wives, fathers can lessen the intensity of the mother-daughter relationship and help girls obtain the emotional space they need to emerge from their mothers' shadows and separate emotionally.

Nurturing Femininity

Even tweens who withdraw from their mothers' hugs may still be receptive to hugs from Dad. Affection from a father can be especially reassuring at a time when a girl is worrying about her attractiveness to members of the opposite sex. In fact, it is common for older tween girls to relate to fathers and father figures somewhat coquettishly, although girls are not conscious of doing this.

Ideally, fathers will respond to their unintentional flirtations by gently helping their daughters understand what behaviors are acceptable. By letting them know that they are indeed attractive young ladies, fathers can affirm their daughters' femininity and reassure them that they are what they hope to be: delightful women-in-the-making whom men are destined to fall in love with some day.

As a father responds to his daughter's flirtatiousness, he can simultaneously help her understand what is acceptable and what is overly provocative. Many girls more readily accept such limits and nudges toward modesty from their fathers than from their mothers. However, most fathers feel a bit overwhelmed and may not know how to set limits without alienating their daughter. In that case, a mother may need to step in to insist on more modest behavior, simultaneously affirming the fact that the daughter is turning into a young woman.

ALERT!

Fathers and father figures play a unique role in their tween daughters' lives, and they nurture their development in important ways. Girls who have a solid relationship with a father are more assertive, do better in math and science, and are more self-confident during adolescence.

It is important to remember that even tweens who relate to their father or brothers in what appears to be a blatantly sexual manner aren't trying to be seductive or test limits. When they come galloping out of the bedroom in their nighties, run to and from the shower wrapped in a towel, and don a skimpy bikini for a family beach outing, it never occurs to them how adults might react to their blossoming figures. To treat your daughter like a temptress can simultaneously shame her, confuse her, alienate her, and damage her self-esteem. Worse, she may begin to live the part you have assigned her. Remember: Tween girls are simply being what they are—young girls with bodies that are maturing much faster than their concept of themselves. (E)

Chapter 3

Boy Tweens

Ask tween boys about their favorite pastime, and if you expect them to vote for video games, you're in for a surprise. Throwing dirt clogs ranks number one; skipping stones and hurling rocks are close seconds. Understanding those particular choices is key to understanding boys.

An Excess of Energy

Every time James turned around, he found himself in trouble. True, the scrapes he got himself into were mostly minor, but they were constant. He had a hard time making it through a school day without getting his name on the blackboard for getting up from his seat without permission, talking out of turn, and failing to keep his hands to himself. At home, his mother had tried withholding privileges and instituted various reward systems to motivate him to do simple things, like hang up his towels after a shower, pick up his toys, and do some small chores. Everything worked for a while. Nothing worked for long.

Some of James's more outlandish behavior made his mother afraid he might have a more serious problem. He was becoming increasingly disrespectful toward her, arguing about everything and even yelling at her if she tried to ground him or send him to his room. He was fascinated with fire, and a blaze he had set in a nearby field had gotten out of hand to the point that the fire department had to put it out.

James loved anything that went "bang," from cap guns to cherry bombs. He made a stink bomb with his chemistry set that had made their house nearly unlivable for a whole week. Then he mixed up a concoction that created an explosion big enough to put a hole in the basement wall.

Both Parents Got Involved

James's mother suspected that he was hyperactive or had attention deficit disorder, and his pediatrician suggested they try him on medication. James's father, who worked long hours and left most of the parenting decisions to his wife, nixed the idea of medicating their son. He insisted that "boys will be boys" and claimed that James wasn't much different from the way he had been when he was young. After they discussed the problem in a counseling session, his wife agreed to wait six months to see if his more active involvement with their son would help.

James's father dedicated the time he usually spent watching the nightly news and checking his e-mail messages to helping James with his homework. Otherwise, they spent the time wrestling or playing catch.

He took James with him to the gym when he worked out and insisted James accompany him on other in-town errands. James complained at first, but he became more enthusiastic as their relationship improved. He even accompanied his father on a short business trip, spending the day working on his school assignments while his father was in meetings.

Before age eight, most boys are closer to their mothers than to their fathers. During the tween years, boys seek out adult males and look to them as role models so they can work on an important developmental task that will occupy them for many years: learning what it means to be a man.

James's father also laid down the law about being disrespectful to his teachers and "my wife." At the end of six months, the improvement in James's behavior was dramatic enough that medication was never discussed again.

Common Myths and Misconceptions

For three decades, professionals made a concerted effort to eliminate the sexism that led to discrimination against America's girls. Now professionals have begun taking a closer look at America's boys to discover what ails them. Although no one has been able to tease out exactly how much of typical boy behavior is due to biology and how much is a result of environmental influences, it's clear that too many boys are growing up in environments that are poorly suited to their needs.

The number of tween boys being diagnosed with hyperactivity, attention deficit disorder, oppositional behavior, and various learning problems has reached epidemic proportions. So have the percentages of those who end up in trouble with the law or diagnosed with a behavior disorder in later adolescence.

Hyperactivity

Difficulty sitting still, restlessness, and fidgeting are symptoms of hyperactivity. They are also symptoms of anxiety. The prospect of having to sit still when they need to move, or of getting into trouble for moving, makes lots of little boys very anxious. Many boys end up tuning out all of the naysayers who seek to contain them, running circles around the classroom during the day and around the living room in the evening. If adults have difficulty penetrating the protective armor boys erect to fend off criticism, some boys can be diagnosed with attention deficit disorder with hyperactivity.

Meanwhile, boys who make a Herculean effort to contain themselves often find sitting still such an energy-consuming task that they can't think about much else. They fade in and out of their daydreams and lose track of what is happening around them as they retreat to the more interesting world of their fantasies. This makes them ripe for a diagnosis of attention deficit disorder without hyperactivity.

The common treatment for boys who display problems with attentional disorders and/or hyperactivity is medication. The hundreds of thousands of children standing in line outside of nurses' offices each day are overwhelmingly male. Labeling masses of tween boys "behavior disordered" and administering millions of doses of mind-altering drugs to control normal albeit difficult behavior is a national scandal.

ALERT!

The most commonly prescribed medications are chemically related to "speed." Although researchers have found that hyperactive boys who are medicated for long stretches during their tween years are less at risk of juvenile delinquency and drug addiction later in life, practicing clinicians report that it is common for them to abuse speed.

Many psychologists question the modern belief that hyperactivity is an inherited problem. Parents who lacked appropriate physical outlets and help to contain themselves when they were growing up may not know how to help their own children. These parents often fail to provide child-friendly home environments, sufficient exercise, and help managing anxiety. They don't know how to teach their sons to pay attention and concentrate, often badgering and belittling them for lapses, which increases children's anxiety and makes it harder for them to relax. If medication designed to control behavior is used at all, it should be part of a therapeutic program designed to ensure that children are being helped to come to grips with their underlying problems.

Jocks and Bookworms

Like any group of human beings, it is impossible to discuss boys without stereotyping. Remember that any adjective that handily describes more than 50 percent of young males may not apply to your child. Contrary to what many parents fear, boys who don't fit the puppy-dog-tail stereotypes aren't less masculine than those who do. Boys who prefer the arts to sports won't automatically grow up to be homosexual. From Beethoven to Hemingway to Picasso, most of the great artists have been heterosexual men.

In fact, boys who display behaviors and interests more typical of girls actually have certain advantages that enhance their adjustment. They tend to do better in school and have fewer conflicts at home. However, pressuring them to pursue interests that don't come naturally to them can result in problems. Parents who worry about their boys being insufficiently masculine can make them feel that they don't measure up, causing them to doubt themselves. Boys who follow the typical developmental pattern and adhere to more rough-and-ready interests and styles of relating are likely to have more than their fair share of problems in both settings. Further, it is a myth that a little jock who is "all boy" will be hetero-sexual. Many extremely virile men are gay.

The Love of Violence

Most toddler boys build and topple tall towers, reveling in the crash. During preschool, they crash toy cars, trucks, and trains into walls and furniture. By first grade, favorite pastimes include crashing Matchbox cars and exploding miniature army men. During the teenage years, lots of boys congregate to cheer schoolyard fights.

In between, boys are captivated by the grand crashes and explosions of cap guns, cherry bombs, fireworks, BB guns, and whatever else makes lots of noise or explodes. The noisier and more destructive, the better as far as many tween boys are concerned—assuming no one gets hurt. If they are prevented from indulging in mock mayhem, they draw pictures of aerial bombers decimating schools, tanks rolling over family members, and friends being blown to bits by cannons, adding red crayon drops, spatters, and smears to represent blood.

The penchant for bangs and bombs is a boy thing. But although blowing up anthills, smashing bottles, and setting off potato cannons are not the kind of activities parents want to encourage, they may find themselves helpless to stop them. Pummeling peers and purposely destroying property are problems that need to be addressed.

If you find such behavior distressing, you aren't alone. Psychologists and psychiatrists know that a fascination with violence can be a serious sign of emotional trouble and are quick to diagnose pathology. Lots of fathers are appalled, too, though many sheepishly admit to having done the same during their own tween years.

Lots of parents resolve the problem by making it clear that such dangerous, destructive play is unacceptable. Then, when yet another backyard explosion sends the birds scurrying for cover, parents make a point of pretending not to hear, as they studiously look the other way.

Tween Boys' Development

From the toddler years through puberty, boys develop more slowly than girls. On average, boys walk and talk a few months later. They complete potty training and other developmental milestones more slowly. It takes them longer to learn to express their emotions appropriately, control their behavior, and comply with adult requests. Boys are more active and aggressive and less rule-bound than little girls even during the toddler years.

By the time school begins, the differences between boys and girls are more pronounced. The motor activity, frustration tolerance, impulsiveness, verbal fluency, fine motor coordination, and emotional maturity of the typical first-grade boy are on a par with the average kindergarten girl, so school presents more of a challenge. Boys' greater interest in activities requiring lots of physical movement may enable them to hold their own in recess and gym, but girls are ahead of boys in every school subject except arithmetic, where boys and girls are about equal. Boys' early struggles can readily create a sense of failure, which persists throughout their school careers.

E ALERT!

Parents often resist having their child repeat a year in school or attend special education for fear of stigmatizing him, yet parents tend to be the worst offenders. If you feel good about your child's need for extra help and time, and advise him about how to respond to questions from peers, his social problems should be minimal.

The first signs that boys are approaching the physical milestone known as puberty are an enlarging of the testes and a thinning and reddening of the scrotum, which occur between ages nine and fourteen, with the average being age eleven. Meanwhile, the first signs of puberty for girls occur a year earlier. Girls' growth spurt takes place at age twelve, while boys' sudden stretch doesn't usually start until age thirteen. Only at puberty do boys forge ahead of their female classmates in math. They close the other educational gaps in college; but even as adults, men have more difficulty in the interpersonal and emotional realms.

Developmental Needs

Developmentally, tween boys need an adult male to emulate, but one-third live with single mothers, and the majority live in households where mothers bear the primary responsibility for child rearing. In addition, most boys are in classrooms headed by female teachers, and everything from the school rules to the way the lessons are taught are more suited to girls. Specifically, the emphasis on sitting still, talking quietly, being neat, cooperating, persisting, and concentrating for extended periods is better suited to the average girl than to the average boy. Boys' greater need for physical activity, preference for competitive activities, and aggressiveness don't fit well with modern classrooms. As a group, female teachers and mothers have difficulty understanding and managing boy-style anger and aggression, and many boys are unwilling to accept lessons in comportment and manners from females.

Boys don't fit well with modern lifestyles in general, since sending them outside for free play and to get the vigorous exercise they so desperately need is not an option in many neighborhoods. It's not surprising that boys are reprimanded and criticized far more than girls and are punished more severely at home as well as at school.

Gender Differences in Emotional Development

When it comes to dealing with emotions, boys are at a disadvantage. They have a harder time identifying their own emotions as well as those of others. Just how hard becomes apparent when children are shown pictures of faces bearing different expressions and are asked what the people in the pictures are feeling. Boys misread them, while even very young girls score as well as adults.

This may be due to physical differences in brain structure, since boys' brains are less reactive to emotionally charged situations. The centers of the brain that process emotions are smaller in boys, and they have fewer of those all-important connections that enable them to process feeling states.

ESSENTIAL

Women's brains may have developed better physical capabilities for processing emotional information because throughout the ages, women have played the central role in nurturing children. Modern boys need to be experts at handling emotions, too. Since identifying and coping with feelings may be more difficult for them, they need intensive help.

Boys' difficulty in recognizing their feelings and emotions, which is the first step to learning to control them, may also be due to the fact that adults provide them with less emotional instruction. From birth on, parents spend significantly less time discussing feelings with their boys than with girls and are less sympathetic, compassionate, and helpful when they do talk to them.

Adults are more likely to respond to tearful boys of every age by telling them not to cry, while they ask tearful girls what is making them sad and provide support, reassurance, or comfort to shore them up. Adults tell boys that they are silly to be afraid, but they give detailed explanations to help girls approach a fearsome situation, person, or object. Adults also provide emotional support and encouragement when girls try to be brave and praise them for their courage afterward, while they ridicule and shame boys for having felt afraid in the first place.

Boys are ordered not to hit, yell, or otherwise overpower an adversary, and they are punished if they continue. Girls, on the other hand, are helped to consider an adversary's feelings and point of view and are given suggestions as to what to do and say when they are angry. Adults yell at boys for being too rowdy when too much excitement causes their behavior to deteriorate, but they help girls redirect and channel problematic behavior by encouraging them toward an alternate activity.

Teaching Anger Management

Boys' difficulties identifying their feelings and using words to express themselves make it hard for them to ask questions and explain their problems in ways that others can readily understand. Since people who cannot talk about their feelings tend to act them out, and since boys are primed to act rather than talk to begin with, it is important to teach boys basic anger-management skills.

The first step is to help them identify what they are feeling at the moment. You can do this by simply saying, "You are feeling angry (frustrated, jealous, afraid, cranky, worried, lonely, proud, loving, excited)." The next step is to provide support and reassurance via a hug or words of comfort and encouragement. For instance: "I know you really want to watch a video right now." Just having someone empathize with them can often reduce their aggression. The third step is to teach boys how to express their feelings in an acceptable manner. For example: "Maybe punching your punching bag will help you get some of your anger out."

ALERT!

Be sure your boy has ways to discharge anger, such as a punching bag to punch, a beanbag chair to wrestle with, or something he can safely throw stones at. Parents may not appreciate the noise, but asking your son to step outside and yell at the top of his lungs can help him, too.

Counting to ten and taking several deep breaths are good ways to calm down. Pounding a pillow, clobbering a tree stump with a bat, and ripping up a phone book are good ways to discharge tension. So is drawing an ugly picture of whomever they are mad at and ripping it to shreds.

Improving Parent-Boy Relationships

The best way to shore up a relationship with a boy is to treat him with respect and not to order him about. Otherwise, you deliver the kind of blows to his ego that will hurt his self-esteem and induce him to rebel or ignore you. Address him politely, just as you would when speaking to someone outside of the family. It would not be respectful to ask a guest who is sitting down at the dinner table, "What are you supposed to do before you eat?" because that is the same as ordering him to "Go wash your hands!" Try to avoid comments such as these:

- Quit fidgeting!
- Take your coat to your room!
- You can go out, but I want you home at six o'clock.
- I can't believe you did that! You're grounded, Buddy.

Instead, be polite! Remember that while girls worry about germs, boys are convinced that a little dirt never hurt anyone, so be prepared to say to your son, "Please wash your hands" every day for the next few years, and praise him heartily if he ever remembers on his own. Sitting still and identifying feelings are difficult, so tell your son, "It looks like you're restless. Is something bothering you? Would it help to go outside and ride your bike?"

Walk into most bachelor pads and boys' college dorm rooms, and you'll see how uninterested males are in "pretty." They think that "functional" is all that matters and consider storing a coat on the floor as good a place as any, so resign yourself to several daily recitations of "Please take your coat to your room and hang it in your closet."

Anticipating how to keep people happy and relationships harmonious is not easy for boys either, so tell your son, "We are leaving at six o'clock; so you need to be home by then. How will you know when it's time to come home?" It may take quite a bit of experimenting to figure out a solution to that one, although digital watches with alarms are popular with boys and can eliminate the problem of not noticing when it's time to return home or report in.

Male Mentors

Most toddler and preschool boys consider their mother to be the greatest, most wonderful person in the entire universe. They may walk like Dad and follow him about when he does yard work, but they turn to their mother when they are upset, and many plan to marry her when they grow up. Mothers always remain important to boys; but at around age eight, male tweens begin to gravitate toward their fathers.

Fathers and Sons

If the father-son relationship is healthy, boys begin to worship their father as a hero. Even if the relationship seems poor, a tween is likely to emulate his father to the point that he walks like Dad, hooks his thumbs in his pockets, or crosses his arms over his chest when thinking in the very same way. Unless a boy bonds with another male, he will absorb his dad's ideas about manhood, as well as his values, beliefs, and method of flipping hamburgers on the barbecue grill.

Boys without sufficient fathering tend to adopt a very aggressive style of relating. Their discomfort with their masculinity is displayed by their hyper-masculine or "macho" behavior, eagerness to distance themselves from women, denigration of homosexuals, and stereotyped interests in firearms, cars and trucks, and physical strength. Insecure boys work overtime to distance themselves from girlish activities and emotions to cover up their own confusion and self-doubts. In the absence of a real-life role model, they model themselves after the men they see on television programs and commercials, where the typically violent heroes are obsessed with power and sexual conquest.

What boys need to learn from a man is how to be stern as well as tender, both strong and loving. To do this, they need to be the recipients of their fathers' firm rules and warm nurturing. Boys also need to observe fathers asserting themselves appropriately with and being openly affectionate toward their wives.

In the absence of an involved, caring adult male, tween boys who watch a lot of television are more likely to act disrespectfully toward girls, defy their mothers, verbally abuse their female teachers, fight with their peers, overreact to small slights, and strive to distance themselves from anything they consider remotely feminine, including their own tender and compassionate emotions.

Finding a Mentor

Although nothing can quite compensate for ongoing daily contact with a loving, protective adult male at home, spending even an hour a week with a man outside the family can make a huge, enduring difference in a boy's life. If no male mentor is available, your son may well be attracted to a gang. There, the older boys take the younger ones in hand, initiate them into their male society, and give them a strict set of rules to live by. Boys do best with a hierarchy where they know their place, and gangs provide them with a rigid social structure.

The Big Brothers Big Sisters of America, which has been dedicated to the cause of youth mentoring since 1904, expects to have 300,000 mentoring relationships in place by 2004. The results of a recent study examining the effectiveness of its program for both boys and girls were impressive:

- 64 percent developed more positive attitudes toward school
- 58 percent got higher grades in social studies, languages, and math
- 60 percent had improved relationships with adults
- 56 percent had improved peer relationships
- 55 percent improved their ability to express their feelings
- 64 percent had improved self-confidence
- 62 percent were more trusting of their teachers

In addition, children with mentors were less likely to repeat a grade and had fewer unexcused school absences. Depending on your community, waiting lists for mentors can be long. Visit ✐ *www.bbbsa.org* for contact information and get your child on the waiting list immediately if you think he might benefit. Other men who may serve as mentors include grandfathers, uncles, older cousins, coaches, neighbors, Sunday school teachers, ministers, camp counselors, tutors, therapists, scout leaders, and karate instructors. Athletic coaches are the closest many boys get to having a father. If your child isn't into sports, check out the local chess teams, computer clubs, Future Farmers of America (FFA) clubs, Future Homemakers of America (FHA) clubs, and every other club you can think of to see if any of the sponsors are male. Many boys who dislike sports enjoy martial arts such as tae kwan do, judo, karate, and aikido. The most important attributes of a mentor are having the time to spend and a genuine interest in your child.

Check with your child's school counselor to see if your district has a mentoring program in place. Some high schools recruit teen volunteers and send them into junior highs and middle schools to mentor or tutor younger boys.

Some after-school programs offered through YMCAs employ male college students. If your son plays the piano, look for a male piano teacher. If he needs counseling, hold out for a male therapist. If you need a baby-sitter or companion to care for your son a few hours a week, post a help-wanted ad on a bulletin board at a local community college and specify that you are looking for a male student.

Wrestling Time!

One example of what boys miss when no older male is present in the home is wrestling. In cultures all over the world, men wrestle with little boys. Apparently there is more to wrestling than rowdiness for children of both sexes. It's not known whether wrestling helps them to be more assertive, increases self-confidence, stimulates the brain, or improves body awareness. Perhaps it does all of those things. What is known is that girls who wrestle with their fathers as tots do better in math years later.

In *Raising Boys: Why Boys Are Different and How to Help Them Become Happy and Well-Balanced Men*, author Steve Biddulph notes that during rough-and-tumble play with an older male, boys learn their own strength and to accept limits. They develop self-control as they learn to balance fun and aggression. Even if they become angry, they must observe certain rules, such as no biting, scratching, punching, or elbowing. They are being trained in two important social skills that many boys clearly lack: keeping their heads about them when they feel attacked and knowing when and how to stop themselves.

ALERT!

Remembering that living rooms aren't playgrounds is a particular challenge for energetic boys. If your son is running inside, say: "I asked you not to do that. What can we do to solve this problem?"

Boy-Friendly Environments

Once you understand that an energetic boy problem is really a problem of a boy's inability to adjust to environments and acquire habits that are basically at odds with his nature, finding solutions may seem harder rather than easier.

Boy-Friendly Classrooms

A boy's academic achievement before third grade is likely to dictate how well he will do throughout his school career, so it is imperative that your son is successful early on. One solution is to delay entry into kindergarten. Some schools have boosted boys' success by establishing different cutoff birth dates for boys and girls.

Making it school policy for boys to attend two years of kindergarten instead of one to give them an extra year to catch up to girls is another solution, since it is more common for boys than girls to repeat kindergarten. Another solution being tested in some school districts is to put boys and girls in separate classrooms for reading and language arts. Anecdotal reports indicate that this arrangement has met with considerable success. Besides the impressive improvements in reading achievement, boys' attitudes toward reading and their self-confidence are reportedly better, too.

Boy-Friendly Space

Ask your boy for suggestions, and he might recommend stripping the living room of furniture so he can use it for basketball practice, getting some mats for tumbling, installing a punching bag so he can work out his anger, and putting in a hardwood floor so he can play tag. Those are actually excellent suggestions! Boys simply must be able to run and jump. They must not have people criticizing them for acting like boys. If there is nowhere else for your son to play and he's climbing the walls and bouncing off the ceiling anyway, why not search for some creative alternatives?

The living room wouldn't be a comfortable place to watch television and entertain guests if you turned it into a playroom, but television really isn't good for kids, and your son's need for a livable space is undoubtedly more pressing than your need to entertain an occasional guest. Years ago, you toddler-proofed your whole house for him; why not boy-proof one small living room now?

Converting the living room to a playroom is definitely a drastic step and may seem too ridiculous to consider. But if you have no basement and your son's opportunities to play outside are limited, and if you're considering medication to get an energetic, distracted boy to settle down and concentrate, maybe it's time to be creative about the space in the house. Bedrooms can be converted, too. Get rid of the bed and put the mattress on the floor. Put up a hoop for Nerf basketball, clear out as much other furniture as possible, put away breakable objects, close the door, and let him play.

Tween boys do want to please. It's when they feel that to make their parents happy they would have to stop being themselves that emotionally healthy boys give up trying. Finding solutions may not be easy, but the time spent is well worth it.

Chapter 4

Parenting a Tween

When your child begins disappearing into her room and assails you with news about what other parents allow/do/buy, the tween years have arrived full-force. Don't be daunted by the impeccable logic and sophisticated talk. She is young, inexperienced, and still very much in need of your loving presence to teach, guide, supervise, set limits, and enforce the rules.

Parent-Tween Relationships

Theresa was a single mother, so when she found her only child's bedroom door closed and a handmade sign that said "KEEP OUT!!!" taped to it, she had no doubt for whom the message was intended. But why was her daughter suddenly shutting her out? Amanda had been more standoffish lately, pulling away from hugs and saying she was too big for goodnight kisses. She also had grown quite critical and even balked at being seen with Theresa, as if she were ashamed of her mother.

At first, Theresa thought that she must have done something to upset Amanda. But why couldn't her daughter say what it was? Then, anger replaced Theresa's feelings of guilt. A ten-year-old had no right to try to dictate what part of the house was off-limits to her mother. Who paid for that room, anyway?

ALERT!

Tweens need privacy and a space to call their own. Otherwise, they may take refuge in tree houses, homemade forts, basement cubbyholes, and rooftops. Many retreat to a special tree limb, a secluded spot in an empty lot, a clump of bushes in an alley, or a shadowed area under a stairwell or porch.

Instead of barging in and telling the daughter she had bathed and diapered that in this house there were to be no secrets, Theresa remembered how she had felt when her own mother had done exactly that two decades ago. The day Theresa had locked her bedroom door had been an unfortunate turning point in their relationship. Although Theresa had done it on a whim, without any particular meaning or purpose, her mother's rule that it was to remain unlocked had left Theresa feeling invaded and exposed.

Theresa had convinced herself that her own mother was treating her like a baby because she wanted to keep her one. That had catapulted Theresa on a defiant search for other ways to safeguard her privacy. As a result, she'd kept secret many of her thoughts and feelings, even when what she really wanted was to collapse into her mother's arms and sob like a baby. It had taken her a decade to realize that she had cut herself off from the person whose wisdom, guidance, and support she'd needed most.

That memory enabled Theresa to rethink what was happening. As she stared at her daughter's locked door, she realized that keep-out signs, secret diaries, hidden treasure boxes, and private phone calls were undoubtedly normal for children Amanda's age. Her anger and guilt dissipated only to be replaced by sadness. Finding her daughter's door suddenly closed to her signaled that her baby was growing up. Did that have to mean growing away? Theresa hoped not, but that's how it felt.

Parents as Fallen Heroes

Almost every parent reacts unhappily when suddenly confronted with the undeniable signs that their baby is truly growing up. At such moments the road to independence can seem very short and the speed at which your child is hurtling toward the grand finish line of adulthood can seem frightening.

Prior to becoming a tween, your child's principal concerns were learning what you think and feel and deciphering how you do things. Now your child's interest turns to learning about the world outside his front door. It's not easy for him to make sense of the confusing mixture of thoughts and feelings that arise in the course of a day, or even in a single hour. He'll need a lot of time, space, and help from you to sort things out.

Wanting to spend a lot of time alone and becoming more intent on privacy doesn't signal that your child suddenly dislikes you, although it can certainly feel that way when you long for the days when words, smiles, and hugs flowed freely between you. This retreat from the mainstream of family life serves several important developmental functions.

Unlike younger children, whose worlds revolve around their parents and later their teachers, your tween is becoming increasingly aware that different people have different viewpoints, opinions, and reactions. That is to say, he is learning that others' ideas are different from yours. That realization turns his world upside down. In the public arena of the playground, he is likely to remain your champion for some time and haughtily insist that whatever you told him is the absolute truth and that your way is always the best way. However, inside himself, he is no longer sure. Other people have other ways of doing things that seem to work quite well. In fact, the things some parents allow their children to do sound even better. There are other people, he is beginning to learn, who possess knowledge and wisdom greater than yours.

Parents' Fall from Grace

The dawning awareness that parents are far from perfect produces a mix of feelings in tweens that range from very unsettling to desperately disappointing to downright scary. It is a bit frightening to realize that the god who ruled the nursery and could kiss away every hurt is only a fallible human being. The world seems far less secure and certain than before.

Some tweens act as though they believe their parents tricked them, and the result can be an unwillingness to trust that you know anything at all for fear of being deluded again. If so, your tween may seize each opportunity to point out your every wart and flaw, taking exaggerated pains to let you know every little thing you do wrong. What she's really trying to do is remind herself that you aren't perfect. Such nitpicking is a manifestation of a child's struggle not to return to the simpler, more secure days when she knew every problem would be solved because you could fix everything.

Growing Toward Independence

Recognizing parents' fallibility is an important step toward independence. As long as you are all-powerful and all-knowing, your tween has no need to reach outside the family, learn to use his own mind, and grow up. Moreover, your tween's growing sense of personal adequacy comes with the recognition that he knows things that you do not. It may be reassuring to know that your parents are always right, but why bother to use your own mind if someone bigger, stronger, and far more capable knows everything? It's not possible to feel good about yourself while languishing in the shadow of someone who knows everything. People who consider their parents to be perfect linger in a perpetual childlike state.

ALERT!

It is normal for tweens to become little know-it-alls, but it's not acceptable for your child to treat you as if you know nothing! Demonstrate how adults behave by remaining respectful even when he spouts facts that are patently absurd. Insist he communicate his ideas without disparaging yours so he learns how to disagree respectfully.

In truth, your halo may never again gleam quite so brightly as in the glow of your younger child's admiring eyes. It can be sad to discover that your halo is tarnished and slipping, and the urge to polish it and force your tween to admire it once again can be intense. Given the impossibility of controlling someone else's perceptions, even if that someone is your own child, it is futile to try. Your fall from grace may be very hard on your ego, but it provides an important boost to your tween's self-esteem.

Friends versus Family

Your tween's preoccupation with people and events outside the family is natural and you should respect her boundaries, but it is imperative to remain actively involved in your child's life. Too often, peers end up filling the vacuum left by parents who are overly critical or largely absent.

Privacy, Please

Your tween's need for privacy can delude you into thinking she no longer needs you very much, but this is not the case at all. Spending time alone enables your tween to hold the rest of the world at bay long enough to tune into her own thoughts and feelings, but she'll still need you to help her process them. Adults may be able to think through difficult issues even as other activities, conversations, and emotions swirl on about them. Because they have more practice, they can more quickly sort through complicated problems, resolve emotionally trying issues, and recharge their psychic batteries. Tweens are still learning how to do all that.

In actuality, the willingness to devote time to self-reflection is a sign of maturity. So is the desire to control the environment to ensure adequate time and psychological space for thoughtful contemplation. It is hard to focus internally when someone else might come barging in at any moment. Furthermore, just as members of religious orders find it easier to meditate while making a repetitive sound or motion, and just as many adults find it easier to think while listening to music and/or engaging in a simple, soothing activity such as knitting or tinkering on a project, tweens may close themselves off and doodle, listen to music, or build a LEGO castle. Piddling and playing with a mindless toy can serve the same meditative function.

Tween social pressures at school range from difficult to excruciatingly painful, and the games children play can be horrifically cutthroat as they vie to improve their own social status by putting down others. The academic pressures in the classroom can be intense, too. Then there are all of the physical changes tweens must cope with as their bodies develop. It's no wonder they need a lot of alone time to contemplate and recover.

FACT

If you have often held time-outs by sending your youngster to his room with orders to remain there until he's settled down, pondered his behavior, and arrived at a solution to his latest problem, during the tween years he may take the initiative and automatically go to his room when he needs to decompress.

It may be your house, but forbidding your tween the freedom to control her bedroom door is tantamount to forbidding her access to her own mind. If she shares a bedroom, try to help her locate a spot where she can get some privacy. Some tweens gravitate to the bathroom, but that can cause conflicts with other family members. Whenever your tween desires privacy, behave respectfully by knocking on the door and holding interruptions to a minimum, just as you expect your tween to do when you need to be alone. You cannot force your tween to be emotionally close to you, but you can certainly drive a wedge between the two of you by refusing to give her the physical space she needs.

Little Space Cadets

Even if your tween continues to spend a lot of time with everyone else at home instead of staging a retreat from the mainstream of family life, he may often seem to be a million miles away. If he's not preoccupied with some far-flung fantasy, he's probably floating in the ozone. Ask him what he is thinking about and the answer is likely to be, "Nothing." Press him for the truth about what is on his mind and you may well get the very same reply. Don't stop asking what's on his mind, though. Sometimes the blankness within may suddenly assume a form he can talk about.

Spaciness is common for tweens, and it lasts through the teen years. Get your tween's full attention before you speak to her, and give her time to collect her thoughts and formulate a response. For emotional issues, she may need as long as several minutes. Remain patient and squelch any urges to interrupt.

Tweens' tendency to space out at unpredictable moments leads to lots of confusion, misunderstandings, and angry scenes as parents mistakenly conclude they are purposely being ignored. "When I ask you a question, I expect an answer!" "Didn't I tell you to get started on your homework?" "How many times do I have to tell you not to do that?" are common signs that an adult is taking typical tween behavior as a personal slight.

If tweens could explain themselves, the answers they would give are, "I didn't answer because I didn't hear you, then I couldn't think of what to say, and then I spaced out again and forgot what you asked me in the first place." "You may have told me but I was too spaced out to get what you meant, exactly." "You're going to have to tell me again and again and again because I spend so much time lost in the clouds, I forget to pay attention to what I'm supposed to do here on earth." Just as adults engrossed in a book can suddenly hear the teakettle shrieking or a siren blaring or rain falling and realize the noise has been going on for some time, tweens can suddenly realize that someone was speaking and even realize what was being said *after* that someone has penetrated the haze. Demand a fast answer, and you'll probably just end up hearing whatever your tween thinks you want him to say.

The Pull of Peers

A young child's preference for spending time with his parents above anyone else changes as the urge to spend time with like-minded people who share the same interests, concerns, and perspectives intensifies. If you don't love to play video games, hold cheerleading practices, and build backyard forts, you'll need to find other ways to remain close to your child.

When older tweens are tucked away in their rooms, they aren't just studying and hunkering down to relieve stress. A lot of their time is spent talking to friends on the phone and contacting them via the computer. Less sociable children may begin to think of their books and hobbies as their friends and companions. If forbidden to communicate with their friends directly, tweens write notes to them. They think about what their friends said to them today and what they will talk about tomorrow.

The chance to interact and have fun isn't the only reason your tween is drawn to spending time with friends. She has lots to learn about getting along with "colleagues," and peers are the best teachers. However, lots of conflicts and questions are bound to arise, and your tween will need many infusions of help from an older and more experienced "boss" to know how to untangle and manage this confusing and difficult world of peer relationships. To help her with her other relationships, your own relationship with your child must be warm and trusting.

Maintaining Mutual Respect

If you think your tween would gladly trade you for almost anybody else's parent, it's probably because she has let you know through words, deeds, or "attitude" that she doesn't think much of your household rules (too strict), your financial decisions (not enough spent on video games and clothes), your lifestyle (you watch the wrong television shows), your age (too old), your weight (too thin or too fat), your wardrobe (not cool), your hair (not cool), the way you drive (not cool).

It is typical for tweens to criticize or ridicule their parents' hairstyle, clothes, weight, mannerisms, and ideas. It is also common for them to use words or body language to signal that they think their parents are committing a disgusting social blunder by walking the face of the earth. You need to take these comments for what they're worth, which isn't very much, and make sure that your youngster behaves respectfully.

ALERT!

Tweens need to be able to express their personal opinions, but they need to learn to do so respectfully. Hurting people's feelings by dissing them is not a healthy way to relate to peers, much less to parents and teachers.

Tween Slings and Arrows

Although your tween probably does believe that you could stand some improvement, her negative comments may reflect her idea about how tweens are supposed to communicate with others rather than how she really feels toward you. In most tween circles, verbal posturing and put-downs are commonplace. Most of their conversation is a competition as peers jockey and vie for social position.

If your tween mocks your errors and ridicules your mistakes, she may well be mimicking the taunts and verbal power plays she has seen television characters dole out to one another. The attitudes toward parents expressed in many programs targeted to tweens are demeaning. Don't allow parent-bashing shows to be aired in your home, unless you're at her side to help her see them for what they are: unacceptable.

Commanding Respect

Parents are human beings, too, and children must recognize this fact. For your tween to blatantly disregard your feelings is hurtful and can undermine even the strongest parent-child relationship. You need to take immediate steps to stop disrespectful behavior at home while letting your youngster know that mistreating others is not acceptable at home, school, or anywhere else. As she learns to disagree with you and remain considerate, she will learn how to respond to peers who torment her or treat her with disrespect. In other words, by respectfully demanding your child's courteous treatment, you teach her to respect others. Moreover, you model how to command respect from others. Here is what you might tell your disrespectful tween:

- How her behavior made you feel—that she hurt your feelings and/or made you angry.
- That if she is angry about something, she needs to tell you in a direct, straightforward manner rather than treating you disrespectfully.
- That you hope she doesn't treat her peers disrespectfully.
- That although her peers may like, accept, or tolerate such behavior, you do not and will not.
- That if she thinks such behavior is acceptable because she has seen children on television act that way, she shouldn't watch it anymore.
- That you expect an apology.

If your child indicates that she is in fact angry with you about something, tell her you will be happy to discuss it later so as not to cloud the issue at hand: She is not to be disrespectful toward you. If she doesn't think an apology is in order, tell her that your relationship must be a top priority since you're going to be living together for many years to come. Insist that she take time out from other activities so she can give careful consideration to how the two of you are going to get along. Even if her pride won't allow her to apologize to you, tell her you need a promise to treat you respectfully in the future.

What Tweens Need Most

Despite your tween's need to spend a lot of time alone and with friends, you must be careful not to let him pull too far away or lose track of what is happening to him emotionally. A 1995 National Survey of Preteens sponsored by KidsPeace Corporation in Pennsylvania provides a disturbing reminder that they are indeed very young, and too many are beset with intense anxieties and fears that require adult guidance.

The survey found that although 93 percent of the respondents felt loved by their parents, almost half expressed such pessimism about their futures that they sounded more like overwhelmed adults than young people. For instance, 41 percent of ten-to-thirteen-year-olds said they worry that they might end up having a baby out of wedlock. Large numbers are concerned they might get involved in using drugs (41 percent), alcohol (40 percent), or cigarettes (38 percent). Fears of being physically or sexually abused (45 percent), getting AIDS (54 percent), or being kidnapped (50 percent) were also rampant. While 51 percent worry about their own death, a full 65 percent worry about a parent dying. Fifty-three percent fear their parents will not have enough money to pay the bills.

Peer pressure has become a major issue for middle-school youngsters, with 22 percent of those surveyed admitting that they sometimes change what they do or where they go during school hours to avoid kids who might physically threaten or hurt them. Two-thirds of the preteens surveyed said that they would do something they wouldn't normally do if pressured by friends.

FACT

Youngsters share their parents' fears about the dangers that lie ahead, but they doubt their ability to avoid them alone. Although they know they are loved, they doubt their parents' ability to be there for them. Your tween needs your emotional and physical presence.

The vast majority of fifth, sixth, and seventh graders were comfortable talking with their parents about sensitive matters. But among eighth graders, the figure dropped to less than half. Still, preteens were most likely to seek out their mothers' help with problems, even though one-third complained that their parents are too busy to talk, 70 percent don't believe their parents understand what it's like to be a kid these days, and 35 percent find the lack of parental understanding an impediment to communication.

It is important to do what you can to relieve your youngster's anxieties:

- If you are unemployed or beset by financial worries, reassure your child that you will keep him fed and sheltered no matter what.
- Set aside time each week to listen to his problems.
- Accept that antisocial peer pressures are more pervasive and intense than when you were growing up.
- Support your child's involvements with pro-social peers and encourage his participation in wholesome extracurricular activities.
- Focus on teaching rather than punishing to solve behavior problems at home.
- Don't hesitate to pull your child away from peers if family and school responsibilities are being neglected or are overwhelming him.

The challenge for parents is that while helping tweens become independent, they must know when to rein them back in to protect them physically as well as emotionally. Still, it is important to refrain from saying, "I told you so" as you did when he was four, even if he encountered the very hurdles and hurts you predicted. Instead, you must help him glean what he can from whatever difficult lessons life presents and pull him more firmly back into the center of the household when he can't distance himself from friends and pursuits that are too much to handle.

Your New Parenting Role

Although the posting of a Keep Out sign is indeed an indication that your tween is growing up, rest assured that growing up doesn't need to mean growing away. In fact, your child's physical departure during late adolescence doesn't have to mean growing away, either. Whether they are twelve or sixty-two, children never outgrow the need for parents, but they need them differently as they mature.

> can actually become richer and more satisfying
> a gradual transition from an emphasis on
> ontrolling during early childhood, to teaching and
> g the tween and teen years, to advising and
> he adult years.

s to consider your long-term goal. Most parents
relationship with their adult children and continue
do that, parents must be able to relate to them as
treating children as their equals. Now is the time to
opportunities to relate to you like an adult. Affirm
lisagree with you, respect her opinions, make it clear
desires when making decisions, and allow her to
ven though they are not the ones you would choose

ber that when she is an adult in less than 120
onger be able to protect or control her. If you are
relationship, you'll be able to offer your advice, but
or it. If she regards you as a trusted confidant and
ill mean a lot. Sometimes she might even take it.
ant your advice, your continuing support can make
r long-term health and happiness. The time to begin
from protector to friend is now. But make it ever so

Chapter 5

Ⓔ Tween Management

Parents use the terms *discipline* and *punishment* interchangeably, but there is a big difference. *Discipline* comes from the word *disciple*, which means a "pupil" or "follower." As a disciplinarian, you need to serve as your tween's teacher. Good teachers demonstrate, explain, supervise, monitor, give feedback, and serve as role models. Those are the things your child needs most from you.

Teaching Self-Control

When Cheyenne turned twelve, her mother became increasingly frustrated by her daughter's lack of respect. When she asked Cheyenne to do something, her daughter often talked back. Her mother got angry and sent her to time-out, grounded her, or took away a privilege. Recently, Cheyenne had become blatantly defiant, rolling her eyes disgustedly, saying that her mother couldn't tell her what to do, and threatening to go out without permission if she were grounded.

If your tween is difficult to manage, find friends or extended family members to provide support. Other parents with children the same age or older are ideal. However, you need more than just listeners. You need wise people to give advice, even if what they say isn't always to your liking.

With the help of a counselor, Cheyenne's mother decided that if Cheyenne was too angry to be polite, she could write her mother a note to express her opinions, take a walk around the block, or pound on a pillow to get her anger out. The consequence for verbally abusing her mother would be to apologize and restate whatever had been on her mind in a more respectful manner.

In the interim, Cheyenne would be responsible for getting herself to and from school via the bus instead of being driven by her mother and would have to work out her own rides to her other activities if she wanted to go. She would have to make her own lunches, wash her own laundry, read herself a bedtime story if she wanted one, and do her own hair in the morning.

That got Cheyenne's attention, and she settled down as soon as she understood her mother was prepared to follow through. Her mother realized that if she didn't want to be taken for granted, she needed to be careful not to take Cheyenne for granted, either. Her mother was careful to use common courtesy expressions when addressing Cheyenne from then on, saying, "Please," "Thank-you," "I'd appreciate it if you would . . ." and "Would you mind . . . ?" She apologized for becoming cranky with her daughter by saying, "Sorry, Cheyenne. I'm in a bad mood, but I have no right to take it out on you."

After just a few weeks Cheyenne began inserting some *pleases* and *thank-yous* into her conversations, too. Once, after she began issuing demands and ordering her mother about very rudely, she suddenly said, "Sorry, Mom. I didn't mean what I just said. I've just had such a terrible day." That's when her mother knew the problems were under control.

The Tween Challenge

No one questions that parenting toddlers is an extremely draining, exhausting business, and the dilemmas faced by parents of adolescents are an ongoing subject of national discussion. Parents of tweens, on the other hand, receive little acknowledgment of their struggles, far less help, and virtually no support. The popular stereotype is that children in this age group float along without needing much adult intervention, are sufficiently subject to parents' control so that they are easy to protect, and have simple problems that their parents can resolve without much trouble.

The stereotype is wrong! While toddlers and teenagers are often anxious to let their parents know what's on their mind and often do so loudly, tweens remain silent. Often they don't know how to explain the problem to themselves, much less to anyone else.

Your Parenting Style

The primary approaches to child rearing are permissive, strict, and flexible:

- **Permissive parenting:** Parents who rely on this approach are friends to their children. They trust them to make good decisions and believe that children need freedom and autonomy in order to flourish. An advantage of this approach is that the high level of parental acceptance promotes emotional closeness. A disadvantage is that some children have difficulty with the lack of clear structure and direction.
- **Strict parenting:** Parents who prefer this approach believe that since children don't know what's good for them, adults need to make the

decisions and children need to learn to obey. Such parents are careful to keep their world separate from their children's, set clear expectations, and provide a lot of structure. Although children may dislike having many rules, they benefit from knowing that an adult is in control. The danger is that unless parents consider their individual child's capabilities, their expectations may be overly demanding.

- **Flexible parenting:** This approach focuses on using positive teaching methods to help children learn what they need to know so they can follow rules and make good decisions. Flexible parents know it is up to them to have the final say in matters of consequence, but they are careful to consider their children's personalities and solicit their opinions so that they can participate in decisions that affect them. The disadvantage is that considering individual needs can be more taxing.

No style is right or wrong. Each has its pluses and minuses. Ideally, parents will adopt a style that meets their child's needs. Unfortunately, instead of considering their individual child, many parents raise their youngsters the way they were raised. It is important to avoid the "if it was good enough for me, it's good enough for my child" mentality. What works for some children backfires with others. You and your child are two different people!

Some parents believe in spanking younger children, but there is never a reason to hit a tween. He'll learn to handle frustrations similarly. Hitting at school is called "fighting," and your child can be expelled. When a teenager or adult hits, it's called "assault," and the punishment is jail.

Permissive Pals

Parents who adopt a laissez-faire or hands-off approach relate to their children more like friends than authority figures. This approach works well for youngsters who only need a bit of advice now and then to find the right path and stick to it, and some kids flourish with a lenient, anything-goes parent. However, some children need more structure and limits. When given a lot of freedom, they make bad decisions.

Too much autonomy and independence can create a very insecure, spoiled, out-of-control youngster who begins looking to siblings, friends, teachers, and eventually police officers and judges to set limits and enforce consequences. If you are a permissive parent, expand your parenting skills by taking a parenting class or assertiveness training class to improve your ability to deal with conflict.

FACT

Parents who choose permissive parenting may operate more like friends than authority figures. Their strength is their ability to enjoy their tweens as people in their own right, which can lead to exceptionally warm, joyful relationships.

Whether or not you adopt a firmer approach, don't undermine teachers and other adults who impose rules and limits. If people complain about your child's behavior, don't rescue your "poor baby" or side with your tween against them!

A Boot Camp Parent

Very strict parents believe that teaching children to do the right thing and to obey are top priorities. They are conscientious about communicating expectations, providing structure, setting limits, and following through with consequences. While your tween may not like many of your rules and regulations, he has the security of knowing what is expected and the consequences for failing to comply. However, too much emphasis on respecting authority may make it difficult to step out of the parenting role long enough to engage in lighthearted play, which is important for relationship building.

Although strict parents know what they want their youngsters to do and how they want them to act, they may not know how to enforce their rules. Being more comfortable in the role of police officer than teacher, parents may assume that tweens break rules because they are willful or lazy and fail to see that tweens need to be taught. This leads them to punish their children for misbehaving instead of teaching them how to behave correctly. Fearful children may develop an exaggerated sense of their own inadequacy as they fail in their efforts to please. Tweens with bolder personalities become increasingly defiant. To expand your parenting skills, read books on child development, ask others whether they think you're being too harsh and demanding, and accept what they tell you!

Flexible Fixer-Uppers

Authoritative parents believe in taking children's individual needs into account when making decisions. They solicit youngsters' opinions but are careful to have the final say. These parents are flexible, being strict or lenient as the situation dictates. Thus, they can engage in some playful silliness one minute and quickly call a halt to the shenanigans if their tween gets out of hand. They see themselves as teachers and are good at working on one issue at a time instead of trying to tackle everything at once, as strict parents often do, or never tackling anything, which is a problem for some permissive parents.

Authoritative parents' willingness to consider many factors when making decisions can backfire, however, when tweens employ logic and advanced negotiating strategies to get their way. Some parents end up saying "yes" when their hearts tell them that their answer should be "no." It can be easy for them to overlook their own needs, too, and they run the risk of becoming drained or burned out.

To expand your parenting skills, learn to say "no." When your child doesn't accept your reasons, end debates by saying, "because I said so." Put yourself first sometimes. Join a parenting support group. Enlist others to baby-sit.

Spouses with Different Styles

Spouses can complement each other if they appreciate their differences. Otherwise, they may become more extreme and rigid as they try to compensate for what they consider to be their partner's flaws. Hence, an easygoing father may adopt an "anything goes" attitude to try to make up for an overly strict mother. This causes her to be even stricter to make up for his failure to set limits.

When disagreements arise, don't argue in front of your child. Parent discord evokes anxiety under any circumstances; when a tween is the subject of the argument, the guilt is tremendous. Don't allow your child to play one parent off against the other. Discuss your differences in private. Agree to respect each other's decisions if you can and see a family counselor for help if you can't.

Solving Communication Problems

Maintaining a good relationship with your child is important for getting him to do things that he prefers not to do and being able to influence him. Even tweens with an overly developed conscience are still at the stage where they do the right thing to avoid displeasing their parents, teachers, and other authority figures rather than because they can readily tell the difference between right and wrong.

A big problem for parents is getting tweens to listen when they are being spoken to. In fact, many parents are so used to being ignored, they automatically raise their voices when asking their tween to do something, as if speaking to someone who is slightly deaf. Most tweens dislike being shouted at and ordered about. It makes them resentful, and as they mature, they begin speaking in the same disrespectful ways to their parents.

ALERT!

Most tweens prefer negative attention to no attention. If you think your tween misbehaves just to upset you, you could be right! To improve your relationship, make a concerted effort to acknowledge and appreciate any small things he does that you feel good about.

Your child may undergo a marked personality change during the tween years. Rather than overreacting to squelch defiance or assuming that if you do nothing he'll eventually mature, realize that he is beginning to have more opinions of his own and needs to learn to express them properly.

For many parents, the biggest challenges are remembering to treat their child respectfully on the one hand, and demanding that their child treat them respectfully on the other. Modeling is the most potent form of teaching. If you yell and scream out of frustration, apologize later, just as you would expect someone else to do if he lost his temper with your child, and just as you would expect your child to do if he took out his crankiness on you or his teachers. Down the road, he'll need to be able to handle himself appropriately with bosses and employers.

Parents get cranky from time to time. Taking care of yourself by getting enough sleep, eating a well-balanced diet, exercising, meditating or doing yoga, and keeping your schedule under control aren't just ways to pamper yourself. They're ways to make you a better parent.

Respectful Communication

If your child continues to argue and questions your decisions, it is understandable that you'll feel defensive, especially if you are unsure about your decisions in the first place. No parent can ever be 100 percent certain. Child rearing is an art, not a science. Give your youngster reasons for your decisions, but do not argue about the fairness of your rules and whether things are better in other households. To do that is to sink to your child's level. Instead, empathize with the fact that she would like things to be different and use these opportunities to teach lessons about conflict resolution. Remember:

- Allow your child to state her point of view.
- Remain respectful.
- Accept her point of view as valid.
- Insist that your child stick to the issue at hand.
- Insist that she communicate respectfully.
- Let your child know that personal attacks hurt your feelings, which is unacceptable.

- Terminate a conversation that is degenerating or going nowhere and agree to resume it when you both have had a chance to calmly think things through.
- Empower your child by offering several options to choose from.
- Compromise if you can; agree to disagree if you cannot.

Just as an effective way to respond to a toddler's screams for a cookie is to let her choose between apple slices or some cheese, offering tweens choices allows them to save face and gives them a sense of control. If you don't allow coed parties and your tween is demanding one, offer her a choice: girls only or a small family celebration. This won't cause her to be joyous if she really wants boys there, but by letting her choose she participates in the decision. It also enables her to explain to her friends, "I decided just to invite girls," or "Instead of a big party, I decided just to have cake with the family."

Tackling Behavior Problems

Tweens feel guilty when they don't do what they are supposed to do or when they do things they've been told not to do. As long as you remain flexible about bedtime, your tween will probably stay up too late and struggle through his days in a state of chronic exhaustion. Remain flexible about chores, and your child probably won't do them. Be flexible about how much time your child spends watching television or playing video games, and he will probably dedicate exorbitant amounts of time to undesirable pastimes. Be flexible about your child's diet, and he will probably subsist on junk food. Try to shape your tween up by nagging, and you will probably fail. In other words, unless you take charge, neither of you will be happy with yourselves or with each other.

Parents who fail to take charge complain that time is at a premium and usually say they lack the strength to discipline due to chronic stress and exhaustion. They are convinced that getting their child to comply with basic household rules would be an ongoing battle requiring more energy than they can summon. They hesitate to make a concerted effort because they doubt their youngster would ever come around.

FACT

If you communicate the rules clearly, apply consequences consistently, and praise everything your child does right, most behavior problems can be eliminated in less than two weeks. Instead of vacationing out of town, take an in-town vacation while your child is in school. Rest during the day so that you'll have the energy to set limits when she gets home.

While it is true that taking charge requires quite a bit of energy at the outset, most tweens will improve dramatically when limits are consistently enforced for five to ten days. Eliminating behavior problems and ending the cycle of guilt, nagging, and recrimination inevitably improves the parent-child relationship. The savings in time, energy, and stress from the reduced conflict lasts for years; the reduction in guilt and worry can last a lifetime.

Advance Preparations

Begin by listing your child's problematic behaviors, e.g., not getting ready for school in the morning, talking back, watching violent television shows and movies, snacking on junk food, getting too little sleep and exercise, not cleaning his room, arguing with his siblings, not doing his homework, and so on.

When the problems crop up over the next few days, mention to your child that you and he need to figure out some enduring solutions so as not to encounter the same difficulties, conflicts, and clashes again and again. Encourage him to think of what could be done to eliminate them once and for all. Suggest he talk to his friends to see how their families deal with some of the behavior problems. Tell him that you will consult your friends, too.

Spend a few days listing as many solutions as you can think of for each problem. For instance, solutions to the problem of not getting ready for school on time in the mornings without a struggle might include such things as deciding what to wear and laying out clothes the night before, packing his backpack the night before, not watching television before school, and so on. If you can't think of any good solutions for some of the problems, put question marks by them.

Brainstorming Solutions

Next, sit down with your child and tell him that you have been lax about helping him in several areas. Admit that this has made things harder and less pleasant for both of you than necessary. Apologize for not having dedicated enough time to helping him in the past. Announce that you are now ready to eliminate the friction so he can be a happier kid. State that you know it's not good for him to have you "on his case." Share one of the problem areas, present the possible solutions you developed, solicit additional suggestions from him, and add any new possibilities that occur to you during the discussion.

Enlist your tween's help defining exactly what could be done differently to solve a problem. It may be helpful to go along with his proposed solutions even if you are skeptical that they will work. Not all of the problems can be fixed overnight. By taking his suggestions seriously, you can encourage him to engage in the problem-solving process.

For instance, if your child says he could get ready for school on time in the morning if you wouldn't keep reminding him to hurry up, you might try it for a few days. Perhaps his irritation about being pressured has caused him to drag his feet. It might be worth following his suggestions. If it doesn't work, you can follow up with the solutions you believe would work best.

Defining the Rules

The next step is to formulate some new rules. For getting ready for school on time, the rules might be:

1. You cannot pressure him.
2. He is to be ready on time.

Solicit your child's input to decide what the consequences will be for breaking each new rule. For instance, you might agree that if you pressure him to hurry, the consequences are having to apologize to him and put money in the family kitty, which will be spent on a family outing. If your tween isn't ready for school on time, the consequences might be an earlier bedtime on school nights.

Write up a contract for your tween to sign agreeing to abide by a specific list of rules or accept the consequences, which should also be spelled out. Tweens are impressed when treated like adults and are inclined to take contracts seriously. Parents feel better knowing that their child understands exactly what the rules are.

Understanding the Consequences

Consequences for breaking rules should be designed to help, teach, and solve problems rather than to punish. Punishment causes tweens to realize that they have done something wrong but doesn't help them know how to do things right. Too often they end up feeling badly about themselves, angry with their parents, and hopeless about being able to get along better.

Often the difference between a punishment and a consequence is subtle, having more to do with the presentation. You can threaten an earlier bedtime if your tween can't get ready for school on time in the mornings and then be angry when you follow through, snarling that because he "blew" it he has to go to bed early. Alternatively, you can say that he is such a vigorous, energetic, athletic child, he obviously requires more sleep than less active youngsters, and he also seems to benefit from a more structured morning schedule. Your tween might not be happy either way, but perhaps he will get the message that the problem isn't that he's bad but stems from a real need.

A punishment for not getting to bed on time could be being grounded. A consequence might be having to come home directly after school the next day and go to his room to rest without such distractions as computers, telephones, and TV.

As an adult, there will be times when he doesn't get enough sleep but has to put in a full day's work anyway. He needs to know the correct action to take: manage his work responsibilities as best he can, then come straight home and take it easy in hopes he can rest. Parents are often surprised to hear their tween propose consequences that are harsher than they would have dreamed of imposing. It's important to help your child understand that the goal is to find consequences that will teach him what he needs to know to eliminate the problem. Often the best way is to consider what the consequences and solutions would be if the same problem happened as an adult. The consequence of arriving late to work in the morning could be losing a job. The solution depends on what caused the late arrival: not being able to get out of bed, not being able to get organized to leave on time, not leaving soon enough to arrive on time, and so on.

Re-evaluating the Rules

Sometimes a tween doesn't think there should be any consequences for breaking a particular rule because he doesn't think it's necessary and doesn't want to abide by it. Amid the accusations of "That's not fair" and "You're just being mean," conscientious parents will pause to reconsider. At those times, it can be helpful to remember that your duties are to protect your child and to prepare him to become independent.

E ALERT!

Tweens often want parents to abide by certain rules and to suffer consequences for breaking them. A tween favorite is requiring parents to speak politely instead of yelling. A popular consequence is requiring offenders to apologize and pay a fine, with the proceeds designated for a family outing.

Ask yourself whether this rule is needed to keep him safe or to help him to function better as an adult. Having to come home at a particular time for dinner or to call if he's going to be late is important. Showing up late and not calling will definitely create problems when he has a family of his own. Telling your tween you want him to be considerate of you may not carry much weight. Help him understand that you are trying to prepare him to get along with a wife someday, and he may be more motivated to learn to comply with a rule he dislikes.

It is understandable that no matter what you say, your tween may be upset about a rule prohibiting chips and sodas before dinner and fail to see its value. If he plans to live in a messy house, you may not convince him that it's important for him to learn to return his dirty plates to the kitchen after snacking in the den. Nevertheless, as the adult charged with his care, you must set the rules you deem necessary rather than allowing tween logic to prevail. If your tween storms out of the room when you solicit his input regarding rules and consequences, you can either decide on your own what they will be and inform him of them via a written list, which includes a date that the new rules will take effect, or wait until he's calmer to continue the discussion. Either way, begin enforcing some of the rules as soon as possible. If he is too defiant and out-of-control to cooperate, see Chapter 19.

Improving Compliance

When parents set and enforce limits conscientiously, it's hard to predict in advance how a particular youngster will react. Most tweens respond much more positively than their parents imagined, and problems that have gone on for years vanish overnight. Some tweens follow the rules meticulously until the novelty wears off, then they lose motivation and their old habits resurface. Once again they forget to take off their muddy shoes before coming in the house, leave their assignments at school, and leave wet towels in a heap on the bathroom floor. In that case, parents must be careful to enforce consequences for each infraction of the rules, or they will have a difficult time maintaining discipline.

Let your child off the hook one time because he begs, pleads, argues, or whines, and you'll have to start setting limits from scratch. If you feel compelled to back down due to special circumstances, have your child concoct a plan to compensate for having shirked his duties. If you agree to let your child skip his turn washing dishes so he can play with a special friend, a proposal to wash dishes for the next two nights to make it up might be acceptable. Let him come up with a plan. If you agree and he doesn't follow through, be careful about allowing him to wiggle out of his responsibilities again. Rather than getting angry, matter-of-factly enforce consequences. Learning self-discipline takes time.

FACT

Some children know that if their parent adopts a certain tone of voice, they will in fact be held accountable and to protest is useless. At that point the angry protests fade. Contrary to what parents anticipate, most children quickly comply when parents consistently enforce consequences. Thereafter, resistance usually takes the form of some occasional small grumbles and halfhearted whines.

Set Clear Expectations

If your child breaks a rule and promises not break it again if you'll agree not to enforce a consequence, don't give in. When you tell a child, "This rule is important and you are supposed to follow it" and then tell her, "It's okay that you broke it this once," you send a confusing double message. It's like talking a police officer out of issuing a speeding ticket by promising to observe the speed limit in the future. Some citizens do keep such promises, but after learning that they may not be held accountable if they're caught, most speed even more.

If you decide the rules you have established are unreasonable or unfair, change them. Otherwise, enforce them. Whatever you do, don't continue to harp about rules your child disregards if you don't enforce them. The tween years are too short and important to spend in such ongoing misery. It's important that both of you enjoy these precious years to the fullest.

Teaching Money Management

One motivational tool that works wonders for some tweens is money. Although paying children to behave, study, make good grades, and do their chores is anathema to many parents, the possibility of riches gets the attention of some little capitalists better than all of the admonishments and punishments in the world. Needing to pay children reminds parents to reward good behavior, which helps them overcome the problem of noticing when their youngster does something wrong but overlooking positive accomplishments.

Besides being good medicine for behavior problems, providing tweens with some pocket money to call their own has some other benefits. Few schools teach money management. If you continue to hold on to the purse strings and buy all of your tween's toys and treats, you will get lots of practice establishing financial priorities, doing simple math, budgeting, saving, and saying "no" to frivolous requests while your tween gets lots of practice wheedling, whining, begging, and feeling deprived. By providing some discretionary income, your child can start learning the art of money management the way tweens learn best: by doing.

Not all parents are comfortable with this arrangement. Some believe that paying children to behave appropriately, care for their possessions, and participate in the upkeep of the house warps their values. Indeed, when asked to do something extra because a sibling is ill or a parent is in a rush, children who are accustomed to being reimbursed for services rendered are likely to ask, "How much are you going to pay me?" and decline if the fee isn't high enough. Paying tweens for pro-social behavior may in fact have its drawbacks.

QUESTION?

When my child has money, it burns a hole in his pocket. How can I teach him to save?
Help him learn by experience. Give him an allowance, open a bank account, and have him deposit a portion of the money each week for at least six months so he can save up for a big-ticket item.

A Word of Caution

If you do decide to provide monetary rewards for good behavior, specify your exact requirements in advance. If your youngster can earn money by cleaning her room, it will be important to decide exactly what constitutes clean and communicate your expectations clearly. Refrain from charging your child for misbehavior and chores that have been left undone, since a youngster with many behavior problems may end up owing money despite having faithfully made her bed and washed the dishes all week.

It is best not to attach strings to the money your tween earns, but you may need to retain veto power so you can nix plans to purchase a pet, an ATV, a BB gun, or some other item you strongly oppose. One popular strategy is to enable children to earn enough to cover some of the nonessential "extras" they very much want but that parents dislike buying, such as snacks at the movie theater, trading cards, or overpriced toys. Another is to insist that a portion go directly into the bank to be saved for a particular item. That way, tweens have the opportunity to make some real decisions and they learn to save, too.

If you also offer special money-making opportunities for completing above-and-beyond-the-call-of-family-duty chores, or if you advise her on ways to make extra money via lemonade stands, garage sales, dog-walking, and lawn-mowing services, your tween can learn about the joys of running a business, and really will have a chance to learn to budget and save.

Chapter 6

Communication Coups

Don't feel shut out because you can't get past the superficial comments and silliness to connect with your child on a deeper level. What seems inconsequential to you may matter lots to your tween. Don't try to crash through the heavy wall of silence, either. When your tween claims not to be thinking about anything at all, it's undoubtedly true!

The Silent Age

When had Maria stopped being such a chatterbox? Her father wasn't sure. Communicating with her had become difficult since the divorce. She was glad enough to see him for visits, seemed happy enough at his house, and wasn't in a hurry to leave when the visits ended, but her conversation was impersonal and when he telephoned she had nothing to say.

When something was bothering her, he had to learn about it from his ex-wife. Maria said everything was "fine" even when her teacher was replaced by a permanent substitute, said nothing about being tested for a possible learning disability, and only mentioned the death of her dog in passing. After one telephone conversation in which Maria spent five minutes retelling the story of a cartoon that had caught her interest, her mother said that Maria had come home an hour before crying because a neighborhood boy had punched her.

After Maria's father learned more about how tweens communicate, he wasn't sure how to proceed. He finally realized that her comments about seemingly irrelevant things while they were doing simple household chores together did reflect what was on her mind at the moment. As he responded to whatever she brought up instead of asking her about the things he considered important, she shared more.

Conversing with Tweens

It is important to continue talking to your tween about important issues even though he is silent, distracted, and preoccupied with people and events outside the family. Just don't expect him to respond with words—at least, not right away. Tweens often appear not to have heard, but they take in a lot unconsciously. They may respond a week or a month later as if you had just finished speaking a moment ago. In truth, it is hard to predict what your tween will hear and impossible to fathom how he will process what you say.

A common tween complaint is that parents or teachers yell at them too much. They are often very adamant on this point despite their inability to give examples. When pressed, they may bring up something hurtful that was said to them months or even years before, which you may not even remember. Even when your words and meaning don't register, your frustrated tone may get through loud and clear. Avoid using an impatient tone to try to cut through the dazed state that is a hallmark of the tween years. By trying to force your child to listen and pay attention, you may widen the very gap you are seeking to narrow. To facilitate communication, respond positively when your tween does speak by empathizing, sharing your own experiences, sympathizing, and simply listening.

The tendency of tweens not to share much makes it easy for parents to lose track of them in the shuffle of a busy family schedule, especially if more talkative, demanding siblings usurp the conversation. Set aside a few minutes each day to be alone with your tween. Spend the time talking a little and listening a lot.

Talking Through Toys

Even professional interrogators like police detectives and psychologists can't get unwilling tweens to open up and answer questions. After supplying their name and grade in school, they retreat into uncertain shrugs and sighs. Don't take it personally if you have difficulty getting your tween to relate ordinary events. When tweens aren't up for talking, they purse their lips and simply refuse.

Play therapy facilitates communication by enabling tweens to express themselves through puppets, dolls, and toy soldiers. In so doing, they act out the things that are bothering them with toys and games. Reading such nonverbal communication is difficult, however. You cannot be your child's therapist.

Talking to your tween while he engages in an activity can lessen his anxiety. That makes it easier for him to express his ideas, although you must expect his mind to wander. Similarly, letting your tween fidget during conversations discharges some of the tension and can help him think more clearly. Don't reprimand him if he likes to swing his legs or fiddle with a small toy during serious talks.

Doing versus Talking

Tweens love to play duets with their mother on the piano and enjoy the chance to play a game of catch with Dad. If you aren't inclined to do these things, your child will be happy to have you listen while he takes his piano lesson or have you cheer him from the sidelines during soccer games. But forget talking about it later. What is there to say besides "I'm starting a new song," "I scored a goal," "The piano teacher is mean," "Matthew pushed me."

To tweens, it is the doing that matters. If you ask your tween about his day and he relates something funny that somebody did during recess but fails to mention that he got into trouble for fighting on the playground, that he needs to take cupcakes to school tomorrow for the class party, or that he was informed that he's failing math, he's not being deceitful or purposely concealing information. Tweens, especially tween boys, don't much care to talk, but when they do, they share what is on their minds at the moment.

FACT

While teenagers often accuse their parents of "not caring" because they failed to ask about their day or broach an important subject, most tweens prefer to bring up issues themselves. Whether they feel cared about depends on whether their audience is attentive and accepting or distracted and critical.

Often tweens have nothing on their minds. Many parents have a hard time believing that, and their inability to get their child to open up makes them feel as if their child is pulling away or purposely being secretive. Doing things together is a great way to connect with your tween. Shared activities help tweens feel close even if they don't share many words.

Getting Tweens to Open Up

Figuring out how your tween is getting along can be difficult, since children at this stage dislike personal conversation. Questioning helps teenagers to feel that their parents care but may backfire for tweens, causing them to feel intruded upon. If something particularly wonderful or terrible happened during the day, it probably won't occur to your tween that your questions are a way to get her to share it. Try being more direct: "What was the best thing that happened to you at school today? What was the worst?"

ALERT!

Important information is likely to burst forth from your tween when you least expect it, which may be when you are otherwise occupied. Do your best to listen instead of postponing the conversation. Once the moment has passed, it is hard for tweens to recapture the emotions and find the right words.

Children in this age group aren't particularly self-reflective to begin with, so innocent parental questions of the how-are-you/how-was-your-day variety can be as difficult for tweens to respond to as the why-did-you/how-could-you-have/whatever-were-you-thinking barrages to which they are so often subjected. Of course, they quickly learn to go through the motions of a conversation by saying that they are "fine," school was "okay," and anything they were worried about turned out to be "no big deal." It's when parents try to have sit-down talks about something they consider truly important that problems arise.

Combine tweens' difficulty using words to express themselves with their propensity to become overwhelmed during emotional exchanges, and it isn't surprising that they work so hard to avoid personal discussions. If you insist that your tween respond verbally or demand reassurance that he has heard and understood, tensions may heat up and conversations bog down.

Formulating Questions

Questions that have a single right answer and can easily be answered with one or two words are called "closed questions" because they tend to discourage conversations and bring them to a close. Open-ended questions encourage conversation by inviting a more detailed response. Hence, they encourage uncommunicative youngsters to open up. **TABLE 6-1** provides some examples of closed, open-ended, and general questions.

Table 6-1

Closed questions elicit very brief answers	Open-ended questions elicit more complex answers	General questions elicit "non-answers"
"Did your science class start the unit on snakes?"	"What did you learn about snakes today in science?"	"What did you learn in school today?"
"What kind of cake was served at the party?"	"What did the kids do at the party?"	"How was the party?"
"What book did you choose for your oral book report?"	"What was the book about?"	"How did your oral book report go?"
"Did you have fun at recess?"	"What did the girls do during recess today?"	"How was school today?"

Most professionals urge parents to ask lots of open-ended questions to demonstrate interest and caring, and so they can keep up with the happenings in their children's life. While it is important to do what you can to keep the conversations going, you're not likely to reap the promised benefits. Open-ended questions are too difficult for tweens, so they often draw non-answers. For instance, when you ask the question every teacher in America urges parents to ask regularly, "What did you learn in school today?" you're likely to get the typical tween answer, "Nothing," or a shrug.

If you ask a general question and get no meaningful response, try being more specific by following up with either a closed question ("Did you have your spelling test?") or a very specific open-ended question ("Tell me what your class did in science today.").

Nevertheless, there are some good reasons to provide lots of openings for your tween to talk. Engaging your child in conversation will help her develop her verbal skills. By combining easy-to-answer closed questions with the more challenging open-ended questions, you can encourage your tween to share more without overwhelming her. It's good to keep asking, as long as you don't demand a response!

Positive Communication

Don't use negative words to describe your child! In the short run, it will hurt your relationship. In the long run, your child will absorb the negative self-images and may define himself accordingly, even if he tries not to by rebelling. William Carey, author of *Understanding Your Child's Temperament* (New York: Simon & Schuster, 1997), recommends some simple substitutions that can make a huge difference in how you perceive your youngster and how he perceives himself **(SEE TABLE 6-2)**.

Table 6-2	
Negative	**Positive**
Always into something	Curious
Bookworm	Enjoys literature
Can't keep his hands to himself	Physical
Clumsy	Not athletically inclined
Crybaby	Wears his heart on his sleeve
Explosive	Dramatic
Hyper	Energetic
Lazy	Low energy level
Manipulative	Passionate
Never does what he's told	Independent
Never thinks ahead	Spontaneous
Oppositional	Spirited
Overly sensitive	Perceptive
Rowdy	Enthusiastic
Spaced-out	Preoccupied
Stubborn	Determined
Timid	Cautious
Weird	Creative

The goal of remaining positive isn't to paint a smiley face on your child's character flaws, mask problems, or encourage him to feel good about his personal failings. It's a way to remember that some of the traits you both find difficult are assets and strengths if viewed from a slightly different perspective.

It is always easier to build on strengths than overcome weaknesses, so finding the positive serves a useful purpose. For instance, calling your child "manipulative" implies that he's out to get you and reminds you to stay on your guard to keep from being taken advantage of. Hence, if he wants something you are disinclined to give, your primary goal will be to protect yourself. Thinking of him as "passionate" may remind you that he suffers mightily when he cannot have the things he wants, becoming readily overwhelmed to the point that logic flies out the window and his emotionality drives him to desperate lengths. Viewed from that vantage point, it is easier to focus on your child's need for help containing himself when faced with the word *no*.

Similarly, calling a tween a "crybaby" shames him, which makes him feel even worse and gives him more to cry about. It puts you in a critical position, but what a crying baby needs most is comfort. By approaching your youngster as someone who "wears his heart on his sleeve," you affirm his sensitivity and may be able to look at his ensuing upset as something that makes life harder for him but also makes him special. Indeed, exquisite sensitivity is a prime characteristic of great artists, musicians, writers, actors, and creative geniuses even in technical fields.

Taboo Tween Topics

Tweens seem to be of the same mind when it comes to discussing unpleasant subjects: They'd rather not, thank you. If you must sit your child down for a discussion about a difficult subject, you will have to do most of the talking. The lack of feedback may leave you uncertain about what your child heard. It's fine to conclude with, "Now what did I just tell you?" and insist that she summarize what you said. Unfortunately, even if she can repeat your words, there's still no guarantee that your message actually got through. Such is the mystery of the tween mind.

Talking about Tragedies

In the wake of major tragedies such as school shootings and the terrorist attacks of September 11, many school administrators rush counselors into the classrooms so tweens can talk, share feelings, and process their emotions. This practice is of questionable value. When I asked tweens whether they felt upset about September 11, the unanimous reply among younger tweens was, "Uh, no—not really," while older tweens said, "Uh, I guess I should have been—but no, not really." When asked what their teachers and parents might have done to help them feel better about September 11, tweens' replies were immediate and emphatic: "Quit talking about it." "Don't discuss it." "Let us change the subject." "Don't keep making us think about it."

In fact, professionals took to the airwaves to urge parents to turn off the television news broadcasts and to talk about something other than the World Trade Center bombings when it became apparent that school-age children were being traumatized by so much unremitting focus on the crisis. Watching the same video footage of collapsing buildings over and over and listening to the same statements from eyewitnesses and reporters helps adults to process the distressing events but may prove more upsetting than helpful to tweens.

ALERT!

Rather than sending guidance counselors into intact classrooms to discuss upsetting events, it is better to make students' attendance optional and allow them to leave whenever they wish. That way, those who benefit from talking can receive crisis intervention services, and those who find the discussions overwhelming are protected.

Lots of tweens are upset about disasters that strike close to home and display stress reactions afterward. Often the somber tones of television news reporters and their parents' strained voices precipitate more distress than the events themselves. Explanations about exactly what happened are important but fail to address the real problem: the feeling that if parents are so worried, there must still be a threat. Soothing words have limited value as long as those around them continue to feel anxious.

When tragedy strikes, provide your child with a brief explanation of what happened using words he can understand. Tell him why you are upset but reassure him that life goes on and everything will eventually return to normal.

E ALERT!

If simple reassurance doesn't soothe your child's distress, provide toys so he can re-enact a traumatic event or art materials so he can paint or draw his feelings. Nonverbal methods can be more effective for helping tweens discharge tension, relieve anxiety, and regain their emotional equilibrium.

Do leave the door open for conversation by asking your tween if he has any questions and by telling him to let you know if he wants to talk. If he brings up the subject, talk as long as he needs to but minimize his exposure to other people's conversations.

Uncomfortable Subjects

When you bring up something that makes your tween uncomfortable, her ability to tune you out may strike you as nothing short of amazing. Ask your tween a difficult question and she's likely to go deaf, change the subject, space out, or clamp her jaw and refuse to speak. This is frustrating for parents under any circumstances, but it doesn't signal that your child is being purposely defiant. There are a number of reasons tweens remain silent:

- They can't articulate their thoughts and feelings.
- They go blank when an upsetting subject is raised or when they are put on the spot.
- They are afraid to say the wrong thing for fear of upsetting their parent.

Boys tend to be less aware of their feelings than girls, so they have an even harder time processing emotional issues and expressing themselves. Most tweens eventually discover the merits of saying whatever they think their parents want to hear, since it is often the fastest way to end a miserable conversation. Parents may feel better in the short run, but when tweens later renege on their promises to do things differently, parents end up feeling betrayed. Meanwhile, tweens can't even recall having made any promises.

> Tweens constantly complain that their parents don't listen to them. Parents complain that talking to their tween is like talking to a brick wall. Often the problem can be traced to parents' haste in demanding replies. Tweens need a lot of time to compose themselves, figure out what they want to say, and say it.

When you must confront your child or broach a difficult subject, the single best thing you can do is provide adequate time for a reply. Few parents wait long enough. Consider timing yourself after you pose a question and let a full sixty seconds elapse before asking your tween to respond. There's a good chance your tween's mind will carry him off to a safer place where difficult questions aren't asked and he won't remember what you asked. Repeat your question and wait another full minute. If your tween still doesn't reply, avoid filling in the blanks by answering your own questions and talking for him. Instead, tell your tween to give the matter some thought so that the two of you can discuss it later.

Holding Dinnertime Conversations

In many households dinnertime provides the best opportunity for family members to chat together. Because tweens are often immersed in their own thoughts and have difficulty expressing themselves, they tend to be out of the verbal loop, remaining silent as conversations swirl about them. When tweens do interject comments, their contributions can sound a bit strange, somewhat bizarre, or completely off the wall. Besides the fact that what they say is unrelated to the general topic being discussed, they often relay facts and information that they picked up in school, on television, or in the neighborhood, and that are so outlandish it is immediately obvious that they misunderstood or misheard something.

Older siblings love to one-up tweens by making fun of them. Parents are likely to adopt a gentler approach as they point out the flaws in logic and try to correct erroneous information, but the result can be to squelch conversation rather than enhance it. Although some tweens gratefully soak up whatever information their parent offers, the majority don't appreciate being contradicted and having their parents go into teaching mode every time they try to speak. Having parents continually focus on their mistakes erodes self-esteem, and sensitive children may feel hurt and embarrassed.

Possible Responses

What to say when your youngster suddenly announces that grass doesn't have to be watered because the moisture in the air is enough to keep it growing and green? Or when he states that Texas isn't part of the United States but a separate country? Or when he informs you that a friend's mother has subsisted on a diet of 100 percent candy since birth without ill effect?

Although the urge to set your tween straight when he has clearly misunderstood some bit of information is understandable, and although many parents seize such opportunities to deliver brief lessons, parental responses that are either critical or designed to instruct have the unfortunate side effect of discouraging communication. By finding ways to affirm your tween when he shares his thoughts and ideas, you encourage him to talk about whatever is on his mind and open the door to future conversations.

Both critical and controlling responses are designed to convince a child that he is wrong:

- "Where did you get such an idea? I hope your teacher isn't passing out that kind of misinformation. Probably you just heard wrong."
- "Texas is a state, not a country. You must not have been listening."
- "Use your head! Babies drink milk. They don't eat candy."

Responses designed to teach relegate the child to the role of a student.

- "Well, probably in the tropics people don't have to water the grass. Too bad the humidity is so low around here. I get tired of sprinkling the lawn."
- "Texas was under Mexico, then it was its own country, then the United States took it over, then it was part of the confederacy. It's existed under six flags, like the name of the amusement park, though I understand it's flying under the U.S. flag again."
- "I know some of those nutritional drinks that taste like milk shakes are supposed to have enough in them to keep people healthy."

Finding something to affirm in a child's statement encourages conversation:

- "Hmmm. I never heard that before. Probably lots of people water their lawns more than necessary."
- "Well, many people do say Texas seems more like a foreign land than part of the United States."
- "I know some poor kids live on a bowl of rice a day. A lot of them are malnourished, but some grow up healthy enough. Candy, huh?"

Keep the Conversation Going

Instead of leaping in to set your child straight, it can be more helpful simply to express interest in whatever information he has chosen to share. Communicate your own ideas without discounting his. Trying to prove him wrong may only cause him to defend his mistaken notions. At this developmental stage, tweens must learn from people besides their parents, so debunking what he tells you may do more to undermine your credibility than shore it up. Contradict your child's teachers and friends and discount what he learned as silly or flat-out wrong, and whether you deflate his ego and discourage future sharing, you may well diminish *yourself* in your child's eyes.

Tweens learn on the playground that insisting on having the last word is the power play of a bully. If you always respond like an all-knowing parent, you relegate your tween to the role of eternal child. Share your experiences or other knowledge that have led you to a different conclusion but refrain from insisting that you are right. In that way, you model how grownups disagree—at least, when they are behaving like adults.

After a straightforward discussion in which you share your views on the subject without discounting your tween's, there's a good chance he will proceed to try to straighten out whoever gave him the erroneous information by dropping those famous lines, "My dad said . . ." or "My mom said . . ." However, if he felt belittled and demeaned during his conversation with you, he's likely to try to restore his sense of dignity by adding, "But what does *he* know," or "But she always *thinks* she knows everything, and she doesn't!" Having the correct information about trivial things matters less than his willingness to continue to learn from you. Lots of other people will be more than anxious to leap forward to set him straight when he has his facts mixed up.

Certainly it is important to correct misinformation when you fear that your child might act on it to his detriment. For instance, if your son declares his intention not to wear his bicycle helmet anymore because he "heard" that wearing one is more dangerous than going without, he at least needs to be told that wearing a helmet is the law of the city or of your household. Still, you can protect your youngster's ego by expressing interest in learning more about this "fact." Ⓔ

Chapter 7

Quality Tween Time

If your family schedule is terribly hectic, you may feel lucky to be able to eat dinner together, so the idea of being able to spend more quality time with your tween seems like a pipe dream. Rest assured that it could be a reality. The key is to integrate your tween into daily household activities and make the time together pleasant.

Limiting Peer Contact

Mark was an easygoing child whose claim to fame was that he got along well with most everyone. He rarely squabbled with his siblings, was liked by his teachers, had lots of little girls chasing him around the schoolyard, and enjoyed skateboarding and playing foosball with friends at the recreation center. His grades were decent, and although he needed plenty of reminders about starting his homework, cleaning up his room, doing his chores, and getting ready for bed, his parents were able to keep him on track without much difficulty. If he did step out of line, the threat of losing a privilege or being grounded was usually enough for him to straighten up.

Mark's parents sometimes worried that between their own busy work schedules and the shadows cast by his successful older brother and difficult younger sister, Mark wasn't getting his fair share of attention. His brother was an academic superstar and award-winning gymnast who competed at various local and state meets; his sister's difficult behavior and learning problems usurped a lot of their time. However, Mark seemed happy enough and was more interested in being with his friends than with the family anyway.

FACT

Although young tweens enjoy playmates, most prefer to spend time with parents. The developmental process of the older tween years is to establish friends outside the family.

In seventh grade, Mark's personality changed. He would promise to do his chores and then not do them. He said he didn't have homework when he did, picked at his brother and sister, and argued with his parents about every little thing. Mark was constantly losing his telephone privileges and being grounded. Although he protested loudly that his parents had no right to keep him from his shows and friends, they couldn't help but notice the pattern. As long as Mark was serving a "no telephone/no going out" sentence, he studied, did his chores, built model airplanes, and became the cooperative, easygoing boy they had always known. As soon as his privileges were restored, his mood darkened and he began acting up again. It almost appeared as though Mark wanted them to ground him.

When they brought Mark in for counseling, they learned that when tweens need more separation from their peers, they often look to their parents to rein them back in. The counselor recommended they find a family activity or hobby, make better use of the little time they had together, and severely limit Mark's time with his friends outside of school. His parents followed the advice and were surprised that Mark actually seemed relieved.

Mark's mother had always wanted to learn Chinese cooking and decided to take it up and involve her son. He seemed uninterested at first, but the idea of learning to chop vegetables at lightning speed and make authentic Peking duck captured his fancy. A few weeks later he announced that he wanted to be a chef at a five-star restaurant when he grew up. Having him participate as an equal in planning and cooking dinners had more of an impact than they would have believed possible.

Growing Away

Most tweens appear to have little interest in spending much time with parents, siblings, and relatives. Despite complaints of being bored, they refrain from participating in routine family tasks such as cooking, cleaning, and yard work. They resist accompanying their parents on regular errands, too, preferring to hang around the house even if they have nothing in particular to do. Many older tweens don't want to go on family outings and vacations unless they can bring along a friend. Some act as though being seen with family members in public is too much of a humiliation to bear. Parents conclude the obvious: Their tween doesn't need or want to spend more time with the family. However, this conclusion is wrong. Few tweens get as much family time as they need and want.

Growing Up Too Fast

Some tweens actually set themselves up to be pulled back into the family when they sense they are growing up too fast. A tween may want more separation from peers because he is being bullied, feels pressured to do things he doesn't believe in or isn't ready for, or simply feels the need to spend more time at home.

FACT

Of almost 6,000 kids who responded to a ✎ *www.pbskids.org* survey, a third said they wished they could spend more time with their mom; 40 percent wished for more time with their dad.

But tweens can't readily admit that they want to spend less time with their friends and more time with their folks, as that is considered terribly "uncool." Instead they act out, knowing full well that their parents will proceed to ground them. Other children don't know why they manage to get themselves grounded two minutes after the restrictions they claim to despise have been lifted and their privileges restored. Still, the pattern is too obvious to miss. Their behavior is fine as long as they are restricted to the house and deteriorates when they are given more freedom.

The Need for Parents

Survey results consistently indicate that about one-third of tweens feel that they don't get to spend enough time with their parents. Many parents have difficulty believing this because their tween is so vocal about not wanting to spend time with the family. Often the problem is that when family members are together, tweens find themselves embroiled in endless sibling squabbles and the target of too much parental crankiness, so family togetherness is about as enticing as the plague.

Most comments directed toward tweens at the dinner table are designed to get them to sit up straight, chew with their mouths closed, and eat their peas. Parents are so busy and stressed that playing, sharing stories, and joking with tweens have all but vanished.

The Family That Plays Together

You will probably have an easy time remaining connected to your youngster if you genuinely enjoy the video games, skateboarding, carnivals, shopping malls, arcades, and movies that are the lifeblood of this age group. If you're willing to serve as cub scout leader, coach T-ball, or sponsor a club at your tween's school, you will have a positive mutual involvement that can help keep your relationship strong. Carving out time for sit-down parent/tween conversations may not hold much interest for your child, but ask him to start a fire in the fireplace or make popcorn in preparation for a marathon game of Old Maid or Monopoly. That's tween heaven!

QUESTION?

I try to talk to my tween, but he never has anything to say. We're drifting apart. What should I do?
To strengthen your relationship, spend less time conversing and more time on joint activities. That can be anything from a game of Crazy Eights to a drive to the edge of town to see the stars.

See if you can involve your tween in your work by having him help out at your place of business or have him participate in your hobby. Even if he accompanies you to the spa but you don't work out together, you will continue to hold a central place in his life if he feels that it is a shared experience. Riding to the spa with the radio blaring and sending him to the pool to kill time until you're finished exercising doesn't count as togetherness! Try to talk in the car going and coming. Join him in the pool, if only briefly. Change and shower at the same time. Empty your gym bags into the laundry once you're back at home together. In other words, actively look for things you can do together.

If you and your child have no common interests, this is a good time to search for a new hobby, activity, or pastime that you both enjoy. For instance, if you are both music fans, perhaps you can browse the music section of department stores together and learn to make your own music CDs even though you like jazz and your child likes hip-hop. If you've always dreamed of visiting Europe, pick up travel magazines at the library or brochures at a travel agency, and invite your tween to fantasize along with you. When planting a garden, solicit your tween's input about what to grow, have him help shop for the seeds, and make decisions together about what to plant where. If you've wanted to build a real car from a kit, collect information about automobile kits, share it with your tween, and discuss the pros and cons of the various brands, even if you never do make the investment of money and time to actually build one.

Quantity versus Quality

It's impossible to have quality time without a sufficient quantity for your child to feel that you are truly present in her life. Since most parents only talk to their tweens fifteen minutes a day, you can double your contact just by carving out fifteen minutes more to spend together each day. Turn off the TV and take a fifteen-minute walk or short bicycle ride together. Drop into your tween's bedroom and spend fifteen minutes chatting or simply hanging out before she goes to sleep at night. If you're out of town, call home and talk to your tween on the telephone for fifteen minutes. Vow that you will not criticize, admonish, reprimand, or even ask questions during these special conversations. Restrict yourself to listening attentively.

Only give advice when your child asks for it or when you get her permission first. To do that, specifically ask if your child would like some advice and wait until she gives an affirmative reply before plunging ahead. If you feel obliged to pass on some parental wisdom, share stories about how you and other people you know dealt with similar issues during their childhoods. Remember to provide time for your child to respond, enduring long silences if necessary. Tweens take longer to formulate their thoughts and to find the words to articulate their ideas than adults. Whenever possible, let your tween be the one to end the conversation.

Doing Chores Together

For your tween to want to spend time with the family, you must make a special effort to remain positive and find ways to sprinkle some fun into the daily mix of household chores, yard work, and errands. Otherwise, your tween probably won't find the time spent with you and other family members particularly pleasant and will avoid it.

ESSENTIAL

Tweens will gladly participate in activities they don't particularly care for because they involve pleasant one-on-one time with a parent. A child who has no interest in cars may enjoy helping Dad change oil because Dad is relaxed and in a good mood. That makes hanging out together fun.

If you're trying to get the housework over and done with ASAP, your tween's presence may be more of an irritant and distraction than a help. Slow down and enjoy the process so that your child can participate too; soon, your tween will know the procedures well enough to provide some real help. Part of the reason tweens resist helping with chores is because they dislike being rushed and ordered about. Take turns cooking dinner, and when it's your tween's turn, make suggestions but let her be fully in charge. She can be responsible for planning the menu and making a shopping list. When it's time to cook, ask what you can do to help. If she can't think of anything, offer to set the table. And don't forget to compliment the chef! A child who can do fourth-grade math should be able to help you balance the checkbook. When washing the car, begin by putting on your swimsuits. When shoveling snow, take time out to make snowangels and build a snowman. During the holidays, let your child help decide what gifts to get for whom and handle some of the other tasks that leave you feeling overburdened. Too often children are filled with holiday excitement but relegated to the sidelines with no way to participate. Let her help select the greeting cards, address the envelopes, and write the messages.

Running Errands Together

If your tween wants to stay at home and complains when forced to go on an errand with you, see what happens if you leave her siblings behind. There's a good chance she'll be much more amenable to a trip to the grocery store or bank if she gets to have you all to herself.

A Time to Chat

Turn the radio off when you are in the car so you can chat en route to school, the grocery store—wherever. Rather than asking questions to try to get your silent tween to talk to you, share what's going on at your work, relate something you read in the paper that interested you, mention that you need to get the refrigerator fixed, discuss your plans to mow the lawn this weekend. In short, talk about anything!

Don't underestimate how important it is for your tween to hear you relate the trivia of your life. As you remind yourself to pick up the special ingredient you need to make spaghetti, your tween learns that spaghetti contains that ingredient. As you debate whether to make a pizza from scratch, pick up a ready-made one in the freezer section of the grocery store, or stop by a fast-food restaurant to buy one, she learns about the tradeoffs of cost and convenience. As you ponder aloud whether to try to get someone out to repair the refrigerator or break down and buy a new one, she learns what factors to consider in making this kind of decision. By letting your child hear what you think about and how you make decisions, you are preparing her to be an adult.

A Helping Hand

Insist that your tween accompany you on errands, and make it a habit to involve her fully. Consult her about what to fix for dinner and have her help you plan menus when you shop for groceries. At the gas station let her pump gas while you clean the windshield or vice versa, and let her pay for the gas. At the bank, have her fill out the deposit or withdrawal slip before you sign it. Have her tell the postal clerk how many stamps you need and in what denominations. At the dry cleaner, have her announce whether starch is needed, give her name and phone number, and write the check so all you have to do is sign it.

Never criticize your tween in public. If she makes a mistake, don't jump in and make a correction. Say to your daughter, "Excuse me, but I thought we decided to get six bagels and a dozen croissants, not a dozen bagels and six croissants." Then let your daughter straighten it out with the clerk.

Family Meetings

If you can't get enough control of your family's schedule so that everyone can sit down together for dinner, it's a good idea to schedule a weekly family meeting. The meeting can be as short as twenty minutes but shouldn't run over an hour. Create an agenda by posting a sheet on the refrigerator so anyone can note a topic to discuss. A parent should serve as the leader at the outset; then children can take turns when they understand the process. With help, even young children can have turns being in charge.

Appoint someone who is old enough to write to take the minutes by recording any decisions that are made. Try to get everyone to give an opinion on each subject. Since younger children are so easily swayed by older family members, make it a policy to have the youngest member of the household give his opinion first on any issue.

Possible Agendas

Family meetings can be used to plan family vacations, divvy up chores, and solve problems that have cropped up during the week. Should your six-year-old be allowed to ride her bike in the street? Should your teenager go out for football even though his grades are poor? What can be done to help your tween who is being bullied on the playground? Should the family go to the zoo or the park this weekend?

Even three-year-olds can make amazingly astute comments on these issues. Parents will need to make the final decision regarding many issues, but as everyone provides input, it helps the family pull together.

Latchkey Kids

If your tween is like most, coming home to an empty house probably feels very bad to her. Most youngsters spend their home-alone time feeling lost; many are lonely and some are frankly frightened. Small difficulties can escalate into crises if your child panics or makes a poor decision.

A tween may believe she should be grown up enough not to need someone to look after her. She may put on quite a display of bravado, but that doesn't mean she necessarily feels secure staying by herself.

Many tweens lack the maturity to handle time alone. They haven't been sufficiently involved in the daily operations of the household to know how to exercise good judgment when problems arise.

If you are uneasy about leaving your child alone but can't take her with you, make arrangements for her to spend the time at a friend's or a relative's house. Otherwise, hire a sitter. However, your tween may feel awkward about having a baby-sitter. Employing a boy sitter for a boy and a girl sitter for a girl may help.

If you must leave your child home for extended periods, call to check on her frequently and invite her to call as often as she needs to. Even if she doesn't call often, just knowing that she can is likely to be very reassuring.

Balancing Friends and Family

At times your tween will prefer to play with or talk to friends rather than spend time with you, just as you'll want to spend time with your friends instead of with your child now and again. And don't underestimate the value of extended family members for your tween. Whatever differences you have with your own parents, siblings, and in-laws, encourage your tween to develop a relationship with them. There's no substitute for the sense of connectedness that comes with being part of a multigenerational family.

FACT

Fifty years ago, children averaged three to four hours per day interacting with parents or extended family members. Today's children only average about fifteen minutes, and "twelve of those are in a setting of critique, instruction, or criticism," according to Josh McDowell, author of *How to Help your Child Say "No" to Sexual Pressure*.

Remember: If you can relax and truly enjoy your child as much as her friends and other family members do, she won't seek them out to flee the unhappiness at home, and you won't feel so much need for a break from her. The goal should be for all of the time you spend with your tween to be high quality. Believe it or not, it's possible. Ⓔ

Chapter 8

Siblings and Spats

Siblings provide a set of interpersonal experiences that is impossible for your tween to come by any other way. Friends may react to conflicts by staying away, but siblings are there for the long haul, more constant than any friend. They provide powerful lessons about getting along with others.

Siblings at Odds

Eva and Emma Compton looked so much alike it was hard to tell their baby pictures apart, but that was where their similarities ended. They had little in common, and the competition and discord between the girls was constant and intense. They were ever watchful of who got the biggest piece of cake, the smallest helping of salad, and the more expensive presents. They bickered over issues and decisions large and small, like whose turn it was to do the dishes or sit in the front seat of the car. Occasionally, one would accuse the other of cruelty, but the lack of concrete evidence led their parents to suspect there was more exaggeration than truth to such tales.

In an effort to minimize their sibling rivalry and stave off accusations of favoritism, the Comptons were careful not to compare them and worked overtime to treat them alike. The spats were tedious, and it would have been nice to be able to make it through a meal or an errand without listening to them argue. However, when no other playmates were available, the girls sometimes played together quite nicely. Overall, their behavior struck their parents as pretty typical, given that their adult friends recounted similar problems with sibling rivalry. They all imagined that down the road, their children would stop competing and become real friends.

ESSENTIAL

You can't make your children like one another, but if you avoid the words and deeds that discourage them from getting along and actively teach them how to resolve their squabbles and spats, you can help to make family life a lot more pleasant for everyone.

Tensions Between Siblings

Although some tweens are very loving toward one or more of their siblings, youngsters growing up in intact families are notorious for considering their brothers and sisters sufficiently "bad" that they can in good conscience treat them with a decided lack of courtesy or even with cruelty. If you insist that your tween stop the maltreatment, she may apply her creativity to continuing the torment in secret.

Nevertheless, only a very unusual tween will fail to leap to a sibling's defense if someone outside of the family is even mildly unkind to her victim. Such incongruities are beyond tweens' ability to explain and defy adult logic. Does your tween's sudden gesture of friendship mean she loves her siblings deep down? Doesn't the fact that she often plays nicely with her brother and sister suggest she likes them? Ask, and you're likely to be disappointed with her answer.

The black-and-white, all-or-nothing thinking that is typical of this age group makes it hard for tweens to recognize that it is possible to like someone "sometimes." They live so much in the present that the idea of loving someone who is at this moment making them mad is alien. Pressure your tween to admit that she loves one of her siblings, and she'll probably grudgingly agree that "he's okay, I guess." It may take several years for her to arrive at a verdict she can truly believe in. Until then, the love-but-mostly-hate relationship is apt to continue. The exception is when a serious, enduring threat to family unity appears. In the face of death, divorce, or emotionally absent parents, a tween is likely to form strong alliances with whoever is left, even if that someone is a sibling. Otherwise, you will probably need to take concrete steps to help your children develop positive relationships.

Sibling Bonds

Most American parents consider sibling discord a fact of life. They don't realize that the norm in days gone by was for brothers and sisters not only to love one another, but also to like each other. This remains true in most cultures of the world today. Except for a few notable Cain-and-Abel exceptions, historically siblings got along well and actively protected and nurtured one another. Latin American siblings still prefer one another's company to that of other playmates, can't imagine that any child would feel differently, and pity children growing up without lots of siblings.

The cultural differences may be due to the intense bonds that develop among siblings in countries where children are actively involved in caring for a new baby. American parents usually consider a new baby their sole responsibility and feel guilty if they must ask a sibling to help. The lack of contact may preclude the development of the strong bonds that emerge between an infant and its caretakers. When American parents do turn to a sibling for assistance with a newborn, they are likely to turn to the eldest, which may be why the oldest and youngest child tend to get along well, while the middle child is odd-man out.

ALERT!

By having your tween assume a lot of responsibility for a new baby's care, you may help to forge a strong, enduring attachment. When your tween must help a sibling to whom he doesn't feel bonded, he may feel resentful. You will have to work harder to help them reconcile their differences and comprehend the importance of family loyalty.

In Latin America, each child customarily bears the primary responsibility for helping with the next younger sibling, although everyone is expected to help out. Consequently, sibling conflict is virtually unheard of and sibling bonds are intense and enduring.

The Roots of Sibling Conflict

It's not surprising that when two siblings who aren't firmly bonded to each other live under the same roof, they have so much trouble getting along. To help parents comprehend what toddlers experience with the arrival of a new brother or sister, Adele Faber and Elaine Mazlish, authors of *Siblings Without Rivalry,* ask women to imagine how they would feel were their spouse to announce, "Honey, I love you so much, and you're so wonderful that I've decided to have another wife just like you."

Then they are asked to consider how they would react if friends and relatives fussed over the newcomer before turning to the first wife and asking, "How do you like the new wife?" Readers are further asked to think about how the first wife would feel if the husband gave the new woman some of his first wife's old clothes, pointing out that since she'd gained weight, they were no longer of any use to her. What if the husband responded to the newcomer's request to use some of the first wife's personal possessions by urging the first wife to "be nice and share"? It is certainly understandable that older children feel jealous of a new sibling!

The Seeds of Discord

It is understandable, too, that parents are especially nervous about the possibility that a toddler who looms over a tiny newborn like a clumsy giant will accidentally hurt the baby. Parents tend to be vigilant, rushing in to protect the little one at the first hint of conflict. This, of course, makes the toddler angry and more anxious to oust the rival who usurps so much parental attention. Parents find themselves having to step in more often to protect the little one. When it becomes obvious a couple of years later that the baby is purposely antagonizing its older sibling, parents chastise the baby. At long last the older sibling sees hope of vindication and begins pointing out each of his sibling's crimes in hopes of besting the little one who has made life such a misery for so long. Once these dynamics are established, they tend to take on a life of their own.

Playing Favorites

It is rare for thinking parents to compare their children, since most realize that this can only breed discord and intensify jealousy. "Why can't you get good grades/cooperate/get along/behave like your brother/sister?" are the kinds of statements that serve to erode sibling relationships, which are often tenuous at best. Tweens who come out worse in the comparison feel compelled to redeem themselves in their parents' eyes to attain the golden position of favorite child. Since they don't know how to outdo their rival by getting similarly good grades and behaving differently, they try the shortcut. They set out to prove that their sibling is not so wonderful as parents think. The way to do that, of course, is to watch for every conceivable error and omission and highlight it.

A sibling problem is usually a parent problem in disguise. The proof lies in the fact that most children can enjoy one another's company and play together quite nicely when their parents are gone. They don't kill or maim one another when they do squabble, and the occasional injuries are typically the results of accidents. When parents are present, however, fights can turn vicious.

Parents as Mediators

Blatantly favoring one child over another harms the self-esteem of the child who comes out on the bottom, even as it harms the preferred child by engendering feelings of guilt. Most parents rightly assume that it is wrong to play favorites. Unfortunately, many take pains to reassure all of their children of their love by bending over backward to treat all of their children the same, which escalates competition rather than lessening it.

> Unfortunately, the strategy of trying to treat all of the children alike is not only doomed to fail, it is virtually guaranteed to increase sibling discord. Children are individuals and need to be treated as such.

Competitive children argue long and hard to be first or receive the choicest morsel of whatever goody is in dispute. Many parents try to settle the issue by having their children take turns on a rotating basis. For instance, if wanting to cut the pie is the subject of contention, parents try to keep track of who got to cut it last time so that someone else can have a turn. If the children dislike having to go to bed and claim that it is unfair to have to go to bed first, some parents set the same bedtime for everyone. Others set bedtimes according to the children's ages so that when their birthday arrives they get the same privilege. When one child is having a birthday party, some parents make sure the siblings each have a present to open and allow them each to invite a friend to minimize jealousy. Some parents go so far as to count the number of holiday presents they bestow to make sure each child receives exactly the same number, or they divvy up the dollars they spend on each child into equal portions. When parents deny their children's differences, children fight harder to assert them.

Equal Treatment

The problem with trying to treat brothers and sisters alike is that they have different needs and wants. To insist they go to bed at the same time despite the fact that they require different amounts of sleep denies their individuality. If an older child happens to need less sleep than a younger one, it makes sense to allow the older child to stay up later. To insist that everyone must go on a diet because one child is overweight denies their differing needs. To apply a set of arbitrary rules to everyone makes the rules more important than the children. The result is that children fight even harder to get parents to recognize their individual needs.

The Favored Child

Despite parents' heroic attempts to avoid playing favorites by treating their children alike, siblings in most families know exactly which child is each parent's favorite. If four siblings are asked in a family therapy session which of them Mom likes best, Mom usually looks shocked and says that she feels the same toward all of them. Meanwhile, three youngsters immediately point to the fourth child, who calmly raises his hand to signal that he is the favorite. It occasionally happens that a group of siblings is uncertain which of them is favored or is quite sure that they are equally cherished, but this is exceedingly rare.

FACT

Favoring a child means liking one child more than another. Playing favorites means depriving one youngster at the expense of another or bestowing special privileges on the favorite child. Having a favorite child is normal and impossible for parents to hide. Playing favorites is hurtful.

Siblings can't help but notice Dad's lingering smile when the favored child is talking. They hear the special lilt in Mom's voice when the favored child tells a joke. Even if the punishments are the same for breaking particular household rules, children see that their parent quickly recovers from being angry with the favorite. They hear the extra sharpness in their parent's tone when a sibling is being chastised. The truth is, parents may not love one child more than another, they may make heroic efforts not to favor one youngster over the other, but it is rare for them to feel equally close to them all. Each child has a different personality, so it is natural that a parent will be more compatible with one than with another. Often the favorite is the one who has a similar personality type, since people who are alike in fundamental ways have an easier time understanding each other and can more readily relate to each other.

Confronting Sibling Issues

Honesty can sometimes do a lot to relieve tensions and can lead to more in-depth discussions: "I do feel closer to your brother. I think we have similar personalities. Often you're a mystery to me, and I can't understand why you do certain things and don't know how to meet your needs. But this bothers me terribly, because I do love you very, very much. I wish I could understand you better. It might help if you could talk to me more."

E ALERT!

The route to treating children with fairness is not having the same rules and giving the same privileges, presents, and praise to each. Fairness means—or should mean—making thoughtful decisions about each child's needs.

Ending Squabbles

A younger sibling is screaming that she wants to go into your tween's bedroom. It is easy to accuse your tween of being selfish when he can't explain his need for privacy. Trust that his need to relax and reflect while engaging in some quiet activity is equally pressing. Teach him how to set gentle but firm limits with intruders—including with you.

The fastest way to end sibling conflict is to stay out of children's arguments and refuse to take sides. For many families this is only step one, however. If you are present when your children bicker, you may be forced to get involved, either because you can't bear to listen to them anymore or because they escalate until it becomes obvious that someone really might get hurt. In that case, you need to proceed to step two: separating them until they can cool down and figure out how to get along. Like conquering any other problem, tackling sibling conflicts takes quite a bit of time and energy at the outset. Here is what you need to do:

- Teach your child that it always takes two to argue but only one to stop an argument.
- Forbid hitting and fighting.
- Don't try to sort out who-did-what-to-whom, who started it, or who had it first.
- Don't take the side of the child who owns the toy that was taken or the child whose space was violated.
- Help each child to verbalize what he is angry about.
- Help each child to verbalize what he is *really* angry about if you think other problems are driving the conflict.
- Suggest solutions if you have any, but let the children decide how to proceed.
- Separate combatants by assigning a time-out until they can come up with a proposal they both can agree to.
- If they prefer to let the matter drop, insist they take responsibility for their part in the conflict and apologize, if appropriate.
- Express pride in their ability to work out their differences.

You can't make your children like one another, but by avoiding the words and deeds that discourage them from getting along, and by teaching them how to resolve their squabbles and spats, you can help to make family life a lot more pleasant for everyone.

There is a difference between sharing your impressions and giving your opinions about how to solve sibling disputes versus imposing settlements and solutions. Do express concern if one child always seems to defer to another. Rather than taking his side, teach him to be assertive so he can hold his own, not only with his sibling but with other children.

Express your concern to the child who always seems to win every battle by hook or by crook. Help him understand that giving in and compromising are the true marks of a winner when he's playing on a team—and a family is a team.

There is no guarantee that your kids will suddenly become great friends or like one another as adults, but siblings who enjoy one another reap some special rewards. Although their memories and impressions of their childhoods will necessarily differ, no one else can come so close to understanding what it was like way back when. By virtue of having shared parents and so many formative experiences, brothers and sisters help one another remain connected to their pasts. That, in turn, connects children to themselves.

Teaching Family Values

An important family value is helping and supporting one another even when things get tough. Learning to put other people's needs first sometimes is part of growing up and becoming an adult. As your tween matures, you need to teach her that pulling together as a family is important. This lesson will serve her when she has a family of her own one day.

Sacrificing for a Sibling

To pretend that it is in everyone's best interest to follow a rule developed for one child is unfair. Even if the goal is to minimize sibling discord, engaging in this kind of deception is wrong and usually backfires. Accordingly, don't pretend that canceling the family vacation is best for everyone when the truth is that you are canceling it so that one youngster can attend summer school, participate in a dance camp, or receive ongoing medical treatment.

Similarly, if one of your children needs to lose weight, explain to everyone that you must prepare low-fat meals for his protection and aren't going to create separate menus. State that you will no longer buy sodas and candy bars because his needs must come first right now. Don't pretend that they could all stand to lose some weight if that is not the real issue.

If you want to save money for one child's college education, modeling lessons, or ski equipment, tell the truth: Everyone must sacrifice a summer vacation to Disneyland because you have decided that one child's needs must take precedence right now.

Be Honest

By telling your children that everyone must pull together to help a sibling, you teach an important value: Family members must make sacrifices to help one another. Siblings may resent having to forgo certain pleasures for the sake of one child, but they will probably figure out what is going on even if you try to deceive them. You can help them feel better by acknowledging their sacrifices and letting them know that you are proud of them and appreciate that they are helping out—willingly or not. Doing so reassures youngsters that if they have a special problem, you will mobilize the family to unite on their behalf, too. Ⓔ

Chapter 9

School Daze

Outside of the family, school is the biggest influence in your tween's life. Not all children are academically inclined or do well with the teaching methods used in most schools. You need to be proactive in working with teachers and administrators to be sure that your child's educational needs are met.

Teacher Troubles

Portia had always been enthusiastic about school, but in third grade her attitude changed. She dragged her feet on school mornings, often complained of stomachaches, and wouldn't do her homework. After her teacher noted on Portia's first report card that she needed to improve in a number of areas, her parents sat her down for yet another talk. "What do you need to do to bring up your grades?" they asked. Tears filled Portia's eyes as she replied, "Lose weight." Her mystified parents scheduled a conference with her teacher, Mrs. Jenkins.

In light of Portia's comment, her parents were surprised to see that Mrs. Jenkins was extremely obese. As she shared her observations about Portia, it became evident that Mrs. Jenkins was not fond of their daughter. She stated that Portia turned in mediocre work and put little effort into her studies. When her mother asked about Portia's strengths, the teacher replied that Portia was probably working up to her potential. Her parents were alarmed by that comment. Why would the teacher think Portia was only capable of doing mediocre work when she had been a top student in first and second grades?

Investigating Further

That evening, they asked Portia's older brother why he thought Portia was having trouble in Mrs. Jenkins's class. His reply took them aback. "Mrs. Jenkins only likes the boys and the thin girls," he said. "She's kind of hard on the fat ones." Portia's parents took turns observing in school for a few days. They didn't hear Mrs. Jenkins make any comments about weight, but it was obvious that she had favorites, and none of them were the heavyset girls who sat at the back of the room. She didn't call on them even if they raised their hands, which they rarely did.

During a second parent/teacher conference, Portia's parents shared their belief that Portia might be more enthusiastic about school if Mrs. Jenkins could give her some encouragement. The teacher responded that there was nothing she could do with a student who lacked motivation. They asked what Mrs. Jenkins would suggest that they do, and she said she would think about it and let them know. When Portia returned from school the next day, she reported that Mrs. Jenkins had accused her of whining to her parents.

Even if you strongly disagree with the teacher's policies and procedures, you must help your tween make the best of the situation or assert himself appropriately. That way, if he finds himself in an unpleasant college classroom or work environment, he will be able to do the same.

Since the school wouldn't change Portia's classroom, her parents joined the PTA and attended school board meetings in hopes of impacting the district's employee hiring and retention practices. In the meantime, they took Portia to a counselor. It quickly became clear that Portia had reacted to the problematic relationship with her teacher by losing confidence and giving up. After a few conversations, Portia was able to understand that teachers are people, too. Although her current teacher might not recognize her capabilities, that didn't mean Portia was less of a student than in years past. She was able to see that paying attention in class was important even if she was never called on. Doing the assignments was important so she could learn the material. If she didn't like Mrs. Jenkins, she must be sure to do her best so she could pass to fourth grade. Otherwise, she might have to spend another year in Mrs. Jenkins's class.

To help keep sight of that goal, Portia would put a calendar in her notebook so she could mark off the days. Each day she would grade herself on how hard she had worked, how much she had learned, and note what she should do to improve. When she felt hurt about not being called on and being ignored, she would make a list of all of the people who cared about her. Once the problems had been openly discussed and a plan was in place, Portia felt much better. She was subsequently able to handle the situation with more maturity than her parents would have thought possible.

Life Lessons

It is understandable that you would be upset if your tween's teacher is critical, harsh, disorganized, can't control a classroom, doesn't give clear instructions, or expects too much or too little. When you believe that a teacher is treating your tween unfairly, your protective instincts are likely to switch into high gear, impelling you to dive in to rescue your child. Nevertheless, difficulties offer important opportunities for growth.

ALERT!

Your youngster will encounter some unpleasant people in positions of authority and many frustrating situations during the course of her life. Learning to cope during childhood is as good a time as any. In fact, childhood is the best time, because you are present to provide guidance, advice, and support.

When you believe something is wrong at your child's school, you should certainly advocate for change. For a classroom problem, the first step is to meet with the teacher. Then you can move up the hierarchy, discussing the problem with the school counselor, talking to the principal, meeting with district-level administrators, and attending school board meetings. Join the PTA and consider running for the school board. In the meantime, help your child cope with unpleasant realities. There's much truth to the saying that what doesn't kill us makes us stronger. That truism applies to tweens, too.

Self-Destructive Students

Young tween students tend to assess their capabilities and judge success based on the reactions of their parents and teachers. They commonly respond to teacher criticism by losing confidence, and they are prone to discouragement when teacher approval of their efforts is not forthcoming. Older tweens often respond with anger. They retaliate against a teacher they perceive as critical by refusing to work in his class or by disrupting it. In so doing, they undermine their own academic progress and that of their classmates and may further alienate the teacher in the process. You must warn your tween that such responses are self-destructive and make difficult situations worse rather than better.

Handling School Conferences

If your child is having problems at school, step one is to set up a parent-teacher conference. Ideally, school conferences are a chance for parents and teachers to share information and develop plans for solving a student's problems. It's a good idea to have your child attend all or part of the meeting, too.

FACT

Behavior problems often stem from students being given work that is so difficult they give up or so easy that it fails to challenge them. They entertain themselves by making mischief in the classroom. Consult with the teacher about ways to ensure that the workload is appropriate for your child.

If you believe your child's teachers are assigning work that is too hard or have expectations that are overly challenging, plan to discuss ways he can get extra help or be given a more manageable workload so he can keep up. Similarly, if you believe the schoolwork is too easy and the expectations are too low, see if the teachers can provide more challenging work or make enrichment activities available.

Conference Planning

Advance planning helps ensure school conferences are as productive as possible. Too often, parents hear a list of problems and complaints, and although they leave with a clearer sense of what is wrong, they don't know what to do to help make things better. Since teachers are so busy, school conferences are necessarily short. Therefore, how productive they are depends on your ability to make good use of your allotted time. Prepare a written agenda in advance and review it carefully to be sure that each item is an educational issue. Arrive early so that you have adequate time to park and find the room where the meeting is being held. Being ten minutes late may mean that half the time has been used up before the conference has even begun. When introducing yourself, simply say your name and relationship (mother, guardian, stepfather).

Nervous parents often have difficulty getting down to business, so by the time the initial pleasantries are finished and they feel at ease, there is little time left to discuss their child's educational needs. Remain on track throughout the meeting. Tangents are great tension relievers, but everyone is likely to end up frustrated with the lack of accomplishment unless you remain focused. While it is important to let the teachers know about any special problems or sources of stress that your child is coping with, refrain from asking for advice about child-rearing issues. Teachers are not parenting experts. It is fine to solicit recommendations about where to go to get help for personal and family problems, but don't expect your child's teachers to counsel you.

Productive conferences don't dwell on a student's problems; most of the time should be spent formulating solutions and deciding who will be responsible for implementing them. However, sometimes educators emphasize problems in hopes of convincing parents to take a particular action, such as allowing their child to receive special education services or attend counseling. At other times, the child's problems remain the focus of discussion because no one can quite pinpoint them or knows what to do to help. In that case, an educational evaluation may be needed. Alternatively, it may be necessary to schedule a second conference after everyone has had time to think about ways to address the problems.

Productive Conferences

Before attending a school conference, create an agenda (see the following form). Jot down questions that you want to ask, list any unmet educational needs that you think should be addressed, and note your ideas for improving your child's education. Try to think about the kinds of classroom activities and assignments that have been successful at motivating him and helping him learn in the past.

Take your agenda, extra paper, and a pen to the conference so you can take notes. It is normal to be nervous during a school conference, and that can make it hard to remember later what was said. Record all of the recommendations as well as any decisions that are made.

School Conference Agenda

Information to share: _____
_____
_____
_____

Issue #1: _____
_____
_____

Solutions: (to do at school) _____
_____
_____

(to do at home) _____
_____
_____

Issue #2: _____
_____
_____

Solutions: (to do at school) _____
_____
_____

(to do at home) _____
_____
_____

My child's special strengths: _____
_____
_____
_____

Notes: _____
_____
_____
_____
_____

When it is your turn to speak, list your questions and share your ideas about how to make school a richer, more beneficial educational experience for your child. Share something that your child has liked or appreciated, such as a classroom activity, an assignment, or attribute of the teacher. Positive feedback strengthens the student-teacher relationship while providing important information about the kind of learning strategies that work well for your child. It is easy for teachers to focus on the deficits and difficulties of a problem student, but successful teaching requires building on the student's strengths. Most of the forms schools use for detailing individual educational plans have a space to list the student's assets and strengths, but completing this section is often treated as a mere formality. Be prepared to list your child's positive attributes during the conference, and ask the other participants to do the same. It's a good idea to have your child attend the school conference, too. He should be prepared to describe the kinds of the problems he is having and suggest solutions.

Mediating Student-Teacher Conflicts

Many students say that they are afraid to ask their teacher for help with schoolwork or classroom problems. Often the real issue is that they don't know how to communicate their concerns. Your presence can give your child courage. As a mediator, you can teach her what to say and how to handle herself.

ESSENTIAL

Consider including your child in your conversations with her teacher. That way, she can begin learning how to handle problem-solving discussions. Mediate when your child attempts to communicate with her teacher by helping her express herself clearly and respectfully.

Once you have identified your child's concerns and formulated some possible solutions, have your child provide input as you write a letter to the teacher. For instance, if your child gets in trouble for talking in class but is afraid to discuss the problem with the teacher, you might write a note like the following.

Dear Mrs. Smith,

Susie is having trouble concentrating because a boy who sits nearby talks a lot. Would it be possible to change the seating arrangement?

Sincerely,
Mrs. Jones

The next step is to write a letter with your child's input that you both sign. That way, your child communicates with the teacher more directly but still has your support.

Dear Mrs. Smith,

Susie didn't do her language arts homework because she doesn't understand the difference between adjectives and adverbs. Could you explain this to her again?

Sincerely,
Susie Jones *and Mrs. Jones*

Next, work together to create a letter but have your youngster write it in her handwriting:

Dear Mrs. Smith,

I lost my government textbook. How do I get another one? Can I wait to take the test until I've had a chance to get another one so I can study?

Sincerely,
Susie Jones and *Mrs. Jones*

The final step is to provide suggestions but have your child write the letter, sign it, and take it to school.

Dear Mrs. Smith,

Even though I make good grades on my homework and study a lot, I get bad grades on the tests. What can I do to improve? Extra credit, maybe?

Sincerely,
Susie Jones

Hopefully, by the time your child reaches this point, she will feel confident enough to address her teacher in person. If not, help her overcome her fear and learn how by accompanying her to school for a conference. If you do most of the talking, provide lots of openings for your child to talk. You might say, for example: "Susie needs to discuss a problem but was worried about talking to you by herself, so I came along to help. She doesn't understand what to do for the book report and was uncomfortable about asking you to re-explain it. Could you tell her again?"

Next time, have your tween do most of the talking while you mediate when needed:

SUSIE: It hurt my feelings when you called me a liar in front of everybody.

TEACHER: I did no such thing!

MOTHER: I think Susie is trying to say that she was upset when she thought you didn't believe her yesterday and felt embarrassed in front of her classmates. In the future, would it be possible to discuss such issues in the hall or after class?

Finally, role-play a conversation with your tween, and then have her talk to the teacher alone. If she is dissatisfied with the results, go to school to assist her:

MOTHER: Susie said she talked to you about the problem she is having with some students bothering her in the halls between classes.

The problem has continued, and she has a question she wants to ask you.

SUSIE: What should I do?

Just as you must teach your child to cross the street by holding her hand until she reaches a certain level of competence and confidence, you must hold your child's hand until she has developed the self-confidence and know-how to talk to her teacher.

FACT

Most teachers say students shouldn't listen to music while studying, but many tweens concentrate better while a tune is playing. Extroverts may be able to listen to music with lyrics, but introverts, who concentrate best when they are alone, are likely to be distracted by songs that have words. They may do better with instrumentals.

When you know that your child can ask questions, solicit special help when needed, confront teachers respectfully, and do her schoolwork, you will know that she has what it takes to succeed in school today, college tomorrow, and at work in the years to come.

Teaching Respect

Educators are routinely blamed for our country's ills without receiving credit for its successes. In a society that fails to respect the work of those who labor on the educational frontier, instilling respect in students is difficult. Modern heroes don't toil in classrooms; they dribble balls across a stadium floor or swagger across a silver screen. When success is measured by the size of a paycheck, teachers look like failures. Even as the makers and sellers of widgets and whatnots live in luxury, outstanding teachers may have to moonlight to support a family. Futuristic skyscrapers filled with high-tech information systems dot the landscape of major cities, while teachers in crumbling buildings are given chalk and a blackboard and told to have at it. It is understandable that those who aspire to more would see a career in teaching as settling for less.

It's important to tell your tween that he must respect his teacher, but it's more impressive to seize opportunities to point out in everyday conversation the vital role that teachers play. Let your child know that by educating tomorrow's parents and employees, teachers hold our country's future in their hands.

ESSENTIAL

At their best, teachers not only impart knowledge, they also instill confidence and inspire a love of learning. Support your child's teachers by insisting that he behave respectfully toward them. Even if he doesn't like them, he must not disrupt the classroom.

When a middle school student groused about having so much homework, her mother said, "It's a lot for you and even more for your teachers. With five classes and twenty-five students per class, that's 125 papers to grade! That's a *real* homework load!" Teachers influence students' lifelong goals and are the silent partners in all of their future accomplishments.

If your district can't pay its chalkboard heroes the salaries that they deserve, at least you can accord them the esteem they merit and insist that your tween do the same.

Improving Academic Standards

Just a few generations ago, schools encouraged parental participation in the educational process but didn't consider it a prerequisite for students to progress academically. Immigrant parents, many of whom didn't even speak English, couldn't reteach lessons at home or unravel homework assignments, and they certainly couldn't check them. Parents who worked evenings couldn't supervise their children to make sure they studied. Many found it impossible to attend parent-teacher conferences and school events. Students were responsible for paying attention in class so they could learn, and teachers could hold them accountable if they didn't try.

When they administered consequences to eliminate behavior problems and ensure students did their work, administrators and parents backed them up.

A number of societal changes have altered the way teachers operate. Teachers' authority to teach as they see fit has been severely limited, as well as their ability to enforce limits to ensure that students behave and do their schoolwork. Modern educators are adamant that parents must take up the slack by setting limits at home and being actively involved in their tween's education. Unfortunately, controlling your child's behavior when you are at home or work and he is at school is difficult, if not impossible.

Assessing Achievement

Amid all the complaints of classroom boredom, busywork assignments, dumbed-down textbooks, and the ongoing calendar of classroom parties, assemblies, and school holidays, many parents suspect that not a lot of actual teaching and learning are taking place at their tween's school. How to tell if your child is at least progressing academically? Grades are not always a good way to tell.

In a substandard school, a fourth grader can make straight *A*s although she's only doing math and reading on a second-grade level. Compared to her classmates she's doing great, but since her classmates can barely read or do the most basic math, she can still be far below average compared to other students in her state.

ALERT!

If your child's educational environment is too taxing, he may be reeling under hours of homework each night and become discouraged because he still can't make decent grades or keep up. If his teacher won't reduce the pressure, the best solution may to change him to a less taxing school setting.

Achievement test results are one good indication of how your youngster is doing, because most compare them to other students in the district, state, and nation. The printouts of scores and data can be hard to interpret. In addition, some school districts don't report the state and national comparisons, but principals should have access to this data. If you don't understand your child's results or data is missing, schedule an appointment with your child's school counselor or a school administrator to discuss them in more detail. A child who is in the bottom half of the school scholastically may be in the top half of the nation if the students at her school are exceptionally advanced. Unfortunately, even national comparisons don't give the true picture of your youngster's academic achievements. Students in the United States remain far behind those of most other industrialized countries.

Improving Motivation

Parents have tried every trick in the book to motivate their children to give school their full attention. Some reward students for good grades by paying them for each *A* or *B,* buying them a bicycle, or holding a celebratory dinner. Desperate parents have gone so far as to promise to take their child to Disneyland for passing the year in school. Other parents rely on punishments, forbidding their child to go outside to play during the week until she brings home a better report card, revoking TV-watching privileges, or even disallowing participation in sports or extracurricular activities.

A better solution is to set limits to ensure your child does homework and studies every day. If no homework has been assigned, students can always benefit from reviewing their lessons for the day, previewing the next chapter in their textbooks, reading, or pursuing another educational activity.

Rewards and Punishments

Promising rewards for getting good grades and threatening to ground tweens and take away privileges for making poor ones aren't wonderful techniques for motivating students. A small minority do respond positively, but most are completely unaffected. A common parental complaint is that everything they try works for a while but nothing makes a difference for long. Similarly, most tweens find parents' lectures about the importance of doing well in school tantamount to nagging and soon learn to tune them out. Teachers' warnings that students must learn fractions *now* to be able to handle decimals in the next chapter or grade don't help much, either.

The Past and the Future

Tell your tween about the importance of working hard in school for future benefits, such as getting into honors classes, college, getting a good job, earning a living, and making a contribution to the world. Children need to know this, and some do respond positively. However, don't be surprised if your youngster does not. Understanding how her actions today affect her future may not provide the impetus your tween needs to pay attention in school and do her homework over the long haul. Unlike adults who spend a lot of time ruminating about yesterday and obsessing about tomorrow, tweens spend most of their time thinking about what's happening now. In fact, it's ironic that even as adults meditate, practice yoga, read self-help books, and attend assorted self-improvement groups to learn to leave the past behind them, let the future take care of itself, and open themselves up to the here-and-now, they are desperate to get tweens to "remember what happened last report card" and "think ahead."

QUESTION?

How can I encourage my social butterfly to study and get good grades?
Explain that good students can talk about more subjects and hold up their side of a conversation, so peers find them more interesting and enjoyable. Even if the most popular boys and girls don't make good grades now, that is likely to change in high school. In college and in adult life, intelligence is highly valued.

That is not to say that tweens aren't ever overtaken by memories and never worry about their futures, because they are and they do. When trying to fall asleep at night or stay awake during a boring class, they may worry about the test they took earlier in the day or about the book report due tomorrow. Instead of worrying, tweens need to work! That is why parents need to set limits.

A Popularity Boost

Ask your tween what kind of grades the most popular boys and girls in his class are making. If the most popular students get good grades, you can be confident that some peers he looks up to will support his school success. If your youngster is not doing well in a school where most students embrace success, the possibility of making more friends by improving his grades can serve as a potent incentive to buckle down. There's a good chance he needs tutoring, special education, or help to develop better study skills, and he might be willing to cooperate if he understands that improving his grades could improve his social life.

School Cultures

Even if tweens can't quite grasp how very important an education is for their future, it is hard for them to miss what success and failure mean in the here-and-now. The smiles and frowns from teachers, the lectures and praise from parents, the admiration and jeers of peers let them know if they are succeeding or failing. Just as adults' self-esteem deteriorates and they become depressed if they spend their days in jobs where they continually feel like failures, children can't feel good about themselves if they are constantly struggling with an overly taxing educational environment.

In the past, students who couldn't or wouldn't keep up academically were usually stigmatized on all fronts, but peer culture has begun to reverse the traditional values in increasing numbers of schools. In many schools, misbehavior and failure are actively supported by the prevailing peer culture. Students who cooperate with teachers and apply themselves are shamed and ostracized. In such settings, the most popular students make below-average grades, and those who get good grades take great pains to hide their efforts and achievements.

To combat peer values that support doing poorly in school, you must have a strong, solid relationship with your child. Even then, your tween may not want to risk the peer censure that can come with academic success. If you can't homeschool her, search out extra-curricular involvements so she can interact with pro-social peers.

If the most popular students in your child's class are doing below-average schoolwork, trying to motivate your tween by criticizing her may strengthen her identification with antisocial peers. For your child to do well when the group norm dictates that she not do well, she needs to be an exceptionally independent type, a strong leader, or very much of a loner. The other antidotes to negative peer pressure are extra doses of parental support.

If your child is gravitating toward peers who aren't applying themselves in school, see if the teacher will help her form relationships with students who are motivated to succeed. Perhaps she can be seated next to a dedicated student or be tutored by a student who is applying herself. In addition, help your tween form relationships with other children who share your values by enrolling her in structured activities. Nurture budding relationships by welcoming your child's new acquaintances into your home. Having friends who value education will boost your tween's motivation to achieve academically.

Chapter 10

Academic Boosts

An antidote to a wide range of educational problems, including such nightmares as substandard schools, uninspired teachers, learning disabilities, and chronic underachievement, is to fill your household with learning activities. The right kind of academic boost at home can instill in your tween a zest for learning and ensure that he continues to progress academically.

Uninspired Students

José would gladly tell anyone who asked that the only school subjects he liked were recess, gym, art, and lunch. In his academic subjects, he did as little as possible. His parents were always after him to keep his grades high enough so he would pass.

José was bright enough. He just didn't care about school. He sounded like a teenager when he complained about having to learn "all that useless stuff." Why learn handwriting when soon the whole world would be dictating into a Palm Pilot? Why learn spelling and grammar when his computer had spelling and grammar checkers? Obviously a calculator could handle any math calculation he might want to do. Why learn geography, social studies, or science? If he ever actually needed to know any of that stuff, it was a few mouse clicks away.

José's parents knew that his spelling and grammar were too poor for a computerized checker to sort out. His reading skills were too poor for him to learn much if he did locate online information he considered important. And of course, without some basic math skills, a calculator wasn't going to get him very far. José's parents might have put him in a private school to see if a different learning environment would motivate him, but besides being big proponents of public education, they didn't have the money. Certainly José's academic record was too uninspired to put a scholarship within the realm of possibility.

Life after Television

Instead, José's parents put more emphasis on educational activities at home. Step one was to limit their little couch potato's television watching to an hour a day on the weekends and school holidays and none during the week. Since his favorite shows were aired during the week, he could tape them for later viewing. The next step was to limit his videogame playing to three hours per weekend. His parents moved the computer into the living room so they could verify that he was studying, not playing computer games. They returned to the bedtime-story reading ritual, which they had dropped years ago, and capitalized on José's love of competitive games by incorporating them into educational enrichment activities.

ESSENTIAL

Students who learn best with a different method or at a different pace are viewed as problems. They may dislike school and put little effort into it or have difficulties mastering the material even if they work hard. Fortunately, what matters most is that your child develops a love of learning and progresses academically. Those are things you can help him with at home.

At first, José was irritable, bored, and restless, but in two weeks he began enjoying some new hobbies and pastimes that involved academic skills. The results became apparent when José took some standardized tests at school a year later. Instead of hovering near the fiftieth percentile as in the past, he moved up to the seventy-fifth. His biggest improvement was in the most important subject: reading.

The Problems with Traditional Education

It's no wonder that so many modern students dislike school and put little effort into it. The policies and procedures in force at most educational institutions were designed over a century ago during the Industrial Revolution. When laws regarding mass education took effect, society's pressing need was for assembly-line workers. A primary goal was to instill the attitudes and teach the behaviors needed to succeed in the work force after graduation.

The "factory model" of education remains the guiding principle in most modern schools. Accordingly, students are required to sit for long hours in neat rows, are expected to accomplish a fixed amount of work in a fixed amount of time, and must move in unison to the ringing of bells. They even take bathroom breaks *en masse* like factory workers. Creativity and individual initiative, which are incompatible with the requirements of mass production, continue to be minimized. Following instructions precisely continues to get top priority.

Providing Enrichment Activities

The best academic enrichment activities make learning fun. Play games, encourage hobbies, and support projects involving each of your child's subjects in school. Send him onto the information highway to play his way to a better education. Tutoring another student can help solidify his academic gains.

Writing Practice

A great way to encourage children to practice written self-expression is through letter writing. Before mailing a card or letter to a relative or friend, have your tween add a few lines of his own. Don't edit! Relatives will appreciate the personal touch of your son's jumbled sentences and misspelled words. Third graders should write their own thank-you notes for gifts and create their own greeting cards and party invitations. Have your fourth grader address your family's holiday greeting cards.

Help your tween find a pen pal. A correspondent living in very different circumstances helps fire a junior writer's imagination, while writing to a friend who has moved away provides a productive way to reach out and touch the special someone he has been missing.

Kids of all ages learn the true joy of letter writing when the long-awaited day arrives and they open the mailbox to find a letter addressed to them. If necessary, send your child a postcard.

ALERT!

Other Activities

The following activities can help your tween progress academically:

- **Reading:** The single most important educational skill is reading. Have your child read the recipe when you cook. Ask him to help you find a particular brand when you shop. Give him a magazine subscription for his birthday. Take him to the library regularly. When you drive, have him read the map and direct the driver. Encourage him to play computer games that involve reading. When you hike a nature trail, have your child serve as the guide by reading the brochure aloud to you.

- **Vocabulary:** Take turns presenting a word-of-the-day at the start of dinner. Make a game of having everyone slip it into the conversation by using it in a sentence.

- **Spelling:** Play password, Scrabble, and slap card. For slap card: Write spelling words on individual cards or scraps of paper. One person calls out a word. The first person to slap it claims it and tries to spell it without looking at the card. If he succeeds, he keeps it. Whoever gets the most cards wins.

- **Math:** To practice counting, let your child keep score whenever you play cards. When you play Monopoly, let your child be the banker. Play slap card by writing math facts on one side of some cards and the answers on the backsides. Place the cards with the problems facing up. One person calls out an answer. The first person to slap the correct problem gets to keep it. If two problems have the same answers, they can both be slapped and won. Games of logic build the skills needed for higher-level math, so play board games such as Clue, chess, Connect Four, Battleship, Othello, and Pente.

- **Social Studies:** Discuss current events at dinner, check out historical or current-events movies, and visit museums. Take advantage of Memorial Day, Veteran's Day, Labor Day, and Thanksgiving to teach your child what these holidays signify. Stop at every historical landmark in town and on vacations to read the plaques.

- **Speech:** Take turns telling stories. Ask your child to tell you about the movie that he saw or the book he read.

- **Science:** Buy a book about constellations so you can stargaze in the backyard. Visit local museums. Give your child broken appliances to disassemble. Buy a book of science experiments he can do at home.

Computer Games

If you're bored with your child's board games and there's a shortage of siblings and neighborhood children to take up the slack, the computer software version of Monopoly and Scrabble are available from ✎ *www.handmark.com*. Both games can be played with combinations of computer and human contestants on a Palm Pilot. Before you buy such a pricey device, know that your child can find a human opponent online to play Scrabble or a few million other educational games against the computer for free. The main gateway to activities you can trust is located at ✐ *www.pbskids.org,* where the "Zoom" section has dozens of interactive games.

Thousands of games are available at ✐ *www.kidinfo.com.* Most were developed by educators who creatively injected enough history, geography, science, math, and language arts into them so that children get a fun academic boost while they play. Tweens can literally play their way to a first-class kindergarten through twelfth-grade education.

Peer Tutoring Benefits

Peer tutoring has been found to be as beneficial for the young tutors and mentors as for the students being tutored and mentored. Lots of tweens with marginal social skills and less-than-stunning academic records show more maturity than adults could have predicted when they tutor a younger or less accomplished student. The educational benefits and boost to their self-esteem tend to be impressive—the key is to find a good match. See if your tween's teacher, a staff member at his after-school program, a YMCA counselor, or a day care center director will pair your child with a younger student and assign some specific duties, such as reading his young charge a story, helping him with homework, drilling him with flash cards, or even accompanying him to the playground and supervising him.

Repeating a School Year

Repeating a year in school can be a chance for a new beginning, but it is important for your tween to feel comfortable about being held back.

If he equates repeating a year with failure and has stigmatized himself, he may not respond very well when peers mention what is for him a very sensitive subject. He must be able to hold his head high when questioned or teased. This will be easier if your tween participates in the decision to repeat the year.

Point out that if he moves up to the next grade level with his class, he will have to struggle very hard to keep up because he is so far behind. If he repeats the grade, on the other hand, he'll already know some of the material. That should make for an easier year. When your tween raises the inevitable concerns about being separated from his friends and having to make new ones, point out that he'll still see some of his old classmates and will soon make new friends, too.

FACT

Unless your child is exceptionally immature for his age, being a bit older than everyone else will put him at an advantage socially. It may also give him some advantages in P.E. and other sports. In fact, lots of little athletes get such an edge from being older than their peers that their parents pressure school administrators to hold them back.

A Summertime Boost

How can a slow student make great academic strides? You don't need to send her to summer school or hire expensive tutors. Just round up last year's textbooks so she can review them during the summer. To help an average student leap ahead, round up a set of next year's textbooks so she can get a head start. This strategy can turn above-average students into outstanding ones and can give insecure types the confidence they need to strut their stuff in school the next year.

Your tween's outrage at having to study thirty minutes a day during her vacation is likely to all but dissipate when you point out the advantages. Knowing last year's material really well or getting a good head start on next year's lessons will put her ahead of a lot of the other students. Having done last year's assignments correctly or tackling next year's assignments in advance will make school easier in the fall. She should be one of the first students to catch on to new lessons and finish assignments instead of being one of the last. She may even be able to help some of the other students by explaining things to them, too.

Any remaining whimpers of protest will undoubtedly disappear altogether once she sees that you are holding firm on your requirements that she study each day. The frowns will turn to smiles when you point out that she whizzed through a chapter in a matter of days that took her class a whole week to cover last school year. When she does a page of problems correctly, note that she would have gotten an *A* if she'd done that well during the school year.

ESSENTIAL

If possible, have your child participate in deciding when she will study. Scheduling study sessions first thing in the morning after breakfast and/or the last thing before going to bed may pose fewer problems by not cutting into playtime. If your child is attending an after-school program, perhaps study time can be worked into her daily activity schedule.

Money Well Spent

You can eliminate the social stigma of having to study during the summer by paying your child for the time she's putting into academics. That way, she can brag to her friends about all the money she's making. Allowing her to earn a small amount for every math problem she completes correctly and every page in a spelling workbook that is free of errors may turn out to be the best investment in your child's education you've ever made. Chances are, you'll have to put a limit on how much she's allowed to do in a day so she doesn't drive you into bankruptcy.

Libraries offer summer reading programs to encourage reading. Alternatively, consider paying your child a large amount for reading a huge book or negotiate smaller sums for shorter books. She'll have the chance to earn while she learns. As her reading skills improve, she may discover she's more of a bookworm than she knew.

Keep Expectations Reasonable

Be realistic in your summertime requirements. Spending ten minutes a day on last year's math book may be enough to help a third grader master multiplication so she'll be ready to tackle long division in fourth grade. If you're setting up a more rigorous schedule, remember that students learn more by studying in twenty-minute blocks than for one long period. Sometimes it works better to require that your child complete a certain number of pages or problems every day rather than setting a specific time requirement.

Don't discourage your tween from rushing through the work. It doesn't matter how fast she does the problems; it only matters that she gets them right. Always focus on her successes. Grade papers by putting a mark by every correct problem and send her back to fix the rest. When they are all correct, put a big 100, *A+*, and a smiley face on her paper.

Schools can be persnickety about lending textbooks. If you can't borrow them, offer to buy them. Alternatively, compile a list of the titles, authors, publishers, and ISBN numbers. You may be able to locate a used copy through ✍ *www.amazon.com* or another online company that sells used books. Alternatively, order new copies from the publishers.

Workbook Wonders

Workbooks that are lots of fun and very inexpensive are available to help students of all ages practice basic academic skills. With their inviting formats even students who dislike academics enjoy them.

It is important to choose workbooks that are several grade levels behind your youngster's year in school so she can do the work with a minimum of help, get lots of remedial practice on basic skills, and build confidence. A bright third grader can finish an entire kindergarten math or phonics book in about an hour even if she colors all of the pictures. The graded workbooks get harder fast, so a bright fourth grader may find some of the third-grade workbooks challenging. Most students do best starting off with workbooks that are so easy, they feel like play. Once your child has spent time on lessons that make her feel like an academic star, her improved confidence may change her attitude toward school.

To motivate your child to do academic workbooks, buy her a new box of crayons or colored pencils, a new pencil and eraser, and duplicate workbooks so she can play school with her friends. A partially finished workbook can serve as the teacher's manual, and the extra copies can be for her "students."

It's hard to describe the expression of awe and pride on a child's face when her parent points out that it took her only a few hours to finish what kindergartners take an entire school year to do. Follow up by wondering aloud how fast she might do the work that takes first-grade students an entire year. After she corrects errors, shake your head in wonderment as you continue to award the top grade to every page. Suggest she save her workbooks so she can show her new teacher in the fall. She deserves lots of kudos for putting in so much time and effort.

Homeschooling Your Tween

Homeschooling has become increasingly popular as more parents have become disenchanted with the problems of public schools and the cost of private ones. Now that homeschooling is legal in all fifty states, an estimated 1.5 to 2 million children (3 to 4 percent of all students) are being schooled at home. Statistics show that homeschooled children score higher on college entrance exams such as the SAT and ACT. By eighth grade, the average student being educated at home is working on a twelfth-grade level! In truth, so much in-school time is devoted to discipline and administrative matters, studying a few hours a day at home can equal a whole day at school.

Getting Started

Before making a decision to homeschool your child, visit ✐*www.bjup.com* to determine whether you're ready to take the plunge and to find out more about what you're getting into. When you're ready to forge ahead, see ✐*www.homeschoolcentral.com* to learn your state's requirements, then go to ✐*www.homeschool.com* to start stocking up on textbooks and curriculum guides, and to locate online courses. Students can receive an entire online education from kindergarten through twelfth grade for $15.95 per month—with your help, of course. Lots of experts are available online to diagnose learning problems and help when you get stuck.

FACT

The Hooked on Phonics series has successfully taught nonreaders of all ages to read and helped students in underprivileged schools make huge gains in short order. The key to the program is the endless repetition. Some students do have difficulty staying motivated. This method is probably not one of the more enjoyable ways to learn. Nevertheless, it does work.

The following how-to books will cover most everything you need to know:

- *The First Year of Homeschooling Your Child* by Linda Dobson (Prima Publishing, 2001)
- *Home Learning Year by Year* by Rebecca Rupp (Three Rivers Press, 2000)
- *Home Learning Year by Year: How to Design a Homeschool Curriculum from Preschool Through High School* by Rebecca Rupp (Three Rivers Press, 2000)
- *Homeschooling Almanac, 2002–2003: How to Start, What to Do, Where to Go, Who to Call, Web Sites, Products, Catalogs, Teaching Supplies, Support Groups, Conferences, and More!* by Mary Leppert, Michael Leppert, Jamie Miller (editor) (Prima Publishing)
- *Homeschooling Your Child Step-by-Step* by Lauramaery Gold and Joan M. Zielinski (Prima Publishing, 2002)

- *The McGraw-Hill Homeschooling Companion* by Laura Saba and Julie Gattis (McGraw-Hill Trade, 2002)

You can also join the National Home Education Network online at ✎ *www.nhen.org* or write them (P.O. Box 7844, Long Beach, California 90807) for information and to network with other parents involved in homeschooling.

Creative Homeschooling

Some parents have found wonderful solutions to thorny homeschooling problems. One remedy for the problem of having your child at home with you all day every day is to band together with three other parents and homeschool your children together. If each parent chooses a subject, spends one day preparing lessons, spends another day presenting them to all of the children, and works with their own child individually one day a week, each parent still has two days free during the school week. If your school district is amenable, you can have your child attend public school for art, music, recess, gym, and lunch, thereby solving the problem of providing sufficient social stimulation. Otherwise, most communities offer enough extracurricular activities so you can provide daily opportunities for peer interaction. If an after-school program is available in your area, it may be possible for your child to have time for free play in a supervised but less structured environment. Ⓔ

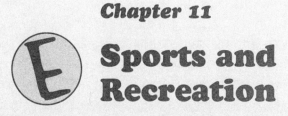

Chapter 11

Sports and Recreation

Like everything else in your tween's life, extracurricular activities should be selected to meet your child's individual needs. Most children do best with a mix of structured activities, opportunities to socialize, and time to call their own so they can kick back and relax. However, what is best for most may not be best for your youngster.

Leisure Activities

Jessica had always made straight *As* at an academically demanding private school. In addition, she participated in so many extracurricular activities that her parents were amazed she could keep track of her schedule. In seventh grade she was on the swim team (four practices a week plus swim meets), in the church choir (one practice a week plus two Sunday services), and on the student council (one before-school meeting twice a month). She continued the piano lessons she'd begun at age six (one lesson a week plus daily practice) and volunteered as a Candy Striper at the hospital (four hours every Saturday afternoon). She spent one to two hours a night on homework and studied on the weekends, too. Often she went to bed after her parents.

ALERT!

Watch your tween for signs of burnout. Most families find themselves racing from dawn until dusk. They enroll their tweens in too many activities. Seventy-six percent of children are overscheduled, according to Metlife's Year 2000 Survey of the American Teacher.

When Jessica went through a period of moodiness, her parents became convinced that she was doing too much. They said she must drop something, pointing out that she had dark circles under her eyes and cried at the drop of a hat. Jessica said she was fine and explained why each of her activities was critical. When they insisted, she became so hysterical they felt a bit frightened. They scheduled a family counseling session to get help deciding what to do.

A Different Kind of Life

Jessica said that her moodiness of late was due to conflicts with some classmates. They accused her of being a snob because she didn't spend time with them anymore. Jessica liked to hang out with them at school but wasn't otherwise interested in their company. "They're into boys and clothes and rock music," she said. "I'm not into that scene." She admitted that missing sleep was a problem but insisted that each of her activities was important for her future. "If I'm going to get into medical school, I've got to get good grades and show that I'm well rounded," she said.

However, it didn't seem that a medical school admissions committee was what drove her. The bottom line was that Jessica loved everything she was doing. She admitted to sometimes feeling overwhelmed but was generally happy in her life. When asked what she needed to help her feel happier, she replied, "More hours in each day."

In the end, her parents decided to help Jessica pursue her own path. They would take pressure off of her by no longer requiring her to wash the dishes after dinner. They wouldn't insist that she participate in their customary Saturday night video and popcorn feast and would let her decide whether to accompany them to the mall and on other family outings. Jessica agreed to go to bed on time and to forgo practicing the piano if she had more than the usual amount of homework on a school night, making up the piano practice time on the weekends. She might not have a balanced life by anyone else's standards, but Jessica wasn't anyone else. She had more energy than most people and very specific ideas about how she wanted to direct it.

Tween Burnout

Scouting, dance lessons, karate classes, chess clubs, soccer teams, swim meets—the list of extracurricular activities tweens may be involved in is endless. Too many structured activities can deprive tweens of the time they need to socialize with friends, spend time with their families, and have time alone with their books, music, and collections so they can relax, unwind, and decompress.

Signs that a child is stressed from being overscheduled are usually obvious to others. If parents don't see them and continue to push their tween toward too many or the wrong involvements, it's usually because they have an agenda of their own. Perhaps they missed out on certain activities during their own childhood and are trying to live through their tween. Some parents are more interested in impressing other parents than in considering their child's interests. They enjoy the reaction they draw when they tell their friends that their child is a downhill racer or chess champion.

It's important to appreciate your child for who he is. Don't try to turn an academic star who wants to spend most of his free time studying into a jock who must spend most of his time working out, or vice versa.

If you're not sure whether your tween is overscheduled, ask an honest friend's opinion. If you're still not sure, watch for the following telltale signs.

- He dawdles when it's time to leave for an extracurricular activity.
- He often loses his equipment, permission slips, and schedules, and you are more upset than he is.
- He requires continual reminders to practice or prepare for scheduled activities, meetings, and events.
- He forgets to relay information about schedule changes and his need for special equipment and supplies.
- He stays up late to finish homework or doesn't do a good job on it.
- He complains about not getting to do what he wants to do.
- He suffers from performance anxiety, getting terribly upset because he failed to score a goal or feeling ill before a recital or competition.
- He doesn't complain when transportation problems or scheduling conflicts interfere with a scheduled activity.
- Family members can't find time to enjoy one another because everyone is too busy.

Providing a variety of extracurricular activities so a child can be well rounded is admirable, but if your child doesn't enjoy them, there may not be a point to insisting he continue. Many tweens have very definite interests and don't take well to being forced to pursue someone else's idea of fun. A single extracurricular activity may be too draining if your child cherishes his time to play in the neighborhood and hang out at home.

Team Sports

Team sports are immensely popular, and most youngsters are introduced to them at about age eight. Team sports teach teamwork and self-discipline and help to keep your tween physically fit. They promote improved balance, coordination, and body awareness. Being able to play with other children in a supervised group can be especially important for children with poor social skills as well as for youngsters who lack peer contact outside of school.

However, because organized sports place so much emphasis on following rules and winning, it may be better to wait until your youngster is ten years old to begin. Since most children under age twelve get quite upset about losing, it is usually better to downplay the competitive aspects of being on a team. Instead, help your tween understand the benefits of practicing and playing as opposed to winning.

ALERT!

Consider carefully before sending your tween into a game, competition, practice, or lesson with instructions to "do your best." Instead, suggest getting good exercise and having fun. Surveys show that over half of grade-school children worry about making a mistake and not performing well in extra-curricular activities.

Teaching Good Sportsmanship

The usual reason for poor sportsmanship is that children equate losing with being a loser. This can be as much of a problem on the baseball diamond where the issue is skill as when playing a board game where a spin of the dial determines the winner. Try to explain that sometimes luck rather than skill is the operative factor, though tweens are so superstitious they may be despondent because they believe they are "jinxed."

Playing for Fun

Help your child understand the difference between playing to win and playing to have fun by asking him if he's having fun when you are playing a game with him. When you're losing, make a point of mentioning that you're still having fun playing. Add that if you do lose, you'll remember how much fun you're having right now so you won't feel too badly. Deliver the usual reminders that, depending on the game, winning is a matter of luck, or of a mixture of luck and skill, or of mostly skill. Help your child understand that the way to improve in a skill is to practice it.

FACT

As frustrating as it can be to play with a poor sport, putting forth the time and effort to teach your child good sportsmanship is important. It's a basic social skill he needs to get along with other children now and with colleagues in the future.

Model good sportsmanship when you play a competitive game with your child by shaking his hand and congratulating him when he wins. Have him congratulate you when you win. Express pride in your son for being a good sport, adding that his ability to handle defeat gracefully shows that he's growing up—that is especially meaningful to tween boys. When you're on a winning streak, state that you like it best when sometimes you win and sometimes he does because not knowing who is going to win makes games more exciting. Otherwise, it's like playing tag with a two-year-old; there's no victory in winning. It's the uncertainty of not knowing who will win that makes things interesting.

Building Frustration Tolerance

To improve at a sport, your tween must be able to tolerate frustration. Children who throw their tennis rackets when they miss a lob and argue every point may appear to be battling their opponents, but such behavior usually signals they are actually engaged in a heated competition with themselves and have failed to measure up to their own expectations. Tweens with poor persistence have difficulty tolerating frustration, too. Sometimes they don't appear to be upset. They simply lose interest in tasks they find difficult because they don't consider them worth the effort. Sometimes they do feel upset but feign a lack of interest because they feel too defeated to continue. To improve at a game, sport, or anything else, children must be able to persist.

To build persistence, help your child experience the "practice makes perfect" rule by acknowledging your child's efforts and small successes whenever she is making progress with a task she finds challenging.

ESSENTIAL

Avoid kibitzing from the sidelines at your child's games; such distractions will make it hard for him to concentrate. Trying to listen to you at the same time that his coach and teammates are calling out to him will add to his stress and confusion. Such over-involvement is an intrusion onto the coach's turf, which sets a bad example for the players, so behave yourself!

To help your child develop better frustration tolerance, explain that when people try to do something they find really hard, their stomach sometimes feels tense or nervous. When that happens, they need a break before they get overwhelmed. Point out times she is managing to cope with frustration by saying, "That kind of situation would drive me crazy, but you're keeping your cool. How are you doing that?"

It doesn't matter that your child can't answer. You want her to give your question some thought and recognize whatever calming techniques she employed so she can summon them as needed in the future. Some children tear up their drawings because of a single wrong mark and destroy their homework papers because of a lone error or erasure. Developing good frustration tolerance yields academic as well as social benefits. Popular tweens share the characteristic of having better-than-average social skills. Hence, there are several compelling reasons to help your child develop good tolerance for frustration.

Tweens on Wheels

Tweens love speed and motion as much as anyone. Some children heed parents' safety warnings, use good judgment, and are careful not to hurt themselves. Still, they sustain some bumps and bruises as they whiz through the neighborhood on scooters, bikes, and skates. Little daredevils seem to have to learn the hard way and may sustain some nasty injuries before learning what they can manage and what is too much. Taking away your tween's wheels from time to time may be necessary to help convince him to exercise some restraint and caution.

ALERT!

Remember that admonishments not to do "this, that, or the other" are of limited benefit. Teach your child the rules of the road for bicycling, what hazards to watch for when skating, and how to minimize danger during skateboard falls. And make sure she always wears a SNELL- and/or ANSI-approved helmet.

Razor Scooters

Tweens love these updated versions of old-fashioned scooters, but they are controversial due to the many serious injuries they have caused. The consumer product safety commission reported that 9,400 injuries from Razor scooters were treated in emergency rooms in 2000.

Most of the injuries resulted from falling off the scooter. An estimated 60 percent of injuries were deemed preventable or could have been far less severe if the child had worn appropriate protective gear, so they may not actually be more dangerous than bicycles and skateboards. A well-fitted helmet and knee and elbow pads are essential. Scooters with handbrakes are safer than those without.

Scooters are great for sidewalks and driveways but should not be ridden in the street. If your child has a folding scooter, instruct him to be careful of the hinge, which can easily damage fingers and toes.

Bicycle Safety

There's nothing like the sense of freedom that comes with being able to roam the neighborhood on a bike. There's nothing like the sense of power that comes from riding with no hands and doing wheelies. Nevertheless, bicycles have their dark side. They are second only to automobiles when it comes to childhood injuries. In 2000, more than

373,000 children age fourteen and under received treatment in hospital emergency rooms for bicycle-related injuries. Wearing a helmet decreases the risk of head injury by as much as 88 percent! (Data provided by the National Safe Campaign Web site, ✑ *www.safekids.org.*)

Be sure your child knows to ride with the flow of traffic rather than against it, to stop at stop signs and traffic lights, and to signal before turning. Be sure he knows, too, the important clichés: "Better to be safe than sorry" and "Better to be wrong than dead right."

ALERT!

If your tween needs a new bike, plan ahead! Watch for end-of-summer sales on bicycles and other sports equipment at stores and check under the garage sale and merchandise listings in the classified sections of the newspaper. Splurge on a sturdy bicycle pump, spare tubes, a tire patching kit, and a bicycle tool kit.

Skateboards

When it comes to buying a skateboard, quality does matter. More expensive models are sturdier, so comparison-shop before buying. The U.S. Consumer Product Safety Commission reports that approximately 26,000 people make visits to hospital emergency rooms each year for treatment of skateboard-related injuries. The primary culprits are insufficient protective gear, failure to maintain the board, and irregular riding surfaces. Sixty percent of injuries are to children under age fifteen. Prime risks are to children who have had their skateboards less than a week because they fall off, as well as those who unexpectedly encounter an irregular surface while doing advanced stunts after riding for a year or more.

ESSENTIAL

Take the time to read *Child Safe: A Practical Guide for Preventing Childhood Injuries* by Mark A. Brandenburg, M.D. (Three Rivers Press, 2000). This book has been endorsed by the American Academy of Emergency Medicine.

When skateboarding, children should check for pavement holes, bumps, and assorted debris. They should not skateboard in the street, where the risk of being killed in a car crash rises dramatically. Protective padding and helmets should not restrict movement, vision, or hearing. They should be taught how to fall properly to minimize injury.

In-line Skates

Wearing a helmet is an important safety measure for skaters, but it must be of good quality and fit properly to provide maximum protection. Some have cushioned padding inserts that make it easier to adjust the fit. The helmet must fit snugly without restricting hearing or vision. Wrists, elbows, and knees are most likely to bear the brunt of a fall, so children should be outfitted with wrist guards, elbow pads, and kneepads. Skaters should use the same hand signals as bicyclists to signal when they are about to turn or stop. Don't let your tween skate near traffic wearing a Walkman. He needs to be able to hear approaching vehicles.

FACT

Knowing how to swim is not enough. Tweens must be able to tread water and handle emergency situations. Enroll your child in a swim class. If she is too afraid of water for group lessons, get private lessons from a certified instructor.

Winter Activities

Winter or summer, snow or sleet, your child needs exercise each day. There is no reason to keep her inside during cold weather. Humans lived in unheated caves for thousands of years. If children living in northern latitudes were only allowed to go outside on warm days, they'd be stuck indoors ten months out of the year. It is a myth that colds are caused by the cold. Viruses cause colds, not the wind or a blast of cold air. Just take care to ensure your tween is dressed warmly enough and stays dry so she doesn't get chilled or damp. In other words, she can be outside when it's cold, but she shouldn't feel cold. If she does she needs to go inside to warm up.

Chapter 12

Scores of Chores

Long before Tom Sawyer was tricking the neighborhood kids into doing his chores for him, tweens have been wriggling out of their responsibilities with tactics that are both creative and exasperating. If you're wondering whether struggling to get your child to do chores is worth the trouble, the answer is yes!

Artful Dodgers

Cullen's parents brought him in for counseling because their nightly arguments over homework and chores were making everyone in the family miserable. Cullen's only regular duties were making his bed and feeding the dog each day, taking out the trash every few days, setting the table when asked, and cleaning his room when his mother thought a bulldozer would be required to clear a path to his bed if he put it off much longer. In addition, he was supposed to do whatever small amount of homework his teachers assigned.

Losing Battles

When Cullen's mother told him that it was time to do one of his chores, his predictable response was to promise to do it later. "Later" didn't arrive until she had issued several reminders, which made her feel like a nag, or until she lost patience, which meant yelling at him and sending him to his room. Cullen put off making his bed until it was time to leave for school, so he had to wait to make it until he returned home. Then, if his mother said he couldn't go outside until he finished, he would say he was staying inside. When a friend appeared at the door, a real confrontation would ensue as Cullen demanded to be allowed to play with him. If the friend was sent away, Cullen still wouldn't make his bed. Sometimes his mother didn't have the energy to fight with him and would be talked into letting him go out "just this once." He did his in-school work well enough, but his teachers assigned more homework each year. His grades were suffering because he wouldn't do take-home assignments or study for tests.

E ALERT!

Tweens learn self-discipline and responsibility by doing chores, but their "help" may not ease your own workload. It's wonderful if your tween does enough to make a real contribution, but monitoring and supervising may require more time and effort than doing everything yourself.

Cullen's parents tried forbidding him to watch television unless he did his chores without being reminded, but he would say he didn't care and do something else instead. When another family member turned on the TV, Cullen was sent to his room. Spending the evening alone did not seem healthy for him, so his parents sometimes pretended not to notice he was watching TV. In counseling, the therapist asked Cullen why he put more effort into avoiding doing his chores and homework than doing them. Cullen gave the famous tween reply, "I dunno. I guess 'cause it's boring." It seemed like a hopeless struggle.

The Quiet Time Solution

The solution their counselor proposed seemed impossible given the family's busy schedule. Cullen's parents agreed to try it for two weeks and were surprised at how well things went once everyone adjusted. The children and parents divvied up the chores and rotated them on a weekly basis. They rotated supervisors, too, so that everyone took turns policing everyone else. A quiet time was held after dinner each school day for homework, studying, and chores. During that time the TV was turned off, the answering machine stayed on, and no guests were allowed in the house. The children studied in the kitchen so a parent could monitor them while simultaneously cleaning up, making lunches for the next day, or sitting at the kitchen table to pay bills. If a child was doing chores in another part of the house, he requested an inspection from his "supervisor" when he finished. If someone had no homework and finished his chores early, he spent the rest of the quiet time reading.

After the first week, Cullen stopped grumbling. The quality of his homework quickly improved. The other children protested at first but seemed to enjoy the camaraderie of studying and doing chores together. Cullen got so comfortable with the new routine that when soccer season started, he was the one who asked, "But what are we going to do about quiet time?" The children were upset when it was moved to before school in the mornings, because that meant an earlier bedtime. However, a week later they had stopped objecting. Everyone seemed to feel that it was worth not having to go through long evenings of endless arguing.

Why Tweens Don't Do Their Chores

Little neatniks pick up their rooms without a dozen reminders, brush their teeth without cutting corners, and wash their hands before meals without being told. Very compliant tweens dust and vacuum, set and clear the table, help care for younger children, and do other chores without needing constant reminders. However, such responsible types are somewhat rare because they violate the two tween golden rules:

1. If there's a chore that I don't want to do, somebody else should have to do it.
2. If I have to do a chore that I don't want to do, I should be able to do it later.

I Forgot to Do It

Tweens can drive their parents to distraction by being perpetually forgetful about hanging up backpacks, returning empty glasses to the kitchen, straightening their bedrooms, studying, and handling simple chores. If you suspect forgetting chores is a manipulative hoax, you are likely to experience a disconcerting array of emotions: angry, angrier, and angry enough to kill.

FACT

Whining is not an appropriate way for your tween to communicate with you. End whining by telling her to use her regular voice. Otherwise, simply refuse to respond when she whines, then praise her for speaking like a big girl. Reward her by fulfilling her request if you can, or politely explain why you must decline.

Some tweens are in fact very manipulative, but most are sincere when they promise to clean up the mud they tracked inside "in a minute," to rinse the dishes before putting them into the dishwasher "next time," and to study for their spelling test "later." However, as soon as they have made such a promise, they put the matter out of their minds.

It seems respectful to wait until their current TV show ends before

CHAPTER 12: SCORES OF CHORES

insisting, but unless your child has proved his ability to keep his promises, allowing him to procrastinate is likely to backfire for both of you. You end up feeling that you've been lied to; your child ends up upset because you are upset with him. Whether he handles criticism by blaming himself and feeling like a failure or by blaming you for picking on him, being nagged is unhealthy for him—as well as for you.

It is easy to feel betrayed if your tween promises to start his chores "soon" but doesn't come through. On the other hand, it is foolish to continue to trust a tween who regularly breaks such promises. If you continue to trust rather than confront the problem, you perpetuate a negative dynamic. Responsibility is something that every tween can learn, but learning requires a teacher. That job falls to you.

Small Tasks, Big Decisions

Parents inevitably suspect recalcitrance when they assign a very simple chore, such as putting the casserole in the oven at 4:30 P.M., and later discover that their tween didn't do it. How do you believe a ten-year-old who claims he didn't know how, when this same child single-handedly taught himself to program the computer? How do you believe he was "afraid of messing up the casserole" when he wasn't afraid of disassembling the VCR, when he obviously knew nothing about it because he never could get it to work again?

If your tween uses the computer and VCR regularly, he probably considers them to be on his turf. He may feel confident that he can manage the computer because he spends so much time on it, although of course his confidence may turn out to be vastly overblown. He doesn't worry about how somebody else might react if he messes up because he thinks of these machines as his. The kitchen, on the other hand, is somebody else's territory. Unless he's spent enough time there and been given enough free rein to consider it part of his turf too, or unless he's familiar enough with the tasks to have developed good confidence, he assumes that to mess up his parents' property is to commit a high crime.

Tweens can be frozen from the uncertainty about a simple decision, such as whether to leave the casserole lid on or off when putting it in the oven. Is it worse to ruin the lid because it isn't oven-safe, or to ruin dinner because it was cooked without a lid? If a tween was supposed to put the casserole in at 4:30 but he forgot until 4:35, he's already "blown it," so now the question is what will upset Mom more. Would she rather serve dinner late? Perhaps the last time he forgot to put dinner on, they had to grab a fast-food meal on the way to his soccer practice because they didn't have time to wait. A five-minute delay seems like a short time; but being five minutes late to work makes Mom crazy and his teachers mad, so a five-minute casserole delay might be a serious problem.

Don't expect your tween to start chores or do a good job on them without help. Announce when it is time to begin, set limits to ensure she gets started, check her work, and have her correct any deficiencies before she resumes playing. Don't forget to issue enthusiastic kudos for any aspects of the job she did well.

A tween who has been fully involved in cooking for a number of years will be able to make the obvious decision. But a tween whose mealtime contributions have been largely confined to pouring himself a bowl of cereal and setting the table won't know what to do. If parents doubt that such small doubts and uncertainties can immobilize tweens, it is because they don't realize how much information and experience people need to be able to reason their way through problems. Many young adults on their own for the first time and single men with little cooking experience find simple dilemmas about whether a particular lid can or cannot go in the oven equally daunting. To be able to use good judgment, people must first have a good grasp of the relevant facts.

Big Projects

When told to straighten her room, study for a test, or do her homework, your tween may truly feel lost about where to begin. This feeling may arise because she doesn't know how to break a large project into a series of small steps and organize them. As a result, her approach is so random and unfocused that when she's finished straightening her very messy room, it looks as if she hasn't even started. When it comes to school projects, she may procrastinate and end up turning in work far below her capabilities.

It can be hard to comprehend that an intelligent child doesn't know how to pick up her room, but unless she's had a lot of hands-on help, guidance, and instruction, or unless she is a born organizational expert, this is often the case. Consider that if a twelve-year-old can solve algebraic equations, he didn't achieve this level of expertise without a lot of help. His natural math ability is only the tip of the iceberg. Over the years teachers have given him hundreds of arithmetic lessons. They have carefully explained basic concepts and procedures, anticipated and answered his questions, and helped him reason through problems when he got stuck. They didn't feel sorry for him and do the problems for him when he seemed overwhelmed, since that wouldn't benefit him in the least. Instead, he was given more detailed explanations and lots of practice problems. Teachers checked his work thoroughly and required him to fix errors so he learned everything correctly. By sixth grade a tween may have advanced to the point that he can handle complex mathematical problems that are beyond his parents' ability to solve.

FACT

If your child can't manage to keep his bedroom clean and his possessions and homework papers in order, it's probably because he lacks a natural ability to organize and/or has never received detailed instructions on where to begin and how to proceed. That's where you come in.

Immaturity

The sophisticated verbal skills tweens employ to get out of doing their chores misleads adults into thinking they are more mature and capable than they actually are. If your tween knows how to straighten up her room but doesn't do it, it is probably because she lacks sufficient emotional maturity. Intellect and emotional control don't develop at the same rate.

Even overweight adults may be intelligent enough to comprehend that they should control their diet and get more exercise, but that doesn't mean they can cope with the discomfort of forgoing a donut or mobilize the will to go to the gym regularly. Being able to tolerate the frustration of having to do things that aren't fun and being able to delay gratification are related to emotional maturity, not intellect. If your tween cannot tolerate frustration well enough or delay gratification long enough to do her chores and homework without a lot of trouble, she needs your help to develop self-control.

An Important Part of Growing Up

Doing homework and chores are basic responsibilities for every child. They help tweens master school lessons, handle household tasks, and develop some of the emotional skills needed to become independent adults. Chores teach the following basic skills your child needs:

- How to organize personal space and care for personal possessions.
- How to tolerate frustration and develop self-discipline.
- How to cook and clean, do yard work, and participate in the upkeep of the home.

Assigning Chores

Assigning a chore your child dislikes and requiring him to do it for years on end makes things needlessly unpleasant; so there is much to be said for allowing your tween to participate in choosing his chore if it is to be the same one every day. By rotating chores, children can practice a variety of household tasks. However, be aware that very disorganized children who need a long time and a lot of help to be able to handle a simple task may benefit from the structure of an ironclad, unvarying daily requirement.

Some families assign chores along traditional sex lines, requiring their boys to mow lawns, sweep sidewalks, and take out the trash while the girls cook, dust, and vacuum. The problem with this strategy is that it reinforces the idea that certain jobs are girls' work. Future wives won't take kindly to that notion, and it is imperative for a single man to know how to cook and clean. Similarly, girls benefit from learning to handle yards, trash, and fix-it projects since they're likely to live alone at some point during their adult years.

Every family has its own way of assigning chores. Some parents choose chores and rotate them among the children, so that one youngster cleans up after dinner one night and the other does it the next. Other parents list the chores on separate pieces of paper and everyone draws from a hat at a weekly or monthly family meeting. Some use one hat for daily chores and another for chores that only need to be done weekly, and each child draws from each hat.

Allowing children to trade chores can be a good way for them to hone their negotiating skills and teach them how to deal with one another respectfully, assuming you outlaw bullying and bickering and don't take one child's side over another.

It's a good idea to work out consequences for failing to do a chore. Consider including yourself so that you, too, must serve a consequence for failing to complete your chore. Solicit your child's opinion as to what the consequence should be for someone who doesn't do her job. If Dad's chore for the week is preparing dinner and he doesn't do it, perhaps his consequence can be taking everyone out for dinner.

Teaching Organizational Skills

If your tween doesn't pick up his room when told to, or if the chaos quickly takes over after you do it for him, the best approach is to start from scratch and help him find a way to organize his space that works for him. Set aside at least half a day to help him with this project. Walk him through the steps and give advice, but insist that he make all the decisions. If your tween is accustomed to deferring to you, he needs to realize that you are now turning responsibility for keeping his room clean and in order over to him. He needs to decide where things go so he can find them and put them away without help.

Teaching Tweens to Categorize

The first step to organizing anything is identifying the main categories. For a bedroom, the main categories of items that need to be organized are clothes, toys, books, and papers. Next, your child must establish the subcategories. Those are the groups of similar objects that should be stored together so they are easier to find and put away. Subcategories for clothing might include underwear, school clothes, play clothes, shoes, pajamas, and so on. Socks might be a separate subcategory from underwear if your child prefers to store them in separate drawers, or they could be in the same subcategory if he wants them stored together. Possible subcategories for toys are large toys, small toys, and special collections.

It takes a lot of experimenting to figure out the best way to organize a room. Suggest that your tween may want to move things around several times to find the arrangement that works best for him. Offer to help when he wants to redo it.

Have your tween make the decisions about where to store items belonging to each subcategory by taking into account both the size of the storage area and its location. It's usually better to store frequently used objects in easily accessible locations. Pose the questions he needs to learn to ask when organizing objects:

- Is it better to store school clothes near the front of a closet and the dress clothes he rarely wears in the back?
- Is the drawer he has selected big enough to hold all of his T-shirts and jeans? If not, is it better to select a bigger drawer, or put shirts in one drawer and jeans in another?
- Would it be easier for him to have T-shirts folded in a drawer or hung in a closet?
- Would his models look better on top of his bureau or hung on the wall?
- Would it be easier to keep pencils on top of his desk so he doesn't have to dig through his desk drawer?

While teaching your child to organize, remind him that the point of organizing is to make things easier to find. Accordingly, encourage him to improve on whatever system you devise. All that matters is what works best for *him*.

Maintaining Organization

Tweens' bedrooms quickly fall into disarray unless they have a trashcan and a place to put dirty clothes. Unless your child is responsible about carrying dirty clothes to the laundry immediately, consider putting a basket under her bed and notify her before you do laundry so she can get them to be washed. Pack rats need a drawer for miscellaneous papers, too. A serious pack rat might require several boxes for miscellaneous papers and other small items. Sometimes they can be stored under the bed.

QUESTION?

How can I get my son to take pride in his room so he'll take better care of it?
Let your tween decide how he wants his room organized and decorated to create a sense of ownership. Give advice but let him decide where he wants to keep things.

Once your tween's room is organized, the next step is to teach her to keep it from falling into disarray. The secret to staying organized is not to let the clutter build to the point that it becomes overwhelming. The easiest way is to put away each item as soon as she is finished with it.

A good time to teach her to straighten her room is before bedtime each evening. Pick up an item and ask her where it goes to help her consider what factors to take into account when straightening a room. Provide suggestions, but follow up in such a way that it's clear that it's her decision. The goal is not to serve as her slave, so be sure she's actively participating in the cleanup. An alternative is to sit on her bed and talk her through the steps, but let her do all of the physical work herself.

Supervising Chores

It's an excellent idea to have your tween participate in deciding what her chores will be and when she will do them, although until she can work on her own she should choose a time when you can supervise. When it comes to actually doing chores, plan to remain very involved until she matures. As your child's supervisor, expect to be responsible for the following:

- Announce when it's time for your tween to do chores or start on homework rather than expecting her to remember.
- Don't be defensive or angry if she argues or tries to put you off. Remind yourself that she may have the intellect of an Einstein, but she's still a child. Tell her it's fine to feel angry, but she still needs to get started.
- If she doesn't comply, give her a shadowing time-out (see Chapter 19) until she has her anger under control to the point that she can function. If the time-out lasts until bedtime, so be it. If the situation doesn't improve after several days, contact a local child guidance clinic, mental health clinic, or private therapist to inquire about anger management classes and counseling.
- Have your tween let you know when she is ready for you to check her work. Avoid criticizing poor work. Instead, point out any small thing she did *right*, tell her what needs to be fixed or finished in a matter-of-fact manner, and tell her to call you when she is ready for you to check her work again.
- Congratulate her on having finished and express pride in her accomplishment.

Be polite when telling your tween to help with a chore. Children resent being ordered about as much as anyone. Say, "I need your help mowing the lawn," or "We need to mow the lawn." Don't ask, "Would you help me mow the lawn?" unless your tween is free to say "no."

Never apologize for requiring your tween to help around the house. That communicates you have done something wrong by expecting her to contribute to the upkeep of the household and develop into a responsible adult. Those are definitely the wrong messages to send!

Giving Feedback

The key to keeping tweens on track once they know how to do whatever chores are required of them is to be conscientious about taking time to survey their handiwork and give positive feedback whenever they have finished a task. Don't expect to ever reach the point where your appreciation of a job well done becomes irrelevant. Study after study shows that adults find positive recognition critical to their overall job satisfaction. In fact, employees are more motivated by having their work acknowledged, recognized, and appreciated than by their salaries.

Direct compliments are important, but letting your child hear you tell someone else really has an impact. Comment that you are proud that he is learning to be responsible for his own room, getting better about handling his homework responsibilities, taking more initiative, and requiring fewer reminders to start on his daily chore. Success builds on success, failure upon failure, so keep the warm fuzzies flowing. Make sure the accomplishments you note are real, albeit small.

FACT

If your child sees herself as an irresponsible ne'er-do-well, dedicating lots of time to hands-on teaching and verbally praising each small accomplishment can help her to see herself differently. Avoid criticizing errors and lavish praise for a job well done.

Flexibility and Structure

Schedule conflicts will inevitably interfere with your child's chores. Avoid the pitfall of letting him beg to be excused with vague promises to do his work later. Follow the work-before-pleasure policy if you can. Otherwise, tell him he needs to come up with a plan for making up the missed work, perhaps adding in a penalty, and hold him to it. At some point, you'll undoubtedly benefit from getting some real help around the house. In the meantime, you'll know that all the time you put in supervising and monitoring is a loving gift. Who knows? Someday your child may even appreciate it. (E)

Chapter 13

Fun and Games

There's more to life than watching television and playing videogames, but your little addict may not want to experience other pleasures until you have pried his hands from the remote control and hidden his joy stick. Introduce him to some great fun and new games to help him recover from the high-tech habit!

High-Tech Highs

Zack was an outdoorsy, athletic boy who enjoyed everything from bicycling and skateboarding to hockey and gymnastics. He was the only kid on the block whose parents didn't own a television set or a computer, although Zack was sure that he was the only kid in the world. His parents weren't worried that he'd grow up to be a complete dinosaur, since he spent time in front of the TV screen at his friends' houses and had access to a computer at school and the local library.

When Zack was ten, the only thing on his Christmas wish list was a TV. Since he was such a sports enthusiast and the Winter Olympics were coming up, his parents decided to take the plunge and buy him one. Besides, they wanted him to learn to watch TV responsibly; they envisioned sitting down together to help him get a perspective on the shows and commercials. "You can only watch one hour a day," they told him. Zack readily agreed.

It didn't take his parents long to realize that one hour a day of TV viewing required some major life changes. By the time everyone got home, it was almost 6:00 P.M. By the time the dinner dishes were done, it was seven. Zack spent thirty minutes on homework, watched TV for an hour, and then needed thirty minutes to bathe, get ready for bed, and read or hear a bedtime story for lights out by nine. That meant there was no time for chores, tossing a ball in the backyard, building models, running an errand, or anything else. "I don't get it," his father said. "There aren't enough hours in the day. How do other families manage?"

FACT

Lots of TV watching and videogame playing have been associated with a range of problems: poor grades, obesity, distractibility, aggression, hyperactivity, and increased parent-child conflicts.

"Other kids stay up until ten, eleven, or even later," Zack answered. His disbelieving parents asked around and learned it was true, but they weren't about to let Zack stay up that late. They called a halt to watching TV on school days and restricted him to two hours on weekends and holidays. They bought a VCR so Zack could tape his favorite weeknight shows to watch later. Soon Zack was back to his old routines, which his parents considered much healthier. They were comfortable enough then to buy him a computer, for use two hours a day on weekends and holidays.

The Adrenaline Rush

It's no wonder that kids love videogames, action-packed TV shows, and horror movies. The good ones provide the kind of all-absorbing mental stimulation and repeated adrenaline rushes that are hard to come by any other way. During a captivating game, show, or movie children enter a state of suspended reality. The lines between there and here, then and now, and me and "it" vanish, and time passes at warp speed. Expressions like "time stopped," "mind-blowing," and "zoned-out" come closest to describing the sensations that artists strive so hard to evoke, and which Hollywood directors and game developers have become so adept at producing.

There's no question that TV shows, computers, and high-tech games are great fun for kids or that they learn from them. The problem is, they may learn a lot of things they would be better off not knowing and miss the social interaction that is critical for children this age. High-tech entertainment is not inherently good or bad. It depends on what programs your child watches and what games he plays, and how often.

Addiction Downers

There are occasional headlines about a child who recreates in the real world what he has seen his heroes do on TV or in a videogame, and the result is a horrific copycat crime. Ask your tween if he considers this a danger, and although he may know a youngster who is overly entangled in a high-tech make-believe world, he will most likely insist it's not a problem for him. In fact, it probably isn't. Only a small minority of youngsters lose track of which side of the reality/fantasy line they are on, and they typically show serious signs of psychological imbalance to begin with.

ALERT!

Addicted tweens show signs of going through withdrawal when the TV is on the fritz, the computer is out of commission, and the Sega unit is on the blink. Don't be surprised if your tween is cross, cranky, bored, and generally at a loss as to what to do with herself if you limit her TV-viewing and time spent at the computer.

Still, the fact that tweens commonly have dreams in which their minds replay scenes from scary movies and reproduce menacing videogame characters proves that they are being unconsciously affected. The biggest threat may well be the slow but steady desensitization to violence. Although there are lots of factors contributing to juvenile delinquency, the role of modeled aggression on TV cannot be discounted. Children in the United States are exposed to an estimated 8,000 murders and 100,000 acts of violence by the end of elementary school, according to the National Coalition on Television Violence.

Learning to Live Without TV

One way to help your tween get control of her high-tech habit is to have her withdraw gradually by lessening the amount of time she is allowed to devote to watching TV, playing videogames, and using the computer. Another is to have her go cold turkey. Either way, she'll probably need help adjusting.

After being forbidden to pick on her siblings, she may try to drown her misery in sodas and assuage her jangled nerves with high-calorie comfort foods before deciding that if she is going to have to suffer, the villain who caused her so much grief deserves to suffer, too. At that point, you may become the target of her ill will.

However, rest assured that your child will adjust in amazingly short order if you help her. Here is what you will need to do:

1. Stay firm. Don't cave in to the accusations of unfairness. The typical pattern for tweens is to settle down after limits have been consistently set for about five days. However, expect a resurgence of complaints

when the household schedule changes. If you start setting limits during the school week, she is apt to have difficulties structuring her time during the first weekend and on the first few days of the next week when school resumes.

2. Provide heavy doses of TLC and suggestions about how to relax and work off excess energy. Be sympathetic as you encourage her to ride her bike, ride her scooter, shoot baskets, or run around the block.

3. Teach her to handle leisure time by helping her figure out other fun things to do.

If that sounds as though life is going to be terribly difficult, keep in mind that once the adjustment period is over, it should be much easier than when she was exploding masses of aliens, pummeling kickboxers, and spending hours vegging out in front of the TV.

Imagination Boosters

Many children who spend much of their free time watching television in lieu of engaging in more creative pastimes have a notable lack of imagination. When asked to tell or write a story, they recount a show or movie they saw and are unable to concoct one of their own.

QUESTION?

Which toys are best?
When shopping, check for the Parent's Seal of Approval, an endorsement by the National PTA, or an indication that the product won a Parent's Choice award. When shopping for books, look for Caldecott and Newbury Medal winners. At the library, ask the children's librarian for recommendations.

The following activities can help get your tween's creative juices flowing:

• Put a notepad, pen, magnifying glass, cape, or any other Sherlock Holmes items you can think of in a canvas bag. Tell your child and his friend that each of them should pick an object, hide it, and invent clues for the other child to follow to find the missing object. Alternatively, have young detectives invent a crime, perhaps using stuffed animals or dolls as victims and perpetrators, and create the clues so someone else can try to figure out "whodunit."

• Give your tween a sack filled with items that can be used to make a doll or stuffed animal. The contents could include clothespins or Popsicle sticks for bodies, glue, cotton, and scraps of fabric, yarn, and lace.

• Turn your child into a hand-puppet maker by giving him a sock to slip on his hand. Provide yarn for hair, buttons for eyes, and some red fabric for a tongue. Suggest that he add a bow tie for a boy puppet, a hair ribbon for a girl. Tell him to try the sock on his hand first and mark where everything goes with a magic marker or chalk. When he's made several, suggest he write the script and invite the neighborhood kids over for a show.

• Your child can be a moviemaker if you're willing to let him head out with the family VHS or digital recorder. The place to begin, of course, is by thinking up a story, writing a script, and finding some other children to serve as actors.

• Suggest your child outdo Milton Bradley by making his own board game from some items you've provided—dice, a timer, pennies or buttons for playing pieces, cardboard for making the game board, markers or crayons, and a stack of three-by-five file cards (or have him cut regular paper to size). Once your child has perfected his creation and field-tested it with his friends, let him scan it into a Web page so other children can play. Alternatively, suggest he go online and try to market it to a toy company.

Backyard Fun

One of the best outdoor investments you can make is to buy a couple of basketballs, soccer balls, kick balls, and a good bicycle pump to keep them inflated. Add a couple of softballs, baseballs, Wiffle balls, tennis balls, bouncy rubber balls, and golf balls, too. A few dollars spent on an oversized beach ball buys many hours of fun. It will bounce on grass unless the earth is exceptionally soft. To protect against loss, have your child write his name on all the balls with a marker.

ALERT!

Frisbees, balls, and dogs are perennial tween-pleasers. If no friends are available to play keep-away, suggest your youngster teach Fido to play catch. The trick is to pat and praise a furry companion for doing something *right* and withhold praise when he hides the toy and tries to chew on it.

Tie a rope across the yard and your child has a homemade volleyball net. Hang a bottomless bushel basket in a tree and you've got a hoop. A big piece of plywood thick enough not to warp can be set up on a couple of sawhorses to make a Ping-Pong table. With the addition of a few blankets for walls, it can be readily converted into a fort, playhouse, or puppet theater. Just be sure it's sturdy enough to hold climbers.

When your child is tired of freeze tag and blind man's bluff, encourage him to keep running, bending, and stretching with a game of badminton or croquet. Kids will appreciate them as presents for Christmas or Hanukkah even if they're not much use until spring. Apartment dwellers can easily carry them to play with at a nearby park, and they're great fun on camping trips, too. An even less expensive, more portable toy is a Wiffle ball and plastic bat, which can be used to play either baseball or golf, depending how your tween swings the bat and whether he tosses or rolls the ball.

Kite flying is another traditional pastime that tweens love. Eliminate the upset over a lost kite by suggesting your child make her own. Two sticks lashed together with string, some brown butcher paper cut to size and stapled to the sticks, a big ball of string, and some rags for a tail will do it.

Swing sets are always popular, although older tweens may consider the kinds sold at most department stores too babyish, and in fact they may not be sturdy enough. As with so many things, homemade is best. Suspend a tire or plank from a tree limb for swinging, and set up a thin bar for trapeze artists. The time you spend installing a bar in your backyard won't go to waste, given the hours your child will spend doing gymnastics. Check to be sure wild swinging doesn't cause a collision with a tree or fence, double-check for strength and stability, and check the ground beneath it for hard landings.

E ALERT!

End all the mowing, spraying, and fertilizing by creating a giant dirt hill in your backyard. A five-foot mound invites games of king of the mountain, and kids will find plenty of other ways to entertain themselves. Alternatively, pour concrete so your tween can play basketball and four-square to her heart's content.

End your child's social problems once and for all by buying him a full-size trampoline, which is guaranteed to draw kids from far and near. Even undersized yards can hold one; tall mesh nets can be purchased that attach to the perimeter to prevent a wild child from being catapulted into a nearby tree trunk or onto the sidewalk. Still, don't cancel your child's health insurance or homeowner's policy. As with all sports that encourage kids to hurl themselves about, there is definitely an element of risk.

Rainy Day Fun

Tweens' need for exercise continues even when the weather drips and drizzles, and being cooped up in the house can make them cranky. Some children even resist going outside to play on a bright, sunny day. Luckily, there are lots of tween-pleasing activities to spark their interest.

Indoor Athletics

After you've sent your child outside to taste the rain, slosh through puddles, and play catch with water-filled balloons, you may need to find an indoor activity to keep her occupied. Give her and her friend the cardboard tube from a roll of paper towels to use as a bat, a balloon to use as a ball, and suggest they play a game of baseball—make that "balloonball." Alternatively, tie a long piece of string across a room so they can play balloon volleyball. Obviously you may need to safeguard knickknacks and move sharp-edged coffee tables off to the side.

If you want to join in the fun, hold a rope with a rag tied to the other end. Have the children gather around and try to jump the rag as you twirl it in a circle beneath their feet.

For a great group party game, stretch a string across the floor, put half the kids on one side of it and half on the other, give each a hefty supply of paper wads, and have each team try to clear its side of the wads by kicking, tossing, or pushing them over the line to the other team's side.

Quieter Pursuits

When your child is ready to calm down, consider the old tween standbys from generations past. Jacks and a ball, marbles, a beanbag toss, juggling, jigsaw puzzles, or pick-up-sticks. They're as good as videogames for developing hand-to-eye coordination.

Organizing photo albums is one of those projects parents keep meaning to get around to but continually postpone because it feels more like work than fun. Consider turning the job over to your tween, who is likely to approach it with enthusiasm. Encourage him to bring some creativity to the task by cutting a few of the photos into interesting shapes, making construction paper borders, inserting catchy captions here and there, and adding some hand-drawn designs. For more ideas, give your child *The Kid's Guide to Making Scrapbooks & Photo Albums!* (Written by Laura Check and illustrated by Betsy Day, this book is produced by Williamson Publishing in Vermont.) When he's finished compiling the photo album, it may not look like the usual family album, but who cares? You intended to pass it on to him someday anyway, didn't you?

Suggest he select a few of the photos for a genealogy project. Your tween can tape-record interviews with relatives, research the family tree, contact distant cousins by e-mail, or correspond with uncles and aunts.

When he's finished, have him photocopy his stories and notes, duplicate the audiotapes and photos, and put them in decorated folders to send to extended family members. They'll no doubt consider it the best present they have ever received.

Another great rainy day project is whipping up a batch of homemade Silly Putty. Simply pour one tablespoon of liquid starch into a bowl. In a separate bowl, mix two tablespoons of white glue and two to three drops of food coloring. Pour the glue onto the starch, and allow the mixture to stand for five minutes or until the glue absorbs the starch. Remove it from the bowl and knead it until the desired consistency is obtained. Store the Silly Putty in a sealed plastic bag or a plastic Easter egg.

Classic Games

It's easy to pour money into cheap plastic toys and games that your tween barely plays with before relegating to the back of a closet. Why bother when spending a bit more on a truly kid-friendly game will yield years of fun? Think of the games you enjoyed most as a child. Classic toys have staying power that transcends generations. How about any of these?

- Backgammon
- Battleship
- Checkers
- Chess
- Chinese checkers
- Chutes and Ladders
- Clue
- Life
- Monopoly
- Othello
- Parcheesi
- Playing cards
- Risk
- Score Four
- Scrabble
- Sorry
- Trivial Pursuit
- Yahtzee

Teach your child to care for his games by taking out only one at a time and putting all the pieces back in the box correctly. Once pieces are lost and cards are bent, the games are ruined. Remember, these games are fun for the whole family. They're a great way to spend time with your tween!

Tween Hobbies

Every tween should have at least one hobby. Whether he collects tin foil, builds model airplanes, or writes poetry, hobbies teach skills that are hard for tweens to learn any other way.

Collecting

Some hobbies involve collecting pricey items. Still, they may be worth their weight in gold because collections give tweens such good practice in planning, saving, trading, negotiating, and organizing. Plus, there's always the dream that by acquiring and maintaining their collection for a half century, it will turn out to be worth millions.

Popular collections include coins, stamps, stuffed animals, post cards, trading cards, marbles, toy soldiers, Hot Wheels, Barbie dolls, McDonald's Happy Meal toys, comic books, Nancy Drew books, Beanie Babies, fossils, butterflies, bugs, rocks, silver spoons, and matchbooks. Actually, when it comes to collections, the possibilities are endless.

It's hard to know why tweens get such a kick out of collecting such things as paper clips, bottles, tin foil, rubber bands, pencils, and stickers. Learning to save and organize are important developmental tasks for this age group.

Technical Hobbies

Whether their passion is filling an aquarium with exotic fish, building a terrarium, bird watching, dog training, or stargazing, science hobbies encourage tweens to explore a subject in depth. Spark your tween's interest with *The Ultimate Book of Kid Concoctions* by John E. Thomas. This book will teach your tween to make wild and crazy things out of everyday household items.

Geography hobbies involve collecting information about a particular state, region, or country. History buffs may have a particular time period they like to read about and may collect antique swords or other paraphernalia related to it.

Technical hobbies yield major educational benefits, so encourage your child to check out library books on her chosen subject and explore her area of interest online. Some children manage to become quite knowledgeable in their chosen field.

Arts and Crafts

Craft sets offer budding artists opportunities to make things but are structured enough that children need not be particularly creative to enjoy them. Kits are available for making items such as potholders, jewelry, leather wallets, candles, paint-by-number pictures, Origami toys, soap, and just about anything else. There's nothing quite so wonderful as handmade holiday presents, so suggest your tween create gifts for friends and relatives. Most tween girls love to learn to crochet, knit, and sew. If you don't know how, find someone to tutor your tween to get her started. If you're into pottery, quilting, ceramics, doll making, or have an interest in another craft, the tween years are the time to share your talents.

Your child will soon be old enough to create some real Play Dough statues and figurines, so why not let him whip up a batch of dough? It's easy enough to make finger paints at home, too. Building projects hold special appeal for tween boys, but girls should be encouraged to do them, too. Tweens are the perfect age for LEGOS, where they can exercise their creativity while building. Constructing model cars and airplanes remains popular, as does assembling a crystal radio or motorized rocket from a kit. Some wood scraps and access to real tools is most boys' idea of a wonderful gift, especially if there's enough wood to build a fort. However, keep in mind that tweens need someone older and wiser to teach safety and supervise until they can be trusted to use tools by themselves.

These days, any hobby can be for either sex. Such pastimes as juggling and doing magic tricks hold strong appeal to boys and girls alike. Some tweens become experts at whittling. Carving balsa wood is easy. Carving Ivory soap bars is easiest of all.

With the award-winning Gears! Gears! Gears! Oogly Googly Motorized Building Set, your child can follow the instructions or design his or her own motorized machines. Call (888) 800-7893 or visit ✍ *www.learningresources.com* for more information.

Best Gifts

Start off a new hobby by giving your tween a book as a holiday or birthday present. Boys and girls love how-to-draw books that teach them to make pictures of horses and other animals and create cartoons and caricatures. You can't go wrong with a joke book or a fact-filled book such as *The Book of Lists*, *The Guinness Book of World Records*, *The World Almanac for Kids*, or *Scholastic Kid's Almanac for the 21st Century*. Most children can appreciate a calligraphy set or a blank journal and fountain pen. And, of course, every tween girl must have a diary with a lock. Ⓔ

Chapter 14
Food for Life

Getting your child to eat well and get enough exercise can be a challenge. The processed chemical concoctions created by the multibillion-dollar food industry are better at satisfying a sweet tooth and tickling taste buds than the foodstuffs Mother Nature serves up. Couch potatoes may prefer gulping snacks in front of the TV screen to meals eaten at the dinner table. It is up to you to make sure your child learns healthy eating habits and gets plenty of exercise.

The Breakfast Benefit

For years, Margie's husband had insisted that their daughter Amy needed a nutritious breakfast. Margie didn't eat breakfast herself and didn't believe Amy was being nutritionally deprived, so she wasn't moved to comply with his wishes. Her husband fixed breakfast for the three of them when he was in town on weekends, but on school days Amy had a bowl of cereal and a glass of juice if she was hungry.

Then Margie read a report about the importance of eating breakfast. It said that students who began the school day with a wholesome breakfast had been found to have fewer behavior problems and to make better grades. Amy was an excellent student who was popular with her peers and teachers, but Margie decided it might be best to pay more attention to Amy's diet after all. Since the food served in the cafeteria was heavy on starch and grease and light on fresh vegetables, she began packing a lunch for her, too.

Given that Amy was already doing so well, Margie didn't expect to notice much of a difference. She was surprised when Amy began arriving home after school upbeat and energetic instead of tired and touchy. That's when the true importance of diet began to sink in. Amy has been eating breakfast and carrying a lunch ever since.

Tween Nutritional Requirements

Tweens gain an average of 6.5 pounds and grow more than two inches a year between ages eight and thirteen. Substantial central nervous system development takes place, resulting in improved coordination, balance, dexterity, agility, and speed. Their sexual organs mature as well, transforming them from little children to biological adults. To support such massive physical development requires the right fuel. Even though getting your tween to eat a well-balanced diet isn't easy, it is possible.

Dietary Guidelines

Dietary guidelines can't help you determine how much food your tween needs to consume at any given point in time, and you shouldn't try to figure it out. Allow him to eat as much as he wants at meals or even in between, but limit the selection of available foods and ensure that they are *all* healthy choices. The only way to do that is to be careful about what you bring home from the grocery store. There may be no other way to control a child who is at home alone, and a rebellious tween may do what he pleases even when you are there.

FACT

You cannot know how much your tween needs to eat on any given day because growth patterns differ tremendously from child to child and from one day to the next. While some tweens grow in a slow-but-steady fashion, others alternate between long lulls and dramatic spurts. If you think your child has grown overnight, you may be right. Tweens can stretch by as much as half an inch in twenty-four hours.

The following guidelines are for children up to age eleven. Older children will need a bit more in each category. To calculate your child's weight in kilograms (kg), divide his weight in pounds by 2.2.

- **Calories:** About 70 calories per kg total; 55 percent from carbohydrates, 15 percent from protein, and 30 percent from fats (of the calories from fat, less than 10 percent should be from saturated fat).
- **Carbohydrates:** Five or more servings per day; each serving equals 1 cup of potatoes, pasta, or rice; 2 slices whole grain bread, ¾ cup dry cereal, ¾ muffin or bagel.
- **Fruits:** Two to three servings per day; each serving equals 1 cup canned fruit, 1 piece fresh fruit, ½ cup juice.
- **Protein:** One gram per kg or about three or more servings per day; each serving equals 2 to 3 ounces meat, fish, or poultry; 1 egg; ½ cup cottage or ricotta cheese; 1 to 2 ounces of other types of cheese; ½ cup cooked dried beans or legumes; 3 tablespoons peanut butter.
- **Vegetables:** Two to three servings of cooked or raw vegetables per

day; one serving equals ½ cup of vegetables.

- **Fats:** One to three servings per day of oil, margarine, butter, or salad dressing; one serving equals 1 tablespoon.
- **Sweets:** Four to five servings per week maximum; one serving equals ½ cup ice cream, ½ cup pudding, ⅛ pie, 1 large cookie.

In addition, your child should consume less than 300 mg of cholesterol per day and drink plenty of water, so watch the egg yolks and turn on the tap!

ALERT!

It is not recommended that you try to shore up your child's diet with vitamins unless a doctor recommends them. The best route to getting enough vitamins, nutritionists agree, is by eating a variety of healthful foods.

The Battle of the Sweet Tooth

Contrary to what every parent wishes and too many believe, you cannot count on Mother Nature to steer your tween toward the foods she needs for optimum health. Human beings were designed with a sweet tooth that craves sugar and a palate that desires fat. These were important for survival back in the not-so-good old days before farming and ranching. Food was hard to come by, and preagricultural peoples could store up fat in order to survive the lean times by overindulging when they chanced upon fruit or game. Now that famines have disappeared from the American landscape, there is no longer a need to overindulge. Still, the genetic preference to cram with high-calorie, high-fat foods remains.

To further complicate matters, since modern humans no longer spend their days hunting and gathering, they need less fuel. Today's children have fewer opportunities to burn the calories they consume than generations past. Few spend hours running around the backyard and neighborhood with their friends. After spending the day sitting in school, they come home to sit in front of the TV, computer, and videogames.

The problem with sugar is that it provides calories devoid of nutrition ("empty calories") and fills children up so that they lose their appetite for nutritious foods. The worst offenders are soft drinks, which have no nutrients. Sodium intake from consuming salty foods is another serious problem as it has been linked to high blood pressure. The average two-year-old consumes more than five times the amount required, but not from a saltshaker. Cutting back on salt when cooking foods from scratch won't help the average family. Most sodium comes in processed foods.

Even tweens who know that too much cholesterol and fat are bad nevertheless admit that they consume diets that are high in cholesterol-laden fatty foods. In surveys, tweens say they are tired of being lectured about eating right and tune out their parents' admonishments.

The Sorry Statistics

Seventy-five percent of children exceed the recommendations for total fat and saturated fat. Eleven- and twelve-year-olds average less fiber per day than is recommended. Most children consume less than 100 percent of the RDA of vitamin E, zinc, and iron. Only half of the children get enough calcium, and only 20–25 percent of children consume enough fruit and vegetables. French fries account for one-fourth of all vegetables consumed. Refined sugar comprises 14 percent of calorie intake by adolescents.

Food Preparation

The miracle of preserving and processing food has vastly simplified cooking, but the high-tech convenience is achieved at the cost of losing much of the food's nutritional content. In point of fact, even chemists don't know what all the nutritious essentials are. They suspect that Mother Nature's originals contain more types than they have managed to identify in the lab. What they do know is that little junk-food junkies can be obese and malnourished at the same time. Their cells may bulge from fat even as they are starving for lack of vitamins, minerals, protein, fiber, water, and whatever other, as yet undiscovered, nutrients growing kids require.

Since fat is so bad, should I eliminate it from my child's diet altogether?
Definitely not! Consuming fewer than 25 percent of calories from fat can lead to stunted growth. Restricting your child's diet too much can do serious harm. The key is moderation.

It's not just what children eat but how food is prepared that matters. Canned vegetables lose so many of their vitamins during processing that they are virtually worthless. Frozen vegetables are much better; fresh vegetables served raw or steamed with a tight lid are best of all. The problem with foods made from processed grain is that they are almost completely absorbed into the system, leaving little bulk needed for bowel health. The solution is to serve more whole grains.

Teaching about Nutrition

You need to actively teach your child about nutrition so he can learn to make good decisions. The way to do that is to select items from the grocery shelves based on what the labels suggest is healthful instead of on what advertisers say is delightful. When your child urges you to buy a certain brand of cereal, study the label carefully instead of dismissing it out of hand. Point to the words *fat* and *calories* and their associated numbers so he understands why you're saying "no" and can learn to check labels. Verbalize your thoughts so your child can hear how to make nutritional decisions, and involve him in the search for the products you approve of: "Hot dogs made from beef contain too much fat and cholesterol. We need to find a kind that is filled with turkey, chicken, or vegetables. We need a fresh vegetable to go with them. Broccoli is high in calcium, which is good for your bones, and you're growing so fast right now. Or you could get your calcium from a glass of milk and choose a different green vegetable. Which would you prefer?"

As soon as your tween is old enough to read labels, send him off to find a kind of cereal or loaf of bread he likes that seems to him to meet the nutritional criteria for good health. If he comes back with a product that doesn't fit the bill, don't chastise him. Maybe he's trying to slip something past you or maybe he just doesn't understand. Don't assume the worst. Just say, "Let's look at the label together." Then point out the figures for fat, sugar, and salt, and send him back to look for another brand.

If one of your youngsters lacks self-control, don't worry about the hardship for siblings who can keep their hands out of the candy bowl. Family members need to help and support one another. Maintain a junk-food-free household to help the child who can't moderate his own food intake, and praise the others for contributing to their sibling's welfare. Even if their sacrifice is not voluntary—and especially if it's not voluntary—they deserve kudos for helping out.

Helping with Appetite Control

The best guide to how much your child needs to eat is her appetite, but boredom, anxiety, stress, and depression can trigger or suppress it. Help her separate food from emotional issues by disallowing arguments at the dinner table. Avoid discussing upsetting subjects while your child is eating. Never punish your child by withholding food or use food to reward good behavior. Instead of cheering her with comfort foods, help her find other ways to feel better. If she's bored, help her figure out something else to do. If she's sad, give her a hug or help her find another way to cheer herself up. If she is nervous, suggest a warm bath or a few moments of meditating. If she is upset about a specific problem, help her find a solution if you can; reassure her that everything really does work out in the end if you can't. Emotional eating doesn't solve problems. It creates them.

It's not just the foods your tween consumes on a regular basis that he will grow to love. Surround a rarely served dish with the warmth, joy, and excitement of a holiday or special "let's celebrate" treat, and it will acquire the ability to soothe and nurture. That is the hallmark of a feel-good comfort food. Confine rich foods to the holidays to make the special times truly special.

Don't encourage a picky eater to consume more. Your child needs to be able to recognize her internal sensations of hunger and satiation. She can't do that if she is being pushed to eat because she "should" rather than because she's hungry. Never urge your child to clean her plate.

If your child says she's full, don't even insist that she finish her salad. However, if she is asking for a second helping of something else, it certainly makes sense to require her to eat her salad first. If she won't eat the salad and you're afraid she'll soon want a snack, save the salad and serve it to her when she's ready. If snack time arrives and she still refuses the salad, reassure her that the next meal will be served in a few hours. Don't argue; just remain matter-of-fact. She will either change her mind about the salad or be ready to eat something else that is nutritious at the next meal.

Controlling snacking is easier than most parents think. If you think that by imposing limits you will have to deal with a cranky child, you're right! But if you take the shortcut and let your child eat what she will in order to minimize conflict, you're likely to find she is harder rather than easier to get along with. Poor eating habits can cause the kind of ongoing irritability, hyperactivity, and crankiness that drive the very tension you wish to avoid.

Tween Diets

Forty percent of all school-age children queried in the Kellogg Survey reported having been on a diet, according to an article by Elta Saltos of the USDA Cooperative State Research, Education and Extension Services (*Adapting the Food Guide Pyramid for Children: Defining the Target Audience in Family Economics and Nutrition Review* 12, nos. 3, 4 [1999]). Given that about 20 percent of children are overweight, and 10 percent actually fall into the obese category, they're not very successful. Still, you should watch to make sure your child isn't succeeding all too well. Anorexia is on the rise, and other eating disorders pose a threat as well (see Chapter 16).

Shedding Extra Pounds

The problem with dieting is that after the first few pounds are off, the body thinks a famine is afoot and slows the metabolism so that the few incoming calories stretch farther. That makes it harder and harder to lose weight. In addition, the feelings of deprivation lead to rebound eating, so as soon as the diet is over the pounds quickly reappear. To lose weight and keep it off, children need a change in their lifestyle. Exercise increases metabolism and is a more effective way to lose weight than dieting. Furthermore, the goal shouldn't be to lose weight, but to get in shape by combining a new set of permanent eating habits with regular exercise. Staying fit is a lifetime affair.

Calorie-Cutting Ideas

Nutritionists recommend that tweens drink 2 percent milk rather than whole milk, unless a doctor advises otherwise. Sodas are the worst offenders of all the items in the grocery store that pass for food; most contain calories that are completely void of nutritional value and are very bad for children's teeth. Don't buy them. Try water with a sprinkling of lemon or orange juice. Instead of serving fruit juice, which is very high in calories and which children can down in huge quantities, serve fresh fruits. Because the fiber from the pulp of fruit is more filling, children don't consume as much, so they take in fewer calories.

Some simple dietary strategies can cut lots of calories fast, but unless the changes in diet are permanent, nothing positive will be accomplished. If your tween is upset about his weight, revise the way you shop and cook.

Tweens do need 30 percent of their calories to come from fat, but most get far more than that. Never encourage your child to dip his veggies in sauces or add salad dressing if he can do without. If you do serve salad dressing, stick to vinegar or lemon juice, and use little or no oil. Experiment until you find a combination of spices your family likes;

try mixtures of lemon pepper, parsley, Italian seasonings, salt, and, if all else fails, a dollop of sugar. Broil meat, fish, and poultry and serve them without breading and sauces. Pep up the taste of protein dishes with herbs, too, instead of frying them in fat. If you do serve chips, forego the dip. When you serve popcorn, skip the butter. It serves no purpose to add fat and sugar to *anything* if your child can do without it, unless your doctor says differently.

Avoid fast-food restaurants where the heavy doses of starch, grease, and salt ensure the taste appeals to most everyone, as that usually means the menu items aren't healthy for anyone. If you are taking your child out for hamburgers to celebrate something special, go with charcoal broiled rather than fried. Pizza is always a tween favorite, and it's healthy enough as long as the crust is whole grain and it's topped with veggies and low-fat cheese—that probably means making your own rather than serving store-bought. Pizza is time-consuming and a mess to make, but your child will enjoy helping, and in time will learn to do it alone. Getting him to clean up afterward, of course, will likely be harder. Lots of kiddie cookbooks are available. They make wonderful gifts and can spark interest in tackling the culinary arts.

ALERT!

It's better to have your tween help you cook dinner than do KP duty afterward. You can teach the culinary arts, have fun together, and he is more likely to eat food he helps prepare.

By giving your tween nutritional information and imposing dietary restrictions, you teach him how to make good decisions and give him opportunities to develop good habits during these crucial years of rapid physical development. When he's away from home, he may not choose to follow your directives, and when he's grown, he may not use your gift for years or even decades, but it's there for him whenever he's ready.

Healthy Choices

Limiting your tween to healthful choices is difficult. Busy family schedules,

TV commercials, cafeteria lunches, and fast-food restaurants conspire to seduce youngsters into consuming too much in the way of fat and carbohydrates, and too little in the way of protein and fiber.

Eating Away from Home

You can control your child's access to money so she can't buy French fries at the school cafeteria and snacks from the vending machines, but how can you keep her from buying the less healthful alternatives with her own allowance? You can provide a healthful brown bag lunch and tell her not to trade food with other children, but how can you keep her from swapping her goodies for a friend's chips, cake, and Kool-Aid? The cafeteria isn't the only problem, of course. Tweens encounter foods and beverages laced with chemicals, sugar, and fat in the bowls of lollipops that are free for the taking at the local bank, in the sodas and chips and ice cream in friends' homes, and at the endless school parties.

FACT

Short of lobbying to get your school's cafeteria to serve healthier foods and oust the vending machines, the only thing you can do is to forbid your tween to trade her lunches or to spend her money on food items that aren't good for her. Give her all your best reasons for your firm stance on the matter and hope for the best.

Tell your child that too many parents don't take good care of their kids these days, so they carry poor lunches to school or are forced to eat cafeteria food. They aren't taught that what they put in their mouths makes a difference in their health, grades, and feelings of well-being. Build family pride in your nutritional standards by referring to yourselves in the third person and letting her know that your family's way is the better way: "Unlike some people, we Finleys don't eat junk food." "Other families might eat greasy, starchy, sugary, salty stuff, but not the Guginos. We know better."

If it seems unreasonable to expect a child not to participate with his classmates by eating what they eat, remember that diabetic youngsters and those who suffer from serious food allergies learn to say "no" without having their childhoods destroyed. If your tween is not afflicted with these problems, it may seem heartless to say she can't do what her friends are doing. On the other hand, combine all of the classroom parties, ice cream days, cafeteria breakfasts and lunches, visits to fast-food restaurants during field trips, snacks at after-school programs, and contests where the class reward is a pizza party or candy bars, and you'll realize that students in some schools are regularly filling up on low-quality, high-fat foods.

It really is important to send very clear, consistent messages about what you expect your child to do outside of the home: Stay away from candy bars, cookies, chips, cake, ice cream, pop, and all the other foods whose most important contribution is to finance your dentist's vacation. Will she follow your instructions when every other child is slurping pop and munching candy bars to her heart's content? Maybe not. Will your child sneak in trips to the candy counter at the movies and lie about what she consumed so as not to upset you? Depending on her personality, the answer could be "never," "sometimes," "usually," or "always." Will she know how to eat healthfully if, at age fifteen or fifty, she finally figures out that she needs to clean up her diet? Yes!

Finding the Middle Ground

Some parents fear that taking a firm stance and insisting their tweens follow a healthful diet when they are at school and in the community will cause them to sneak around and lie. Some children will in fact disregard their parent's wishes, and then take pains to keep their dietary lapses secret. Is it better for your child to sneak around, cover up, or even lie, because he knows that what he's doing is wrong? Or is it better to do the best you can to monitor food at home and let him do as he will when he's away from home without expressing disapproval? The danger of the latter is that it can send the message that you don't really care enough to protest. Perhaps a middle ground would be to clearly communicate your expectations and let your child know that you understand he will have lapses.

Acknowledge that the pressure of peers or enticement of sugar will at times win out over good sense. Be appreciative of your youngster's honesty rather than critical when he reports that he ate something that is supposed to be off his menu. Talk about what he was feeling and how else he might have responded to hunger, peer pressure, or problematic emotions; then discuss things he can do to balance his diet for the day. For instance, perhaps he can forgo dessert after dinner on a day when he eats cake and cookies at the class party. If you feel inclined to indulge your child at a restaurant, let him choose to have soda or a dessert, not both.

Problems, Problems

If you get hints that your child is regularly disobeying your directives to refrain from consuming junk food when he's away from the house, trying harder to control what he puts in his mouth probably won't help. It may engender defiance and rebellion. The only realistic solution is to assume he's satisfying his needs for fats and sugars elsewhere and alter the foods you serve at home accordingly. Do *not* argue, threaten, punish, or look for creative ways to force compliance. Just change the menus at home. Being overly controlling about a child's food intake can translate into more serious problems, such as stealing, hiding, and hoarding food. Too many tweens develop serious eating disorders, which may prove more dangerous than consuming a generally poor diet.

ALERT!

If your tween fills up on empty or less-than-desirable calories, she won't have room for healthier foods. Don't feel you are being mean by setting limits, even though most other parents don't. Your child may not like your decisions, but she will understand your intent and will be able to make good decisions when she's grown.

You can't always control what your tween does when he is home alone or out from under your watchful gaze, and you can't force your child to eat foods that he is determined to avoid. What you can do is to control *yourself*. Remember that your child's current and long-term food preferences will include the menu items that you place before him. Whether he grows up with platters of chicken claws or broiled chicken breast, boiled fish eyes or canned tuna, sheep's heads or beef roasts, fried pig skin or French fries, these are the foods he will search out when he leaves the nest and yearns for meals "just like Mom used to make." If you satisfy today's craving for sugar-coated cereal, frozen pizza, or a nutrient-light fast-food restaurant meal, you are helping to establish these items as part of your child's lifelong diet. Accept that there are no shortcuts to parenting, and redesign your life accordingly. Know that your child will not argue with you forever if you hold firm—but if you occasionally give in, the arguing will not only continue, it will escalate.

QUESTION?

My child gets hungry before our dinner hour, which can't be moved up. What are good snacks?
Serve part of the salad, soup, or side dish you have prepared for the regular meal.

Combating Commercials

Watch TV with your child and point out how commercials trick people into buying and consuming foods that aren't healthful by including toys in cereal boxes, pairing pictures of snacks with beloved cartoon characters, offering free giveaway items kids want at fast-food restaurants. Note that if Ronald McDonald were a really good clown, he would broil or bake the burgers, chicken nuggets, and potatoes instead of serving them fried. Point out that commercials advising parents that "chewy stops the chatter" are actually suggesting they stuff children's mouths with candy bars to keep them quiet!

Special Feasts

Tweens cannot live by bread alone. Humans wind treats into their rituals and feature rich foods in their celebrations. We could survive Easter without jellybeans, Passover without matzo, Valentine's Day without chocolate, and birthdays without cake, but special occasions would be a lot less fun without lavish indulgences. Limiting your child's diet on a daily basis doesn't mean you should do it on the holidays. It does mean that the special times will be all the more special. Ⓔ

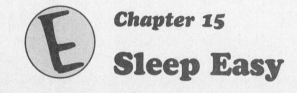

Chapter 15
Sleep Easy

To hear teachers tell it, millions of tweens go to school sleep deprived each day. Many educators say that ensuring tweens get to bed at a reasonable hour is the single best thing parents can do to improve school behavior and performance. And in fact, it is easier than you may think to get night owls into bed and to help insomniacs get some shuteye.

Sleep Deprivation

Like all of his friends, Ruben stayed up as late as he wanted to, which was not quite as late as he bragged to his friends but much later than his parents liked to admit. They had tried to enforce a nine o'clock bedtime, but it was difficult. When he was young, he feared that something would leap from his closet; when he was older, he insisted on staying up to finish homework. Moreover, they weren't certain that he needed more than seven or eight hours. Though he was a demon in the morning and they virtually had to drag him out of bed for school, he was energetic enough during the day, and at bedtime he was so rowdy they had to remind him again and again to settle down. His parents actually felt guilty for even worrying about his bedtime. The truth is, he tended to get so wild that they wanted him to go to bed so that they could get some rest.

Ruben had always been a typical kid and an above-average student, so his parents were surprised to learn that he actually displayed all of the classic signs of a chronically sleep-deprived child. Even his tendency to fall asleep in the car was a typical symptom. A study that compared how the same children scored on the same test after getting enough sleep and getting too little amazed them. Children's performance deteriorated dramatically when the researchers ranked them as sleep deprived, even though the children ranked themselves as having had plenty of sleep.

ESSENTIAL

Don't let homework interfere with bedtime. Your tween needs to start getting ready for bed early enough to get a good night's sleep. If that means he must drop an extracurricular activity to free up time in the evening, so be it. Many tweens are overscheduled. The results are stress, sleep deprivation, and chronic crankiness.

At that point Ruben's parents decided to follow the recommended guidelines by setting a bedtime and enforcing it. They feared they would not succeed and would end up fighting the battle of the bedtime forever after. They were delighted to find that in less than two weeks, Ruben began going to bed without an argument. Thereafter, he still tested limits occasionally by complaining that the bedtime rule was designed to treat him like a baby, and he would beg to stay up to watch a TV show. But his parents were so impressed with the personality changes, they began forbidding him to attend sleepovers and have friends spend the night. Besides the crankiness the next day, after getting so off-schedule, it was hard to get him back into a routine again.

Sleep Facts

It is a myth that by adopting a hands-off approach to bedtime, your child's need for sleep will motivate her to go to bed when she is tired and ensure that she gets enough rest to maintain good physical and mental health. Chronic sleep deprivation is a serious problem that takes a huge toll on large segments of the modern tween population. It is a little-known fact that sleep deprivation can manifest as attention problems and hyperactivity. Contrary to what most people think, it is not possible to make up for lost sleep on the weekends. Once sleep is lost, it is gone forever.

By laying down ironclad bedtime rules, parents can avoid the nightly discussions, negotiations, and arguments that rev kids up when they're supposed to be winding down. However, ordering your tween to get some sleep doesn't teach her how to accomplish this tricky feat. More compliant children may crawl into bed and turn off the light on command, but that doesn't mean they know how to squelch the niggling worries and fears that keep them tossing and turning for long periods each night. In addition to setting bedtimes, you need to teach basic sleep skills and create the conditions your tween needs to get enough rest.

You can't send your child to his room as a punishment during the day and expect him to feel good about being sent there at night. He needs a sleep environment he associates with comfort and calm, not tension and turmoil. Choose another location for time-outs, or use the "shadow" time-out described in Chapter 19.

How much sleep your child needs is influenced by her age, whether she is going through a growth spurt, how much stress she is under, and how much exercise she is getting. Here are some guidelines, but keep in mind that children need more sleep when they are younger, growing, under stress, and getting lots of exercise.

- **Age eight:** 10¼ to 10¾ hours
- **Age nine:** 10 hours
- **Age ten to thirteen:** 9¾ to 10 hours

To tell whether your tween needs to spend more time sawing logs, watch for the telltale signs that she is overly tired:

- Sunken appearance of the eyes
- Difficulty awakening in the morning
- Trouble learning in school
- Falling asleep in class
- Napping after school
- Falling asleep during car rides
- Irritability
- Tearfulness
- Hyperactivity
- Difficulty unwinding at bedtime

Being tired produces a state of tension that makes it hard to relax enough to fall asleep, so it is important to be sure your tween gets to bed when she is sleepy or she may have difficulty unwinding. Watch for yawning, a puffy face, slowed movements and speech, and lots of rubbing of the eyes. Determine the time at which sleepiness typically occurs by keeping track for a week; then have your tween start getting ready for bed early enough so that she can crawl in before she gets tired.

Handling Bedtime Resistance

If you have trouble getting your child into bed at night, you're not alone. Most younger tweens prefer to be where the action is: up with the rest of the family. But there are other factors that drive them to rub the sleep from their eyes and try to carry on instead of turning themselves over to the sandman.

Scary Shadows

Young tweens may resist retiring to a darkened bedroom where ogres appear in the shifting shadows, and where faint creaks and groans as the house shifts and shudders sound like burglars rapping at the window and dinosaurs creeping down the hall.

FACT

Nighttime fears are so universal they may actually be part of the human genetic heritage. A case of the creepy-crawlies probably discouraged cave kids from straying into the forest after nightfall where they would be ready prey for the nocturnal beasts with superior senses of sight, smell, and hearing.

If outlawing violent movies and videogames doesn't help, try dousing fearful shadows in beams from night-lights or a flashlight that he can keep under his pillow. The rays stop predators in their tracks and send them scurrying for shelter. Leave a hall light on and the door open to dispel the darkness, or leave the overhead light on in your child's room and let him fall asleep in the reassuring glare. Who says that people must sleep in the dark?

Often a fear of a nighttime visit from a wild animal or cartoon character can be overcome by outfitting your tween with a special repellant guaranteed to render the nastiest beast harmless. The repellant can be anything from a flashlight to a designated stick to wave like a magic wand. Since sound can banish monsters, provide a rattle your child can shake at the closet shadows and at the branches tapping the window. Placing a protective object in the room, such as an oversized Teddy bear to stand guard, can be reassuring. Knowing that they are being watched over by angels or another divine presence soothes many tweens, so prayers are often helpful.

Night fears are virtually unheard of in countries where families sleep together, and bunking down together is a virtually guaranteed way to eliminate scares. However, sharing sheets with a thrasher and losing precious alone time and privacy with a spouse may create more problems than it solves. A short-term solution is to allow your child to fall asleep in your bed and walk him to his room when you retire or set up a nearby pallet on the floor where he can bed down. However, while such strategies may relieve his fearfulness, they may not solve the bigger problem of learning to relax and fall asleep alone.

ALERT!

If your child watches shows, plays videogames, and reads stories filled with scary images, they can return to haunt him at night. However, many protected tweens envision snakes under the bed, spiders crawling up the walls, and wolves peeking from the closet.

When the Day's Too Short

As tweens get older, their reluctance to retire when told is driven by their wish to socialize with friends on the phone rather than with family in the living room. Fears of being attacked by prowling ghosts are supplanted by ruminations about personal problems and real-life dangers. Many stay up late doing homework.

Some children find it helpful to share their problems at bedtime, so they can get them off their chests instead of having them swirl through their minds after the lights go out. However, talking about problems at bedtime causes some children to feel more upset, making it hard for them to fall asleep afterward. The only way to know what works best for your youngster is to ask him if he continued to worry about his problem after you left the room. If he did, find another time for him to share about his day, such as after dinner.

Some parents don't feel particularly sympathetic when they are tired. When children continue to express fear, plead for one more glass of water, and make other bids for continuing time and attention, some parental crankiness is inevitable. Nevertheless, it's important to communicate three things to a restless night owl: "I'm sorry that you can't sleep," "I have confidence that you can control your thoughts and relax," "Thinking happy thoughts, counting sheep, and turning on some soothing music are activities that can help you. We'll try some dietary and exercise changes to see if they make a difference."

Stress and Depression

Stress and depression, as well as some medications, cause brain waves to change and alter sleep cycles. As a result, a youngster may be tired during the day despite spending long hours in bed. Agitated depression causes hyperactivity and difficulties unwinding enough to sleep. A common symptom of clinical depression is early-morning awakening. Take your youngster for a mental health evaluation if sleep problems persist.

Improving Sleep Through Diet

For your tween to relax enough so that sleep is possible, he needs to stick to menu items that have calming properties and avoid foods and beverages to which he is allergic or that function like stimulants.

ESSENTIAL

Don't just say "no" to bedtime snacks containing additives, sugars, and stimulants. In fact, don't just say "no" or "yes" to your tween about anything. Share the "whys" behind your decisions so he can make good decisions when he's grown and you aren't present to tell him what to do.

Read the labels on carbonated beverages and teas and forbid caffeinated beverages, especially after dinner. Even decaffeinated coffees contain small amounts of caffeine. Some blended teas contain black tea, which contains caffeine, too, so stick to herbal. Chocolate is a stimulant, so it should be avoided.

Instead of the usual chips, cookies, and ice cream, offer a bedtime snack high in tryptophan (an amino acid found in meats, fish, poultry, cottage cheese, and peanuts) combined with a complex carbohydrate (found in whole grain breads and crackers, pasta, and rice). Together they induce feelings of well-being and slow brain activity. Sliced turkey on crackers, an egg and cheese on toast, or some leftover tuna casserole are good choices.

Serve bedtime snacks with a relaxation-inducing beverage. Try a glass of warm milk or a cup of chamomile tea.

Food Allergies

Many parents are not aware that their child suffers from allergies that interfere with sleep. Allergy testing is one way to make this determination. Another is to keep a journal of everything your tween eats at home and have her record whatever she consumes away from home in a journal of her own. If your tween doesn't follow through, interview her when she gets home to find out what she ate that day. Note in the journals the time at which she feels tired, sleepy, cranky, nervous, "hyper," ill, sad, or has any physical symptoms, such as hives, itchy skin, sneezing, coughing, runny nose, difficulty breathing, constipation, or diarrhea. Compile a list of suspect foods and begin an elimination diet. To do that, cut out the most likely culprits altogether, and reintroduce them at the rate of one every few days while continuing to track her symptoms. Many children are affected by refined sugars, milk, eggs, soy, wheat, and fish. Consult the labels on processed foods. Dried eggs, powdered milk, sugars, and refined wheat are included in lots of foods you wouldn't typically think of as containing those ingredients.

Other Sleep Aids

After shoring up your child's diet, try some other quick fixes to help ensure your child falls asleep quickly and moves through the sleep cycles properly so he can get the kind of rest that makes it easier to start the day with a smile and keep a positive mood until bedtime.

Aromatherapy

Inhaling certain scents may not cure cancer as some people claim, but studies show aromatherapy can in fact produce short-term relief from anxiety and induce sleep. In a study of geriatric patients, lavender oil dispersed in the air enabled them to sleep as well as when they were on prescription medication, falling asleep quickly and sleeping without a lot of restlessness.

Assuming your tween doesn't have allergies, put a drop of lavender oil on her nostrils before tucking her in, or add several to her bath at night. Just be sure the oil contains real lavender. It is possible to mimic the smell synthetically, and the effectiveness of artificial lavender has not been researched.

Soothing for Snoozing

"Trying" to go to sleep doesn't work since it creates the kind of tension that works against achieving the relaxed state needed to fall asleep. If your child complains of insomnia, begin by reassuring him that just resting in bed is enough to ensure he'll feel refreshed the next day. Then try some relaxation enhancers. Help an auditory tween calm his thoughts by turning on some restful music. A visual child may do better visualizing a restful scene, such as lying on the beach, sitting in a meadow, or gazing at stars. A verbal youngster may benefit more from counting sheep or engaging in another mental task that is repetitive but innocuous. If you're not sure what kind of tween you have, suggest he try all three to see which works best.

Alternatively, teach your child a standard meditation technique by having him concentrate on his breathing. Talk him through the process in a hypnotic voice, instructing him to breathe deeply by inhaling through the mouth, holding it in for the count of five, and exhaling through the nose. Tell him to imagine that feelings of relaxation are entering his body when he inhales and that tension is leaving each time he exhales.

Physical exercise releases tension and induces feelings of well-being through the release of endorphins, so be sure your child gets plenty of daily exercise. However, rowdy play and strenuous activities that increase physical arousal should be avoided an hour before bed, as should conversations and stories that create excitement or anxiety.

FACT

Even tweens who no longer like hugs and kisses may be amenable to a back rub or a massage of the hands, feet, or neck. Whether you use a sweet-smelling lotion or just your hands, be gentle rather than vigorous to enhance relaxation.

Helpful Bedtime Rituals

As long as you remain flexible about bedtimes, your child will probably press to have them postponed. The best way to eliminate nightly arguments is by establishing ironclad bedtime rules and instituting a regular sequence of bedtime preparations. Once your tween can re-enact them like a ritual, he will automatically begin relaxing as he moves through them. The secret is consistency. Have him move through the nightly chores of eating a bedtime snack, brushing his teeth, taking a warm bath, putting on pajamas, reading a story, saying prayers, and exchanging good-night kisses in the same order every night.

When it comes to choosing a bedtime story, offer limited choices to ensure that whichever book your child selects will be soothing. Boredom can help lull children to sleep, so if your tween wants to hear the same story night after night, it's wise to go along. However, if this is your only time to read together each day, more variety is called for. One compromise is to read a different story or chapter of a book each night, then let your child read her favorite story to herself before lights-out.

Tweens are so mature and capable in so many ways, it is easy to underestimate their needs for your direction, limits, and supervision. They can tuck themselves into bed, but most will stave off sleepiness to the point of total exhaustion rather than retire. They spend the school days fidgeting because they can't bear to sit still, and then sit in front of the TV during evenings and weekends. At bedtime they can't get to sleep because they never did get enough vigorous exercise. Teaching your tween what he is supposed to do is important, but it's not enough. He needs you to keep him on a healthy track.

Other Sleep-Related Problems

Millions of tweens continue to wet the bed at night, with about 15 percent outgrowing the problem each year. Contrary to what many people think, depression doesn't cause chronic bed-wetting. On the contrary, bed-wetting puts tweens at risk for depression because they can't do many things other youngsters do, such as attend camps, slumber parties, or because they are made to feel ashamed by being punished and treated harshly.

Hereditary factors are thought to be involved in bed-wetting, since most bed wetters have a parent who wet the bed. The problem usually stems from an inability to awaken when the bladder sounds the alarm and tries to rouse the sleeping brain.

ALERT!

Bed-wetting can also be a symptom of other sleep disorders, like apnea. If your child wets the bed, it's a good idea to have him screened for a sleep disorder.

Brief bouts of bed-wetting can occur when a tween is overly tired, stressed, or depressed because the sleep cycles are disturbed. The altered brain waves prevent the sleeping brain from detecting signals from the bladder, so the child fails to awaken. In that case, you can expect the problem to disappear as soon as your tween is back on an even keel. Since punishments increase stress and depression, be kind or you may perpetuate a problem that might have cleared up on its own.

Sleepwalking

It is not unusual for tweens to sleepwalk. Although most outgrow it, fatigue and sleep deprivation are thought to precipitate it. Tweens can injure themselves if they rise from their beds and cook in the kitchen or go outside for a midnight stroll, so take steps to keep them contained. It's a myth that it's dangerous to awaken a sleepwalker. It is common for tweens to talk in their sleep, too. It's doubtful you'll be able to pry any secrets from his sleep-loosened lips, however. Few of their comments are comprehensible and those that are tend to be pretty mundane. E

Chapter 16

Tween Health and Safety

After the raging fevers of the toddler years and endless runny noses that afflict kindergartners and first graders, having a hale-and-hearty tween can be a big relief. Still, a few health and dental issues will require your attention. Moreover, your tweens' increased independence raises new safety issues that you should be aware of.

Health Care Decisions

Mrs. Richardson was leery of Western medicine in general and had done her best to avoid taking her daughter Hannah to traditional doctors. Instead, Mrs. Richardson had taken Hannah to naturopaths and alternative practitioners who successfully treated her minor ailments with herbs, homeopathic remedies, and vitamins. Mrs. Richardson declined baby shots for Hannah, but when the public school refused to enroll her without them, Mrs. Richardson decided to break down and have her daughter receive the basic required vaccinations rather than fighting the district's rule.

ALERT!

Some children need booster shots between age ten and thirteen in order to have continued protection against measles, mumps, tetanus, and rubella. Check on whether flu, meningitis, and hepatitis A vaccinations are needed, too. The consequences of contracting a communicable disease range from difficult to devastating.

When Hannah was twelve, the school sent home a note saying that she had been exposed to chickenpox. Mrs. Richardson investigated the subject and was distressed to learn that since Hannah hadn't contracted the infection or been immunized, she was at risk, and the repercussions could be serious if she caught the disease. Pneumonia was a common complication, and scarring from lesions is worse for older children. Moreover, if Hannah were eventually to become infected during a pregnancy, the results for the fetus could be disastrous indeed.

That incident caused Mrs. Richardson to have her daughter vaccinated and to take her to a "mainstream" physician for annual wellness checks. As a responsible mother, she would consider recommendations carefully rather than blindly following anyone's advice. But rather than dismissing Western medicine out of hand, she would make sure that Hannah benefited from the best that both Eastern and Western practitioners have to offer.

Growing Pains

Leg pains are common between ages eight and twelve when children are growing by leaps and bounds. Pain typically centers in the calves, behind the knees, and the tops of the thighs, often intensifying in the evening and disappearing in the morning. An over-the-counter pain reliever can help, as can heating pads, warm baths, and a leg massage. Doing some gentle stretches may provide some relief, too.

Scoliosis

About 3 percent of the population suffers from scoliosis, a curvature of the spine that develops after age nine. Five times as many girls as boys are affected. Treatment options for scoliosis depend on the severity of the curvature. Very mild cases just need to be watched; orthopedic braces may be used for moderate cases; and severe cases may require surgery.

A symptom of scoliosis is one shoulder blade being higher than the other, which makes skirts appear a bit uneven. However, less severe cases can be difficult to detect. Have your child screened for scoliosis by a nurse or doctor.

Shoulder, Neck, and Back Pain

A common culprit in tween pains of the upper trunk is carrying backpacks that are too heavy. The rule of thumb is that they should weigh less than 10 percent of your child's weight. If your tween has lots of heavy textbooks, help him figure out ways to lighten his load. Another important factor is how he carries his backpack. Advise your child to use both straps rather than slinging the pack over one shoulder, since he will automatically raise one shoulder and shift his weight to achieve better balance. Be sure the straps are wide enough so they don't dig into your child's shoulders.

Ear Protection

Earphones aren't necessarily a solution to the problem of a tween whose music is blasting you out of the house. Unless she turns down the volume, she can damage her ears. Temporary hearing loss can result from just fifteen minutes' exposure to loud noise. More prolonged exposure can result in permanent hearing loss. If your child goes to a concert, be sure she takes along some earplugs.

Vision Problems

Many children get their first pair of glasses during the tween years. The common symptoms of poor vision are sitting too close to the TV, holding a book close to the face, squinting, having difficulty seeing objects at a distance, and not being able to read the blackboard in school. Schedule an eye exam, but know that sitting close to the TV and holding a book close to the face don't necessarily indicate myopia. Children are more able to focus on near objects than adults, so sitting near the tube may simply be a habit.

Dental Health

Second permanent molars appear during the latter tween years. Because they are very prone to decay, an application of plastic sealant can do a lot to protect them. Except for the wisdom teeth, the last permanent tooth should make its appearance by about age thirteen. Any teeth that haven't appeared could be embedded and lack the force needed to push out the baby teeth. Overcrowding from the permanent teeth may cause impaction. Be sure your tween has regular dental checkups.

Your child's dentist may recommend an exam with an orthodontist to see whether braces are in order to straighten crooked teeth. Although metal braces are still used, many youngsters are able to wear the kind that are clear or the same color as their teeth. Some use rubber bands that are available in funky colors and are popular with the tween crowd these days. Wires on braces help move the teeth, while rubber bands correct the alignment. Tweens should avoid popcorn, gum, hard candy, and hard or sticky candy while wearing braces. They should also floss after eating and brush their teeth after eating or drinking anything containing sugar.

ALERT!

Expect to have to help your young tween floss his teeth until about age eleven, when children can master the movements. However, flossing can become more difficult as the teeth continue to shift closer together, so he may still need your help to remove all the plaque.

The length of time children need to wear braces differs, but the average is about two years. Subsequently, youngsters may need to use a retainer for another six months to two years. Retainers should be cleaned daily with toothpaste and a toothbrush, or they can be soaked in denture cleaner or mouthwash. They should not be allowed to dry out, as that creates a risk of cracking, and they should be kept away from heat, which can cause them to warp.

Eating Disorders

Many girls are distressed about putting on so many pounds as they pass through puberty, and many boys become concerned about not having the grand muscles of the athletes and stars they admire. You need to help your tween appreciate her body instead of falling victim to feelings of worthlessness because she doesn't have a figure she considers ideal.

Compulsive Overeating

The first way that babies feel nurtured is by being fed. The stimulation of the lips, tongue, and palate, and the sensation of a full tummy are enjoyable and satisfying. Many parents continue to soothe their children's upsets by offering them food and drinks. They continue to reach for food to restore a sense of well-being instead of reaching out for a hug, putting on some soothing music, taking a time-out, talking to a

parent or friend about whatever is bothering them, or finding another
way to relax. The primary complication of compulsive overeating is
obesity. Besides the social stigma, the physical complications of obesity
include diabetes, high blood pressure, heart disease, osteoarthritis, and
gall bladder disease.

Combating Obesity

Dieting alone is not likely to combat obesity because children gain
back the weight they lost as soon as the diet ends. The better way is find
a diet and exercise program your child can follow long-term. To eliminate
nervous eating, reduce the stress to which your child is subjected. Learn
to recognize signs of tension, point them out to your child, and help your
child find alternative ways to relax and nurture herself that don't involve
food. Exercise may not feel nurturing at the time, but it is a proven way
to relieve stress.

QUESTION?

My child is a bit overweight. How much exercise does he need?
Studies indicate that it is possible to reduce risk factors for heart
disease with twenty to thirty minutes of aerobic exercise three to
four times a week. Ask your pediatrician to formulate
recommendations for your tween.

If your child really wants to do something about her appearance, take
her to a nutritionist to work out a diet and exercise plan that will work
long-term rather than attempting a short-term diet. Avoid expressing
concerns about your own weight so your child doesn't absorb your
preoccupation, and never tease your youngster or make comments about
his body that are even mildly disparaging. Record numbers of tweens of
both sexes are suffering from eating disorders.

Anorexia Nervosa

Anorexia has a high mortality rate because sufferers can literally
starve themselves to death, continuing to perceive themselves as fat even

when their hair is falling out from severe malnutrition and they look like concentration camp inmates.

To maintain such a rigid restriction of diet (and often compulsive exercising) requires tremendous self-control. Youngsters with overcontrolling parents seem to be especially at risk, as are young models and athletes involved in sports where weight is an important factor (for example, wrestling and gymnastics).

As anorexic girls lose fat, they stop menstruating and their secondary sexual characteristics disappear. Hence, girls who have been sexually abused and those with serious conflicts about growing up are also at risk for developing an eating disorder.

In general, girls who have been criticized for being heavy or praised for losing a bit of weight are at risk. They are already under tremendous pressure from peers and from the images of beauty presented on TV and in magazines, so be careful what you say about your pubescent daughter's weight gain. Girls acquire an extra layer of fat during puberty, but instead of being delighted to become a curvaceous woman, many are distressed about their altered appearance.

FACT

Once a very rare disorder, anorexia has traced a path from the United States to other countries that have imported American pop culture via movies and TV shows. It is more common in cultures that have adopted Western values.

Bulimia Nervosa

Tweens suffering from bulimia alternate between consuming huge quantities of food and purging their systems to get rid of it, either by vomiting or taking laxatives. Like anorexics, victims think about food obsessively and deal with it compulsively; often they cannot stop eating. Bulimic children may be of average weight, and since they go to great lengths to hide their activities because they feel ashamed and out of control, many parents don't realize what is happening.

If your child has an eating disorder, don't try to manage things yourself. Get professional advice from a therapist with expertise in the area, or contact the American Anorexia/Bulimia Association at ✆ (212) 575-6200 or Overeaters Anonymous at ✆ (505) 891-2664.

Strangers and Other Dangers

Media reports of children who have been snatched strike terror into every parent's heart, but it is important to keep these widely publicized horrors in perspective. Of the thousands of kidnapped children, the vast majority are the victims of parental custody disputes. In 2001, strangers approached about 4,600 children, but only about 300 were snatched and either found murdered or never found.

Meanwhile, thousands were killed in automobile, bicycle, skateboard, and gun accidents. While you must teach your tween to protect herself from dangerous strangers, don't overreact to inflammatory press reports. Make ironclad rules about wearing seatbelts and helmets, and keep guns out of the house!

Auto Safety

Children under age twelve should sit in the backseat of moving vehicles. Make sure the lap belt lies across the lap and fits tightly. The shoulder belt should fit snugly, crossing the chest and shoulder and resting on the collarbone to avoid abdominal injuries. Children under 4'9" should use a booster seat that faces forward, constructed so that both the lap and shoulder belts run through it.

When your child can sit all the way back in the seat, bend his knees over the seat cushion, and rest his feet on the floor, he no longer requires a booster seat. Air bags are dangerous for children and should be turned off if your youngster sits in the front seat. Contact the Auto Safety Hotline at ✆ (888) 327-4236 for additional information.

Pedestrian Safety

All the time you spent teaching your kindergartner to cross the street safely may go out the window when she turns into a distracted tween at age nine and a cocky daredevil at age twelve. Remind her of the basics: not to chase a ball into the street, to wait for a traffic signal to give the go-ahead, to look before crossing, and to be aware of speeding cars that appear out of nowhere. Most important, your tween should always remember that cars have the right of way—whether she likes it or not.

Fire Safety

Fire is the leading cause of unintentional death to children under age fourteen, with nearly 600 deaths and 40,000 injuries each year. Keep matches and lighters under surveillance. Have your child wear tight sleeves if he's cooking, building a fire, or lighting a candle—loose sleeves easily catch fire. Keep flammable objects away from heaters and radiators, and don't store flammable liquids such as gasoline inside the house. Check for electrical cords and wires that are loose or frayed and replace them immediately. Don't hide extension cords under carpets and rugs.

Don't block an exit to your home with furniture; that could block an escape route. Hold fire drills to be sure your child knows how to get out of the house in the event of a fire. Since 50 percent of home fires occur at night, hold a night drill as well as a day drill once a year. Require everyone to meet outside at a particular spot so that if a real fire happens, you can readily ascertain that everyone has made it out. Don't call for emergency help until after everyone is safely outside.

Install smoke detectors on each floor of your home and in every sleeping area. You will decrease the risk of death by half and cut your insurance costs, too. Remember to test the smoke detectors once a month and replace the batteries once a year. Smoke detectors should be replaced every ten years.

Since most deaths from fire are actually caused by inhaling smoke, instruct your child to crawl beneath it rather than trying to walk through it. Explain how to smother burning clothing and hair by stopping, dropping to the ground, and rolling—running in fear would only fan the fire.

Gun Safety

If you think you've succeeded at hiding your gun, think again. Studies show that 75 to 80 percent of children know where the family gun is hidden. Moreover, when they stumble across it or decide to show it off to a friend, they cannot resist the temptation to pretend to aim and fire. Over 1,800 children age fourteen and under were treated at hospital emergency rooms in the year 2000 for gunshot wounds, and many of the wounded youngsters died. The little gunslingers were always oh-so-sure it wasn't loaded.

I'm Lost!

When separating at a mall, fair, concert, beach, or other crowded place, be sure your tween understands exactly when and where you are to meet. To lessen misunderstandings, have your child repeat your instructions. Be sure he knows, too, that if a problem arises he should never, ever leave the area to go to the car. Instead, he should explain the problem to a police officer, security guard, or employee so he can be taken to the lost and found.

If he is lost in an area where there are no employees, he can ask an adult for help contacting the police, but if he must approach a stranger, he should look for parents with children. The next safest are older couples and single women.

Phone Home

By age eight your child should know how to place a collect call. He should know how to spell his name, his home phone number and address, parents' work numbers, and whom to call in an emergency. If that's too complicated—and complicated it is if you're trying to teach about the need to dial the area code when calling from certain long-distance locations—be sure he knows how to dial the operator, ask to be connected with the police, and explain his dilemma so you can be contacted. Your tween needs to know how to spell your last name, and the name of his city and state. As an added precaution, keep your telephone number listed.

Home-Alone Safety

Be sure your child knows basic safety rules before leaving him at home alone. On arriving home to an empty house, have your child telephone someone to check in. Be sure he keeps the doors locked and does not open the door to anyone but another family member; even friends should not be inside the house unless an adult is present. Provide a list of emergency phone numbers, including someone else he can call if you can't be reached.

In the event that he will be alone for an extended period, have him check in with you or someone else once an hour and call if he has any sort of problem. Tell him to trust his intuition and call if he thinks something is wrong even if he can't pinpoint what it is. Make backup plans for the inevitable problems that crop up when your latchkey kid is on his own: He could lose the house key, need help in an emergency, miss the school bus, or get stranded.

Sexual Abuse

While parents worry about perverts leaping from the bushes to attack their child, in 80 percent of sex abuse cases the child knows and trusts the perpetrator. The distressing truth is that fathers, stepfathers, and other adult relatives are the most common abusers. While parents oust homosexual teachers from classrooms for fear they will harm their sons, 90 percent of the perpetrators against boys are heterosexual males. Children age ten to twelve are in the second-highest risk group for being sexually abused.

Familiar Danger

Signs that a child has been sexually abused include having a venereal disease; being suddenly shy around men; not wanting to be alone with their father, stepfather, or a particular male relative; sexual acting out or a compulsive interest in sex; marked withdrawal from peers or aggressiveness toward them; and decline in school grades. Having an emotionally available mother provides a protective factor for girls even if the mother is physically absent much of the time. Girls are more at risk if they are emotionally needy.

FACT

In a 1998 survey by the Commonwealth Fund, 7 percent of girls in grades five to eight said they had been sexually abused. Thirty-four percent of the perpetrators were family members and 59 percent were acquaintances. Only 7 percent of the perpetrators were strangers to the victim. (Sexual Assault of Young Children as Reported to Law Enforcement. Washington, D.C.: Bureau of Justice Statistics, U.S. Department of Justice, 2000.)

Be sure your child knows that no one is allowed to touch her in a way that makes her uncomfortable, and that includes teachers, neighbors, coaches, and other family members. Be sure she knows, too, that if someone swears her to secrecy, she must not keep the secret under any circumstances. Tell her that if someone does touch her she must tell you, and promise to stand by her if it happens.

Forewarn her that abusers try to manipulate children in predictable ways. They say that no one will believe her if she tells (which is ridiculous, since people are very aware of the problem of child abuse these days), and they threaten to harm someone she loves (which is impossible, because the parent would contact the police immediately).

Take seriously your child's claims that a family member or friend has abused her. Either something has really happened or her invented accusations are a sign that she needs psychological help. Instead of trying to sort out exactly what happened, contact the local police for help so that a professional trained to interview children can speak with her. The police will notify the Department of Human Services so that a social worker can take a statement and advise you how to proceed.

Stranger Danger

The good news is that it is highly unlikely that your child will have to cope with a truly dangerous stranger. Still, you need to keep track of your tweens' whereabouts, teach him his phone number and address, show him how to place a collect call, tell him who to contact in the event of an emergency, and establish a family code word or phrase for use in emergencies. The phrase can be anything (such as "After dinner I will walk the neighbor's dog"). You can share the phrase in an emergency when you need someone your child doesn't know well to provide emergency transportation.

When teaching your tween the following don'ts so he can protect himself from stranger danger, remind him that bad people who hurt children are actually very rare. You don't want your youngster to live in fear. You do want him to know how to protect himself in the highly unlikely event he runs into someone who might want to harm him.

- **Don't answer the door unless an adult is at home.** If it's important, the visitor will return later.
- **Don't let telephone callers know that no parent is at home.** Instruct your child to say you are sleeping, busy at the moment, or indisposed.
- **Don't walk alone at night.** Instead, your tween should call for a ride. Be sure she knows how to place a collect call.
- **Don't walk or ride bikes alone in secluded areas.** Your youngster should have a companion.
- **Don't let a stranger separate you from a group of children.** Everyone should lock arms and run away together. It might be possible to carry off one child, but it's almost impossible to take off with two if they resist.
- **Don't accept candy or toys from strangers.** Explain that normal adults give presents to their own child, to young friends and relatives,

or donate to charity. They don't walk up to people they don't even know and offer gifts.

- **Don't fall for common ploys, like "I need help finding my lost dog/cat" and requests for directions.** Emphasize that adults who truly need help ask another adult or the police, not a child.
- **Don't let a stranger touch you under the area that would be covered by a swimsuit.** Scream, "No! Help! Police!"
- **Don't go off with a stranger or get into a stranger's car unless he or she knows the special family code word or phrase.**

Teach your child that if a stranger approaches him, he should say, "No! I'm not allowed to talk to strangers! Don't talk to me!" loudly enough to attract attention while crossing his arms tightly in front of his chest so he can't be grabbed. Someone who meant no harm will respect his wishes and back off, as will dangerous strangers since they are afraid of getting caught.

Handle stranger-danger discussions in as reassuring a manner as possible. People who jump out of the bushes to assault and abduct children make big headlines but are actually rarities. Tweens cannot live happily when they are living in fear. Moreover, they need to be able to reach out to a stranger for help if they do run into a serious problem.

If a stranger persists after being told to go away or tries to force your child into a car, separate him from friends, or lure him into an isolated area, he needs to run away and should scream, "Help!" and "Somebody call the police!" to attract attention. Once he has escaped, he should look for a city worker, mail carrier, or utility-repair person. They are ideal in an emergency since most carry cell phones and can readily notify the police. Otherwise, an endangered child should run to any nearby public place, such as a store, restaurant, gas station, or playground if other people are there, and insist that the police be called immediately. In a residential area, any house can be approached, but it is best if someone is home. If it looks like no one in the neighborhood is at home, tell him to run toward the back door of the nearest house as if it were his own, knock or ring the bell, then hide in the yard and wait to see if someone comes to the door. He should tell whoever answers to call the police but should wait on the porch until help arrives rather than going inside a stranger's house.

If someone actually grabs your child, he should collapse to the ground so he'll be harder to carry, yell and scream to attract attention, and bite, kick, and scratch so as not to be carried off.

Online Safety

If your child surfs the Internet, participates in chat rooms, and sends e-mail, you must supervise what she's doing. It's best to keep the computer in a family room so you can see for yourself what she's up to when you walk by.

E ALERT!

Contact your Internet service provider to see what services are available to prevent children from visiting sites containing unsuitable material (blocking) and to screen out objectionable e-mail (filtering). Like movies, many Web sites are rated for suitability.

The number-one safety rule is for children never to give out personal information, not their names and especially not their addresses or phone numbers. To reduce temptation, help develop information for a fictitious character so that your child can give it in lieu of personal information. Have her invent and write down a first and last name, address including zip code, phone number, age, and an online name she can use each time she's asked. Otherwise, she's likely to forget what pseudonyms and other identifying information she gave to which sites. That adds to the temptation to use real information since it's easier to remember.

Your child must never send her picture unless you approve it and must not meet face-to-face with an online friend or acquaintance unless you physically accompany her to meet in a public place. Online sexual predators may pretend to be children. Warn her that being asked to keep something secret from her parents for any reason is a sign that something is wrong, so she should always tell you immediately. It is easy for a twelve-year-old girl to develop a crush on a boy she has met online or become best friends with an online pen pal and agree to meet him in person, never guessing her correspondent is a middle-aged male.

FACT

According to the Census Bureau, approximately four out of five tweens spend time online. Computer literacy is a must for every child. There are enough educational games to provide a first-class K–12 education. The Internet puts the best and the worst of the world at tweens' fingertips. Supervise carefully.

Advise your youngster never to respond to e-mails or messages in chat rooms that contain anything sexual, obscene, threatening, belligerent, or angry, and to tell you about anything that makes her in any way afraid or uncomfortable. Any child pornography that either of you stumble into should be reported to the Center for Missing and Exploited Children's Cyber Tipline by calling ✆ (800) 843-5678 or visiting ✍ *www.missingkids.com/cybertip.* Ⓔ

Chapter 17

The Birds and the Bees

As tweens develop an interest in members of the opposite sex, they become intent on learning the facts of life, and learn they will—the only question is who will teach them. You may find sex hard to talk about and your child may find it hard to listen to you discuss this topic, but if you remain silent, peers will fill the conversational vacuum.

What Schools Don't Teach

Tommy was looking forward to seeing the movie about puberty with the rest of his fifth-grade class. Afterward, the boys would go to a classroom with a male teacher for a discussion while the girls met with a female teacher in another room. Tommy ended up pretty disappointed. Although the movie was interesting enough, the discussion turned out to be worthless. The kids were giggling and acting as though they already knew everything. Tommy didn't dare ask the questions that had been on his mind. He swallowed his disappointment and did his best to joke around like everybody else.

Tommy's mother tried to talk to him about sex a few months later, which was so totally gross and embarrassing that he didn't hear much. Actually, his mom seemed as embarrassed as he was. She gave him a book to read and told him to ask if he ever had any questions. He told her that he already knew all that stuff, but as soon as she was gone, he read the book from cover to cover. It explained a lot, but one thing worried him. The book said that a "queer" wasn't just "a dork" like he'd always thought. *Queer* was a slang word that actually meant "homosexual."

Now when somebody called him a queer, he wished a hole would appear and swallow him up. Once he turned beet-red, and some girl said, "See Tommy blush? That proves it!" He wondered if it was true. In fact, he was very worried. He sort of liked girls, but maybe he didn't like them enough. Since his dad hadn't given him the sex talk, there was no way Tommy could just go up to him and start asking him questions.

The Hardest Conversation

When they were growing up, most modern parents were told that sex was dirty, bad, or wrong, and little more. They vowed not to be so negative and moralistic with their own children in hopes of helping them develop healthier sexual attitudes and keeping those all-important lines of communication open.

Some parents did manage to teach "penis" or "vagina" while helping their toddlers to learn the names of parts of the body. Some managed to respond to their preschoolers' "Where do babies come from?" questions with answers about Daddy's seeds and Mommy's egg. A few parents even explained to their five-year-olds how the baby gets out of Mommy's tummy. But when six-year-olds asked how Daddy put the seed inside Mommy in the first place, most parents postponed further discussion until later. In too many families, "later" never arrived.

ALERT!

Surveyed tweens say parents influence them more about dating and sex than friends. Although most adolescent respondents would prefer to talk to their parents, they report that they usually end up talking to their friends, so it is very important that you keep the channels of communication open.

From Books to Conversation

There are some excellent books for kids of all ages (see Appendix B), and it is a good idea to buy at least one for your child. However, she needs to be able to ask questions, discuss concerns, and share her thoughts about sexual matters with a trusted adult. She may think that being handed a book means that you expect her to learn on her own. One possibility is to read the book together, perhaps taking turns reading sections aloud. As awkward as you and your child may feel, she will probably begin asking questions. As you answer, conversing will get easier. Like anything else, practice makes perfect.

Education as Part of Life

Another approach to sex education is to integrate it into your daily household conversation. This may be the best approach for a tween who is too uncomfortable to hear or remember much from a single sit-down conversation. Presenting information in bits and pieces can also establish sex as something that can be freely discussed. Here are some ideas:

- When you see an ad for deodorant on TV, are picking up some antiperspirant at the store, or are perspiring on a hot summer's day, comment that soon your child will perspire a lot and need deodorant, too. Explain that during puberty the hair under the arms begins to grow and the sweat glands produce more sweat.

- When taking your tween for a haircut or helping her comb her hair, take the opportunity to mention that during puberty the hair on the rest of her body will begin to change by growing longer and thicker. Like many girls, she may want to shave off the hair that grows on her legs. Alert her that when the hair grows back in it will be darker and coarser, and she'll probably feel obligated to continue shaving regularly. So she should consider carefully before shaving for the first time. Boys confront the same dilemma during puberty. They end up with dark stubble shortly after shaving their beard and moustache for the first time.

- When changing your son's sheets, tell him that he shouldn't be surprised if he awakens one morning to find them wet. Explain that about a year after a boy's penis and testicles start to grow, his body begins making sperm and it is common to have wet dreams. That means that while a boy is asleep and dreaming his penis has an erection and ejaculates sperm, which is a clear, sticky substance. Once his body is producing sperm, if he were to have intercourse with a girl who has gone through puberty, they could produce a baby.

- When your daughter is washing her face or hair, comment that when she enters puberty they both will get oilier. She'll have to wash more frequently, her hair to keep it shiny and her skin to keep from getting acne.

- When folding your daughter's underwear, tell her not to be surprised if she finds a bit of blood in it one day, because that is what happens when girls turn into women. It is called having a menstrual period. It doesn't hurt, though some girls get a bit of a tummy ache. She will need to let you know so you can give her some sanitary napkins to wear so her clothes don't get messy.

Besides encouraging questions and conversation, another advantage to dispensing information gradually is that you can pre-plan what you want to say.

Sex Education for Young Tweens

It is much easier to have the birds-and-bees talk with a tween who is young enough to respond with interest instead of embarrassment. Linda and Richard Eyre, the authors of *Teaching Your Children Values*, recommend incorporating sex education into your eight-year-old's birthday celebration. They suggest building some anticipation by telling him that now that he has reached this important age, you will have a special dinner without his siblings and teach him about the "most wonderful and beautiful thing on earth."

ESSENTIAL

Diagrams can help your child better visualize what you are explaining. You can print out drawings from ✑*www.puberty101.com.* The book, *Where Did I Come From?,* is designed for younger children but could be a good present for an eight-year-old. See Appendix B for other suggestions.

By describing how men and women participate in the miracle of creating a baby before peers have convinced him that sex is dirty, you will have a much more receptive audience. If your child has already turned eight, consider choosing another special time, such as when he is exactly eight and one half, on the solstice, or on some other special occasion.

Begin by explaining that sex is personal and private, and many people are offended if bad words are used because they consider sex to be sacred. State that he needs to be considerate of other people's feelings.

Basic Words and Concepts

How much technical vocabulary and detail you use depends on your child's level of understanding. If your child doesn't know the correct terms for the genitals, this is the time to explain that boys have a penis and testicles, which start producing millions of tiny sperm at puberty. Sperm are kind of like seeds, but they have tiny tails and can swim. Girls have sex organs inside their bodies beneath their stomachs and a small opening between their legs that leads into a tunnel called the vagina. The vagina connects to a sex organ that releases a new tiny egg every month.

Sometimes when a man is feeling very loving toward a woman, his penis gets longer and harder until it is the perfect shape to fit inside a woman's vagina. When he puts his penis into her vagina, the sperm come out and swim toward her egg. If one of the man's sperm gets inside a woman's egg, a baby is created. The baby grows inside the mother's body in a place called the uterus until it's ready to be born, and then it comes out through the opening between the woman's legs.

Changes to Expect During Puberty

Explain that as boys turn into men they get more hair on their arms, legs, faces, and around their penis and anus. Their voices deepen. Their sweat glands start to work, so they perspire a lot. Many get pimples on their faces. Their testicles wrinkle and darken in color, and their penises grow and have erections.

Meanwhile, girls grow more hair on their arms and legs, anus, and in the pubic area. The area around their nipples wrinkles and darkens and then they grow breasts. Their breasts will fill up with milk when they have a baby so they can feed it. Every month their bodies build a special sort of nest inside to hold a baby. The nest is made of blood and tissue. Every month their bodies produce an egg, too. If no sperm joins with the egg to make a baby, the nest isn't needed and the body spends about five days releasing the blood and tissue. When it comes out through the vagina, it is called "having a menstrual period." Even though there is blood, this is not painful. It is messy, though, so girls wear a sanitary napkin to catch the blood.

E ALERT!

Don't wait to let your tween learn about sexuality in health class, which typically takes place in fifth grade. If a girl begins her period before then, she may suffer the trauma of thinking she is dying when she discovers menstrual blood. Boys are often fearful about their physical changes, too.

Sex Education for Older Tweens

By the time children are nine, they are too busy giggling and trying to change the subject to be able to have a conversation about sex. Don't believe your tween's claims that he "already knows all that." Tweens use many sexual words long before they know what they mean. At age eleven, most children still think an "ass" is a donkey and admit to wondering why it's bad to mention these poor creatures in public.

By holding an elaborate coming-of-age ceremony, it may be possible to eliminate your tween's embarrassment so that you can have a serious conversation about sex. Choose a date a month or two away, explain that during his special event you will reveal the truth of what it means to be a man. Tell him that afterward everything will change for him, because you will begin preparing him to assume adult responsibilities so that he will be able to have a family of his own one day. Of course, you would do the same with a daughter.

For the ceremony itself, create a mood with candles, incense, and music. Be ready to present a speech about what it means to be a man and what makes men special. For example, "Men are strong but loving; they care for their bodies, their minds, and their souls; they cherish the mate they choose above all others; they love the children they bring into the world; they honor God; they protect the earth and all living things." Tell your daughter what it means to be a woman and what makes women special. Then proceed with a discussion about how men and women make babies and about the physical changes boys and girls go through during puberty.

Teaching Sexual Values

Tweens need to know about the deeper meanings of sex, too. What you say will reflect your personal values, so it may be helpful to consider what you would have wanted your parents to have told you. If you believe that people should only have sexual intercourse to produce babies or that only married couples should enjoy it, be sure to give your reasons. Children who have been exposed to pop culture will know that few people believe in premarital abstinence and monogamy. If you believe that only people in a committed, loving relationship should have intercourse, be prepared to explain your values.

In the tween world, sex is viewed like a baseball game—a competitive endeavor in which boys struggle to overcome girls' resistance, so they can get to "first base" in hopes that they can "score" and are disappointed if they "strike out." Many boys and girls maintain this competitive mentality through high school. Some, of course, maintain it throughout life; but by young adulthood, most are able to form committed relationships based on emotional as well as physical intimacy.

FACT

Every third joke in a TV sitcom contains a sexual comment or innuendo. In most TV dramas, couples have sex outside of wedlock. Despite what you say, your couch potato will learn that making love is a way to relieve a physical itch that entails no special responsibilities to oneself or to one's partner.

Depending on your beliefs, you might tell your child that sex involves being physically as well as emotionally close to someone toward whom he feels attracted. How much people do together sexually should depend on how much of their hearts and bodies they can safely share. Many kids think sex just has to do with the body, but the truth is that normal people can't separate their bodies from their minds and hearts, so sharing your body means sharing your feelings, too. It's important to protect your own body and heart as well as your partner's.

Holding hands or giving someone a little kiss is like sharing a small secret. You might share a small secret with someone you like but don't know all that well. If the person later betrayed you by telling your secret, you would probably be disappointed and a bit angry but not crushed. Petting and deep kissing is like sharing a big, important secret because you're sharing more of your body and your heart. You have to be careful because you could end up getting really hurt. Even if you weren't in love at the outset, if the petting feels good you might start to fall in love. If the other person didn't love you back, you could end up feeling crushed.

If the other person fell in love with you but you didn't fall in love, that could crush the other person.

Having sexual intercourse involves sharing your body with someone else in the deepest, most intimate way possible, so it is like sharing your deepest, most important secret. There is also serious physical risk involved, since you could catch a disease or make a baby. You can lessen those risks by taking precautions, but there is a huge emotional risk, because when people have intercourse, they often develop a very strong attachment. If you later realize you don't like that person anymore or decide that the person is wrong for you, you may have a hard time ending the relationship because when you gave your body, you gave your heart, too. Then, when you do break up, you may feel very unhappy and need a while to heal emotionally. If you end up falling in love with someone who breaks up with you, your heart could feel as if it's breaking. If someone falls in love with you and you end the relationship, you could devastate your partner. Eventually you both will recover, but until then either or both of you can be truly miserable. Therefore, before having intercourse, it's important to know your partner very well so you are sure that the person and the relationship is safe for both of you. Usually it's hard to be that sure of yourself and of someone else until you are at least eighteen and are both willing to say, "I do."

What Parents Need to Know

The first sign of puberty for girls is breast budding, which occurs between the ages of eight and eleven, with the average age being ten. Menstruation begins an average of about two years later, but one study found that 30 percent began menstruating before age eleven (Lisa Miller and Marav Gur, "Religiosity, Depression, and Physical Maturation in Adolescent Girls," *Journal of the American Academy of Child and Adolescent Psychiatry,* vol. 41, no. 12 [Feb. 2002]: 206–209).

Body fat triggers the pituitary gland, which plays a role in puberty, so lack of exercise and excess body fat may explain why heavyset girls get their periods before lean girls. Race is also a factor; black girls mature an average of seven months earlier than whites. The father-daughter relationship may also play a role. Girls who are close to their biological fathers from birth to age five go through puberty later. Exposure to the scent of unrelated men such as stepfathers may accelerate puberty while exposure to the scent of a biological father inhibits it, as is the case for other mammals. Psychological pressures on girls to grow up quickly may prime them to develop faster, too. Here are some other facts every parent needs to know:

- Fifty percent of sexually active teen males had their first sexual experience between age eleven and thirteen.
- The birth rate in 1998 for children aged ten to fourteen was one birth per 1,000 girls.
- Thirteen percent of all U.S. births are to teenagers. Approximately three-quarters of teenage mothers are unmarried.
- Each year, 20 percent of sexually active teenage girls become pregnant.
- A sexually active teenager who does not use contraceptives has a 90 percent chance of becoming pregnant within one year.
- The mortality rate for infants born to teenage mothers is about 50 percent higher than that for those born to women over age twenty.
- The U.S. teenage birth rate is the highest in the developed world. This is due to fewer comprehensive sex education programs, less access to contraception and abortion, and fewer confidential services for teenagers.
- Every year about 25 percent of sexually active teenagers acquire a sexually transmitted disease.
- The risk factors for having sex during the tween years are poor self-esteem, poor academic achievement, a poor parent-child relationship, and poor peer relationships.

FACT

From a single act of unprotected sex with an infected partner, a teenage woman has a 1 percent risk of acquiring HIV, a 30 percent risk of getting genital herpes, and a 50 percent chance of contracting gonorrhea. Up to 29 percent of sexually active teenage girls and 10 percent of teenage boys tested for sexually transmitted diseases had chlamydia.

While the emotional and physical dangers of sex cannot be denied, neither can its pleasures, as your child will soon discover. In helping your son comprehend the workings of the human body and unravel the mysteries of sexual love, you are ushering him into the world of adults. It can be hard to have your baby grow up, but if you're lucky, you may someday be rewarded with grandchildren. With your good influence and guidance, that "someday" won't come too soon. Ⓔ

Chapter 18

E Preserving the Innocents

Lots of eight-year-old girls have boyfriends. Nine-year-olds go on dates and attend coed sleepovers. Ten- and-eleven-year-olds go steady. By age twelve, lots of kids are "doing it." Drugs, sex, and gangs lurk in the shadows of many middle-school playgrounds. Even in schoolyards where they have not penetrated, they are the subject of tween curiosity and debate.

Growing Up Too Fast

Rosalind was at a loss as to how to slow her daughter's headlong race to grow up. Rosalind thought she had won the battle over makeup when Iva was age nine, only to discover that she carried it in her backpack and put it on at school. Rosalind refused to buy Iva skintight pants and skimpy tube tops, and then discovered she was borrowing them from friends to wear at school. After Iva attended a girlfriend's slumber party, Rosalind was shocked to learn that it had been a coed party. While chaperoning at a school dance Rosalind was appalled to see the children freak dancing, which involved rubbing one another's genitals via full-body bumps and grinds.

Iva's moods swung from high to low, depending on whether a popular boy or girl had or had not talked to her that day. Then Rosalind intercepted an e-mail in which Iva mentioned smoking pot. Rosalind met with the school principal and learned that makeup, skimpy clothes, and drugs were common in schools across the country, as was escalating violence. More tweens were getting pregnant and having babies, too. His ho-hum attitude was not reassuring.

Parents Unite

The PTA agenda was set for the year, but the president agreed to an emergency meeting and sent out the flier Rosalind made. It announced a meeting for "Parents United Against Peer Pressure" and said parents would meet to discuss rules for clothes, makeup, dating, movies, TV, gangs, and drugs. Rosalind personally telephoned the parents of Iva's friends to invite them.

Only a handful of parents showed up. Rosalind presented the rules she wanted her daughter to follow. After a brainstorming session, everyone agreed to forbid gang involvement, drugs, coed sleepovers, dating, R-rated movies, music with parental advisory labels, and freak dancing. The opinions about makeup, clothes, and PG-13 movies differed. Some parents wanted youngsters limited to videogames and computer games rated for everyone; some approved of the games rated for teenagers. Each parent created a rule list for his or her own tween. Someone suggested giving copies to their children's teachers, so the parents added rules about behaving in class and doing assigned work. The teachers couldn't keep track of each family's rules, of course, but their tween's compliance should improve just knowing that their teachers had the list and could potentially report violations to their parents.

Help your tween fight peer pressure by helping him understand the meaning of true friendship. Being popular may not feel very good if it entails doing things he doesn't believe in. He may be happier with just one or two friends who really respect him.

Back at home, Rosalind went over her rule list with Iva and had her sign it. Iva seemed to feel relieved that some of her friends would have similar rules. Apparently she'd felt torn between her peers' and her mother's expectations. Rosalind made a flier for a second PTA meeting listing all the sample rules the parents had come up with at the first meeting. The turnout was huge. Rosalind felt confident that together they would change the school culture so the students could have a few more years to be kids.

The Disappearance of Childhood

Childhood is actually a recent phenomenon. Prior to its invention in the mid-1800s, children worked beside their parents at home, on farms, and in factories and rarely had time to play. They nurtured younger siblings instead of dolls, wore the same clothes as adults made in smaller sizes, enjoyed the same music and books as their parents, worried about the same family problems, and did what they could to help out.

After child labor laws were enacted and mass education was instituted, children were freed from home and work responsibilities and were segregated from adults in schools. Suddenly they were surrounded by same-age peers all day, and the culture of youth came into being. Companies responded by making special clothing, toys, furniture, music, and even foods to appeal to young people's unique tastes.

Adults saw these changes as creating a definite improvement in children's lives. Professionals maintained that childhood was a special time that youngsters should enjoy to the fullest. Involving children in household duties and responsibilities so they could learn to manage families of their own would deprive them of what young people were now believed to need most: a carefree period during which their only responsibility was school.

Childhood changed dramatically. Children couldn't work to help out financially. If they tried to relieve their parents' burdens by helping at home, they made a mess of things because they lacked experience with chores and household responsibilities. Exposing tweens to adult concerns blurred the lines between children's and adults' worlds, made children feel upset about their powerlessness to make a difference, and confused them about their role in the family.

Childhood Transformed

In the 1950s tweens regained entry into teenage and adult life via the TV, and in the 1980s taped movies began recounting adult joys and sorrows in living rooms across the country. Modern tweens average five hours a day watching the goings-on in the wider world depicted on the screen, so it's no surprise they began emulating the styles of dressing, talking, and relating of their media heroes. American industry responded by creating video and computer games, movies, music, books, clothes, and toys attuned to tweens' central preoccupations, which mirrored the central themes of shows and movies: sex and violence. Tweens cannot know that the stories about the fascinating world outside their living rooms do not reflect reality. They do not realize that the characters are stereotypes and caricatures. They only know that the people on the screens appear to be living life to the fullest while they can only watch.

Not surprisingly, tweens want the toys and foods the media stars recommend and try to match the weight, physique, wardrobes, and style of their heroes. Through video and computer games, tweens participate vicariously in the more fascinating aspects of adult life they have seen on TV: driving cars, shooting guns, maneuvering spaceships, besting enemies, and solving crimes. More and more tweens are now living their fantasies. They fight, have sex, drink, smoke cigarettes, take drugs, and commit crimes like the exciting, powerful characters they have come to know and love.

FACT

When young actors appear in commercial shows and movies, they are typically portrayed as heroes, while adults are depicted as boobs and dolts who know little and understand even less. In most tween PBS productions, vibrant, powerful, intelligent kids play all the parts, and adults have been ousted altogether.

It may look as though childhood is disappearing as a separate time of life, but children continue to inhabit a separate world. Never having worked or been responsible for helping their families to survive like their counterparts throughout history, modern tweens remain extremely immature. Older tweens can fall in love and have babies, but unlike children from the days before childhood was born, they are unaware of love's responsibilities and can't even care for themselves.

Changing Tween Values

It is virtually impossible for a child to watch an ongoing stream of commercials about the horrors of bad breath, foot odor, acne, uncontrollable hair, freckles, thin lips, crooked teeth, and extra pounds without becoming painfully self-conscious. Parents need to help tweens appreciate their bodies even though their physiques don't match the pop ideal.

Contradict your child if he complains about his appearance and he may conclude you just don't understand. Instead, empathize and help him put his feelings into perspective. No, he doesn't look like Arnold Schwarzenegger, but few people do.

Never tease your youngster or make comments about his body that are even mildly disparaging. Record numbers of tweens of both sexes react to "lookism" by taking drastic but largely ineffective measures to try to control their weight via extreme diets.

Tween Fashions

Lots of parents are shocked by modern tween fashions, which from their perspective are overtly sexual. However, tween girls aren't necessarily trying to seduce boys when they don skimpy Spandex dresses, skintight pants, short shorts and skirts, and T-shirts that bare their midriffs. Tweens want to dress like the heroines in rock videos, movies, and magazines.

ALERT!

American third graders average thirty hours per week watching TV and only two and a half hours reading. In a year students spend about as much time in front of the TV as in they do in school.

A century ago, a flash of female wrist or glimpse of ankle was racy enough to leave boys panting. Now bare legs, arms, and stomachs aren't considered the signs of a fallen woman. Tween boys appreciate the modern fashions but don't find skimpy outfits especially erotic because they see them all the time.

Still, letting tween girls wear revealing clothes can cause problems. Grandma will probably be shocked and more conservative parents will disapprove. A developed ten-year-old may appear provocative to male members of the older generation, and teenage boys may think she is their age. As long as she is surrounded by her peers, she looks like everyone else. Outside this safety zone, she may end up with more attention than she can handle.

When Tweens Dress Like Teens

Don't take the position that only bad or promiscuous girls wear revealing clothes or makeup—that will confuse your tween. If some of her perfectly nice friends wear that style, you may end up losing credibility. Don't suggest that she must be bad or promiscuous for wanting to wear certain clothes, either. She may define herself accordingly and live out the role you assigned her.

Rather than arguing and criticizing your child's choices, teach her how to make good ones. Tell her the following:

- "That skirt is too tight for you. Find one that fits looser."
- "Your nipples show through that top. If I buy it for you, you would have to wear something under it."
- "Those pants are too loose at the waist. They're sliding down in back."

Don't foist the fashions you loved during your tween years on your child. If she rejects your suggestions, agree to disagree until she can find something she likes that you are willing to spend money on. That way, she still gets to choose her clothes, but you can veto items you disapprove of.

FACT

If your tween becomes upset about your refusal to buy certain clothes and storms about, that doesn't mean you have to do the same. Just explain your reasons, be clear about your rules, and stick to them. If you decide to change them, explain your reasons and be clear about the new ones, too.

Understanding Tween Conformity

Learning to conform is part of what the tween years are all about. As tweens learn to conform to the rules, demands, and expectations of teachers, family members, and friends, they learn to get along with others.

Peers versus Parents

Conflicts may develop if your expectations and demands differ from your child's peers. To conform to your desires, she must care more about what you think than about what they think. That will be difficult if she spends all day with her friends at school, comes home to an empty house, and only sees you when you are exhausted and irritable from a long day at work. If you are too critical, she may stop trying to conform to your wishes, believing she will never please you.

You will need to spend a lot of quality time with your tween and have a very strong relationship before you can hope that she will resolve her peers-versus-parents dilemmas in your favor. See Chapters 4 and 7 for suggestions. Another solution is to surround him with friends whose values coincide with yours. To that end, look for an activity he enjoys that you approve of.

ESSENTIAL

> To lessen criticism and negativity, turn each "no" into a "yes." For example: "Mom, can I go out on a date?" "Yes! When you're fifteen." "Mom, can I wear makeup to school?" "Yes! Lip gloss now; blush next year." "Mom, can I watch TV?" "Yes! As soon as you do the dishes."

The "Just Say No" Fallacy

If your tween is like most, he swears he won't smoke, drink, take drugs, or have sex until he's married. He has learned that these things are very bad and can easily recite what happens to people who indulge in these evils: They end up addicted, with a baby, or dead. Before you relax too much, though, keep in mind that in a few years he will outgrow his black-and-white mentality. Before he's sixteen, he'll have proof positive that people can smoke without dying of cancer, drink without killing anybody in a car wreck, take drugs without getting addicted, and sleep around without getting HIV or producing a pregnancy. Then he'll consider the "just-say-no" promises and the "Don't worry, Mom, I would never, ever . . ." commitments he made back in middle school to be null and void. After all, he only made them because he was so seriously misled by the string of half-truths adults feed little kids.

The "just say no" principle may work for younger, compliant tweens whose loyalty to parents reigns supreme, but it fails when the call of peers and tweens' own desires for excitement and love begin to take precedence. Before tweens can say "no" to anyone else, they must be able to say "no" to themselves even when the temptation to say "yes" is great. In other words, they must be able to control their impulses and assert themselves.

Impulse Control

To teach your child to control his impulses, you must say "no" to him when he cannot say "no" to himself, help him cope with feeling deprived, and praise him heartily for succeeding. Any time you deny your child something or ask him to wait, empathize with his disappointment. Let him know that you understand that it is difficult to wait until dinnertime to eat, to finish homework before watching TV, or to postpone playing until he's straightened his room. Be sympathetic that he must wait until he is fully independent to ride a dirt bike or do something else of which you strongly disapprove. That is, after all, a *very* long time to wait.

When your tween is upset because he can't tolerate the stress of having to wait for something he wants *now*, help him find ways to calm himself. Suggest he take deep breaths, try to think about something else, or find another way to occupy himself. Let him know that you are proud of him for managing to contain himself and settle down even though he is probably still feeling upset. Allow him to have his own feelings, even if they are angry or resentful but insist that he express them appropriately.

Tween Assertiveness

Some kids benefit from hearing exactly what they can say to resist peer pressure. Role-playing is a good way to teach your child to say, "I can't—my parents won't let me" and "No, my folks don't want me to do that." Most younger peers and pro-social older ones readily accept such statements.

However, some will consider such statements the mark of a "baby" who has yet to emerge from her parent's shadow and will tease her. Instead, it might help for your tween to say, "No, I'm not interested in doing that," or "My parents don't want me to and I'm tired of them hassling me." Invite your child to use you as the fall guy at any time. What matters is that she finds ways to say "no" to activities and involvements that strike her as wrong or that she isn't ready for. When role-playing, let your child act the part of a peer so you learn about the pressure she is up against and can give her suggestions that apply to the problems she faces. The good news is that most children are glad to have the necessary verbal weapons to withstand peer pressure and make the decisions they know will keep them safe.

A Pound of Prevention

As an enlightened teenager who feels invincible enough to be undaunted by risk, your child will be making life-altering decisions. As you teach about the dangers of drugs, gangs, and sex, help your tween understand why some people go for them anyway. Soon enough, he will be spending time with those people.

Help your tween learn to evaluate and contemplate risks in a more in-depth fashion instead of just telling him to avoid them at all costs. He will need to be able to answer the hard questions when tempted: What are the real risks to me personally? Why say "no" when I want to say "yes"? Why alienate friends and perhaps the love of my life by not going along with the crowd? Help your tween think about the pros and cons of engaging in risky behaviors by discussing the issues that affect him now.

FACT

Teens with a strong religious faith are more able to resist dangerous temptations than the average young person. If your child hasn't been attending organized services, the tween years are a good time to begin. Seek a church or synagogue with an active youth program so she can develop some friendships.

Children who are accustomed to being respected won't take to peers who don't respect them, so allow your youngster to have opinions different from yours, and respect his views even as you expect him to respect yours. For instance, discuss the pros and cons of seat belts. Is it worth the bother and hassle when car accidents are in truth rare? People often emerge from accidents unscathed even though they weren't wearing a seat belt. Whatever his views on the subject, he must still wear a seat belt, of course. Citizens can work to change laws but must not break them, and it's important for him to learn the difference between thoughts and actions. Talk about what he can do if he's in a car with a parent who is breaking the law by speeding or drinking. Is it best to live and let live so everyone does his own thing? Role-play some conversations so your child knows it's acceptable to get out of the car and round up another ride. If he can say "no" to an adult, he'll be more able to say "no" to another child.

Coed parties may be fine if an adult will be present, but coed sleepovers are an invitation to trouble. There's nothing wrong with a tween girl having a boyfriend if it means talking at recess and sitting together at lunch. If they go to the movies, make sure your tween understands that they must go as friends, not as dates. Think carefully before allowing your child to attend school dances. Between the intense social pressure and the sexually stimulating contact of some modern dance styles, it may be better to wait until your tween is an official teenager. Perhaps she can have a party the same night where she can have more wholesome fun.

Tweens and Violence

An entire generation is being systematically desensitized to violence via television shows, music, and video and computer games. If you don't outright forbid PG-13 and R-rated movies, sexy sitcoms, dramas filled with blood and gore, and cartoons with adult themes, screen them before letting your tween watch them. Alternatively, watch them with your child so you can discuss them. Similarly, listen to tapes and CDs that bear parental advisory labels before buying. Don't let your tween buy or play video and computer games rated T for "Teens." Stick to those rated E for "Everyone."

ESSENTIAL

Use software that prohibits entry into Web sites that haven't been approved for children. In many states, exposing youngsters to sexual stimulation beyond their developmental level is considered by child welfare officials to constitute abuse. Accordingly, pornography and adult magazines should be strictly off limits.

Avoid buying violent toys, too. That may mean that your tween will pick up a stick and pretend to shoot it, imagine that a clump of dirt is a grenade, and picture his rival's face while pummeling a punching bag. These are normal tween boy pastimes that may help them harmlessly discharge some of their pent-up aggression. That doesn't mean you have to buy replicas of semiautomatic guns so your child can get a more realistic sense that he is killing others and wreaking mass destruction.

Gang Troubles

It is no mystery that so many older tweens are attracted to gangs. They provide lonely tweens with a sense of family and belonging, and a child who lacks friends may prefer joining a pack of troublemaking peers to being alone. Fatherless boys appreciate the clarity of gang rules, the rituals, and the initiation into manhood. Gangs offer protection from bullies, though often gang members are the bullies who intimidate other children into joining.

If there is a gang at your school, notify the school administration and local police. If your child is in a gang, seek counseling for him immediately, find a same-sex mentor he can bond with, and sign him up for some extracurricular activities where he can find friends and a sense of purpose and belonging.

Bullies out of Control

"I'm having a party, and you're not invited." "I'm going to tell everybody that you said Sheri is a no-good, and they'll believe me." "Don't play with her! She's got germs!" While boys typically bully through physical intimidation, girls are more prone to engage in psychological warfare, relying on the power of the spoken word to devastate their enemy of the moment.

Bullying is as normal for tweens as rush-hour traffic jams and accidents are for adults, but that doesn't reduce the cost to everyone involved. The victim suffers shame, humiliation, fear, helplessness, and loneliness. The emotional battering has precipitated many tween suicide attempts and has been implicated in school shootings. Children not directly involved in bullying learn the terrible lesson: Say the wrong thing, antagonize the wrong person, and you could be next.

Here are the common signs that a child is being bullied:

- Depression (typical signs include difficulty sleeping, loss of appetite, difficulty concentrating, sadness or irritability, deterioration in grades).
- Not wanting to go to school.
- Bruises or clothing that is dirty.
- Lost clothing, school supplies, books, and/or money (due to items being stolen).
- Excessive hunger after school (due to food or lunch money being stolen).
- Excessive hurry to use the bathroom after school (due to fears of using the bathroom at school).

Some children inadvertently make themselves targets of bullying. They need to learn to say, "I'm sorry" if they inadvertently hurt or antagonize someone and must not be too quick to take offense when teased. Since bullies thrive on the reaction they get, delivering the old standby "Sticks and stones can break my bones, but names can never hurt me" and walking off can often deter them. However, some bullies up the ante, escalating until they wear down their victim. Contact your child's teachers, principal, and the local police.

Bullies can only function as long as the children who know someone is being mistreated are too intimidated to step in. Zero-tolerance policies help. School-wide programs that teach children to take a stand against bullies by banding together and that impart the skills needed to thwart them are very effective.

Bob Kanegis and Liz Manual of Future WAVE (Working for Alternatives to Violence through Entertainment) recommend teaching the *Ha-Has* approach to dealing with bullying:

- *H* **is for** *help.* Tweens should be told to seek help from an adult if they can't handle bullying on their own.

- *A* **is for** *assertiveness.* Children should clearly tell a bully that they don't like being called names or mistreated. "How would you like it if someone said that to you?" is a good comeback.

- *H* **is for** *humor.* Always a good way to disarm an adversary, joking can diffuse a tense situation. When teased about his small stature, one boy said, "My mom predicted this would happen if I didn't eat my spinach, but I can't stand the stuff. If your mother serves it to you, I'd suggest you clean your plate." When called a chicken, another boy flapped his arms and clucked.

- *A* **is for** *avoidance.* Advise your child to stay away from a bully.

- *S* **is for** *self-talk.* To avoid being beaten down by insults, tweens need to remind themselves that bullies try to make others feel bad because they are unhappy people. They learn to bully by being bullied, usually by their parents.

FACT

The verbal sniping on sitcoms and commercials teaches youngsters how to dis one another. It may be hard for them to understand that what is funny in the staged make-believe electronic world isn't funny in real life. If they don't, pull the TV plug.

Taking Teasing in Stride

Unlike bullying, teasing is meant to be humorous and isn't meant to wound, threaten, or intimidate. It stops when a child says, "That hurts my feelings," "Don't call me that," or "I don't like being teased about that." Other children aren't afraid to intervene if the teasing gets out of hand, whereas they are reluctant to intervene during bullying for fear of being attacked. Helping your tween to ward off teasing today can help her ward off bullying tomorrow.

A few children take teasing in stride, but most tweens get their feelings hurt and more sensitive souls are deeply wounded by it. Trying to toughen children by criticizing their reactions to being teased or blaming them for having provoked someone into teasing them usually causes them to feel that everyone is against them, with the predictable result that they become more rather than less reactive to perceived slights. Trying to stage a rescue is also problematic because it communicates that your child cannot cope with being teased. The way to strengthen your tween is to provide empathy, support, and/or reassurance. Concrete advice about how to handle being teased can help, too. Negative responses will probably make your child feel as though you're against her, too. Positive responses help to strengthen your child so she is less hurt by teasing.

- **Empathizing:** "It sounds as though she hurt your feelings."
- **Supporting:** "It used to hurt my feelings when kids teased me about wearing glasses."
- **Reassuring:** "Personally, I think your freckles are cute. Perhaps they tease because they're jealous."
- **Advising:** "Maybe she's trying to joke with you and doesn't realize that she's hurting your feelings. Ask her to please stop."

Chapter 19
Troubled Tweens

Increasing numbers of tweens are seriously out of control. They swear at their parents, fight, vandalize, steal, and bully others. Beneath the bravado are frightened kids, many of whom are battling depression. Address your child's problems before the teenage years arrive. Work to strengthen your relationship through lots of affection and limits.

The Day Care Generation

Veronica was well liked by her teachers, and her friends' parents wished their youngsters could be equally polite, well behaved, and respectful. Veronica got along well with her peers, too. She was on the cheerleading squad and was one of the most popular girls in her sixth-grade class. No one would have suspected how extremely difficult she was at home. In truth, her parents would have been embarrassed for anyone to know how she defied them, even going so far as to yell obscenities if they tried to prohibit her from doing something she had set her mind on. If they insisted she do something she didn't want to do, Veronica could fly into a rage and break things.

The pattern had been the same for as long as they could remember. Her day care teachers gushed over such a well-behaved tot, while her parents struggled with her screaming fits and breath-holding tantrums at home. How could they not feel to blame when she got along with everyone but them? They had read that lots of youngsters who had grown up in day care were more tightly bonded to their peers than to their parents, and they considered it quite possible that this was the case with Veronica. Such children do fine with superficial relationships but have difficulty with more intense relationships. Although her peers' opinions always mattered more to her than her parents', she could turn on her best friend in a flash and react to people she supposedly cared about with amazing cruelty.

ESSENTIAL

For the past decade, child development specialists have been concerned that societal changes undermine the quantity and quality of time parents spend with their children. Weakened parent-child attachments put large percentages of children at risk for engaging in antisocial behavior that is increasingly serious as they mature.

Veronica had the kind of superficial charm and excellent social skills that made her a leader in her class. However, her parents couldn't help but wonder if she maintained her status through bullying other children.

They took Veronica to several therapists before finding one who saw through her veneer and took their parental concerns seriously. After an evaluation, it was concluded that she had attachment problems. That meant she didn't really trust anyone else and had to be in control to feel safe. Her self-assured appearance notwithstanding, she was insecure; beneath the bravado was a frightened child.

Fearing that in a few years they would lose the little influence they had, her parents decided to make more of an effort to be affectionate toward her to strengthen their bonds. At the same time, they worked harder to hold her accountable for her actions. Veronica's first reaction was to become more defiant and oppositional than ever. However, it didn't take long for her to settle down, and they felt a fundamental shift that went beyond her more compliant behavior. She began expressing some genuine affection toward them, became more receptive to hugs, and began turning to them for help and advice. Time would tell how she would do as a teenager, but for now, she was finally becoming the loving little girl she'd taken such pains to hide.

Attachment Problems

Psychologists and social workers have long been mystified by the serious emotional and behavior disorders so common among abused and neglected children. They noted that many foster and adoptive children could not form secure attachments even when placed in stable environments with loving families. It was later suspected that the trauma of abuse and neglect was only partially responsible for their difficulties, because youngsters not subjected to harsh treatment were vulnerable to developing similar problems if they received inconsistent nurturing or lost a primary caregiver before age five.

Day Care Dilemmas

The need for both parents to work in order to make ends meet means that large numbers of youngsters end up in full-time day care at extremely young ages. Although there are many excellent centers where little clients' needs for consistent nurturing are met, many operations are definitely substandard.

The revolving door of poorly paid caregivers with overcrowded classrooms prevents the formation of adequate bonds. Estimates of employee turnover in day care centers range from 25 to 50 percent per year! If a youngster does become attached to a staff member, the deep sense of loss when the relationship abruptly ends can make little ones leery of trusting the next person to head the classroom.

FACT

Day care kids have been noted to have better social skills on average than those who spend the preschool years with a stay-at-home parent, but they are also significantly more aggressive both at home and with other children. Many show signs of being more bonded to their peers than to their parents.

Moreover, parents who feel guilty about the lack of time and energy they are able to devote to their youngsters and the quality of care they receive in day care are loath to spend their few precious hours together tangling over rules and limits. They try to overlook as much as they can only to explode when they can no longer tolerate their child's misbehavior. As a result, many children miss the predictable affection and consistent limits they need to trust that their parents have their best interests at heart and are truly there to help them learn to behave properly.

Children of Divorce

Losing caregivers affects the parent-child relationship as well. After all, if all the other adults keep disappearing, how can a child trust that his parent won't leave, too? In fact, huge numbers of parents do disappear. Fifty percent of marriages end in divorce. The offspring of disrupted marriages display subsequent difficulties with intimacy and commitment, as demonstrated by the fact that children of divorce are twice as likely to divorce as those reared in intact families. They are at serious risk of abusing drugs and alcohol, delinquency, dropping out of school, and having a baby during the teenage years.

The TV Factor

Television has served to weaken parent-child bonds as well. Children are likely to spend most of their time at home in front of the screen instead of interacting with their parents. Even toddlers are <u>more</u> influenced by what commercials say they should have than by what their parents say. By preschool, youngsters scream for the breakfast cereals, sodas, and toys they have seen on TV; they also complain to their day care friends about their parents' refusal to buy them certain toys and wage battles at home over whether they will go to school dressed in what their parents have chosen or wear the fashions popular with their nursery school classmates. By the tween years, many parents find their opinions hold little sway. Corporate advertisers rule their children's minds.

Victims of Depression

If your tween has lots of mini-crises, finding ways to reduce stress, shoring up his diet, ensuring he gets lots of sleep, and involving him in an activity he enjoys may be sufficient to relieve the pressure and restore his emotional balance. However, if your tween threatens to act out by hurting himself or someone else, seek an immediate mental health evaluation. Most people equate depression with despondency and sadness, but depression can manifest in other ways. Should any of the following symptoms last for more than a month, take your child for a mental health checkup:

- Chronic feelings of boredom.
- Deterioration in grades.
- Disturbed appetite (loss of appetite or overeating).
- Disturbed energy level (either too little or too much energy).
- Disturbed mood (sadness, despondency, and/or irritability).
- Disturbed sleep (insomnia or sleeping too much).
- Loss of interest in friends and previously enjoyed hobbies.
- Unexplained headaches or stomachaches.

A chemical imbalance is only one theory on what causes depression. Many youngsters who are very angry turn their anger inward, directing it against themselves. Millions of children are now taking antidepressants, but since pills do not teach children how to cope with their emotions or solve their problems, therapy remains the treatment of choice.

ALERT!

All suicide threats should be taken seriously, including those that appear merely to reflect a desire to manipulate parents. The fastest-growing age group of people attempting suicide is children ages ten to fourteen, and too many of them succeed. Contact a crisis line immediately and get your child into therapy ASAP!

Even if your child is getting professional help, you remain your child's closest confidant and primary teacher. Attend parent counseling sessions or a parenting class if you don't know how to help your child. Fortunately, even serious troubles that develop during the tween years often can be readily overcome.

Behavior Problems

Aggressive children with difficult temperaments tend to become increasingly challenging to manage as they get older. During the latter half of the tween years, they can get physically big enough to just say "no," and their parents can no longer control them. Tweens who are very oppositional and defiant are at risk for escalating. They go from tearing up household possessions and raging at family members to unleashing their venom in the community. In school they disrupt classrooms, defy administrators, fight with their peers, lash out at their teachers, and vandalize property. Gang members and loners alike set fires, shoplift, and terrorize people of all ages.

A Challenge to Parents

Youngsters with attachment problems thwart their parents' efforts to be close to them or enforce consequences due to their inability to trust and their terror of being vulnerable. Other common characteristics are being exceptionally manipulative and refusing affection except on their terms.

Attachment research remains in its infancy, and some controversy exists regarding every aspect of this emerging field, from the nature of bonding itself to the best way to help children who completely reject adult authority. It is clear that they must learn to cope with limits and rules, but the customary methods of setting limits and enforcing consequences require some cooperation on the part of the child.

When a tween adopts a stance of "I won't cooperate and you can't make me," the customary disciplinary methods fail. An attachment-disordered child may feel so threatened when a parent or teacher tries to take charge, she will fight as if her life hung in the balance.

Most youngsters are relieved when their parents express an intention to tackle problems head-on and help them become more disciplined. That doesn't mean your out-of-control tween will let you know that she welcomes your attempts to curb her difficult and unruly behavior. Rules may frighten her if she doubts her ability to adhere to them. If she has trust issues, she may feel frightened of what will happen if you take charge. If she is accustomed to having consequences only enforced when you are angry, she may feel you are merely trying to punish her and require many reminders about what you are trying to accomplish.

Most tweens understand intellectually that certain behaviors are wrong, feel badly about misbehaving, and recognize that limits are supposed to help them even if they don't feel helped. They have learned the value of rules at school, and they accept their importance even though they don't like them or feel inclined to follow them.

If she has been able to circumvent or ignore rules by displays of sadness, she may think that you are holding firm because you don't love her any more, so your affection becomes even more important. She may even be angry that you have neglected to attend to her problems in the past. If so, she may confront you with lines like, "Where were you when

I was a little kid and needed these rules?" Such statements can make parents doubt that they will ever get things right.

Difficulties Setting Limits

Attachment-disordered tweens can be very astute about the subtleties of family dynamics. Some know that if they cooperate with new rules for a few days, their parents will soon lose interest and they can then regain control. Others have learned that if they raise a ruckus for a few days, their parents will become too upset to continue enforcing rules, and the whole matter will soon be dropped. Still others know that by hurling some nasty insults, slamming a few doors, breaking some toys, or putting their fists through a wall, they can intimidate their parents and get them to back down.

Distraction works to subvert rules and avoid consequences in some households. Accordingly, children may challenge their mothers' authority to enforce dietary rules by accusing her of overindulging. They may insist their father has no right to limit their TV watching because he watches TV. They may raise accusations of favoritism ("You didn't treat my sister this way when she was my age") or of having ruined their lives ("You divorced my Dad and everything has been terrible ever since"). It is easy to get sidetracked, but it is important not to miss what is going on. Her very method of trying to convince you that she doesn't need limits and consequences only goes to prove how very much she does need them.

Physical Containment Strategies

Tweens are old enough to be reasoned with and should not be spanked. If your tween loses control to the point that it is impossible to reason with him, you need to use disciplinary methods that will help him develop better internal controls so that he can eventually control himself. Parents who believe in hitting children need to remember that soon their tween will be big enough to hit back. When that happens, the parents lose their ability to control their child, and a child who hasn't learned to control himself is at risk for serious trouble.

Shadow Time-Out

Despite the popularity of sending tweens to their room for time-outs, this procedure has some drawbacks. The point of a time-out is supposed to be to provide a cooling-off period so your child can calm down when he is losing control, think clearly enough to discuss the problem with you, and come up with a plan so the same problem doesn't happen again.

In practice, children are often sent to their rooms as a punishment and are allowed to come out once their parent is no longer angry. Many youngsters are more than happy to go to their rooms. They play, nurse their resentment, lick their wounds, or simply put the problem out of their mind.

Being sent away can make tweens feel rejected and confirms an attachment-disordered child's core sense of not being lovable. In truth, most parents handle time-outs in such a way that their only real use is as a cooling-off period for the parent. This is important when parents need a physical separation to calm down but isn't otherwise helpful.

A better time-out procedure is to require your youngster to shadow you as you move about the house. Instruct her to remain nearby until she can calm down and either do as she is told or come up with a solution for the current problem. Meanwhile, tend to other children, talk on the phone, and continue your normal activities. Studiously refuse to engage in any verbal exchanges until she is willing to talk calmly. Do not comfort your tween when you release her from time-out. Once she is settled down, be sure to discuss the problems of defiance or other manifestations that she lost control. Don't divert to the issue that she acted out because she was angry about this, that, or the other. Keep to the topic at hand: Defiance, cursing, breaking things, and similar actions are unacceptable under any circumstances. The relevant problem is how she can refrain from losing control of her anger in the future. For help with anger management, see Chapter 5.

Containing an Out-of-Control Child

Some children escalate to the point that parents can't even enforce a shadow time-out. Your child may leave the area, destroy property, or try to hurt himself or other family members. You must take concrete steps to end such destructive behavior, but do not resort to yelling or hitting. Some children thrive on being yelled at, and having two out-of-control people solves nothing. Your tween is fast approaching an age when it won't be possible to yell or hit to get him to settle down because of his physical size. Soon he will be willing to strike back to defend himself.

One solution is to take a behavior management course to learn physical containment ("holding") strategies. Many mental health professionals and therapeutic foster parents enroll to learn how to contain volatile youngsters. Contact the Crisis Prevention Institute at ✆ (800) 558-8976 or visit ✍ *www.crisisprevention.com*.

The Basket Hold

One containment strategy, the basket hold, is a measure of last resort after other, less drastic disciplinary techniques have failed. Again, treatments for out-of-control children suspected of having attachment problems remain controversial, and parents would do well to take a course and consult a child guidance professional before proceeding. The controversy stems in part from some well-publicized cases in which children were injured or even killed during the containment process. The following description is *not* a substitute for taking a course in physical containment techniques, because there is indeed a risk of injury.

This technique involves physically containing an out-of-control child to ensure that she doesn't harm herself or anyone else during a rage. It is to provide her with the experience of being physically overpowered so that she can learn that in becoming completely vulnerable and letting her parent take total charge of her, she will not be harmed. Instead, once the tantrum has run its course and she collapses into an exhausted heap, she is to find that the same parent at whom she was raging is holding her lovingly.

The basket hold is not appropriate for every child and should only be done under the supervision of a trained professional. Tweens' tantrums can be extremely violent, and as they swear and curse, and try to kick and bite, it is easy for parents to become enraged and use too much force, which results in injuries. Further, adults can easily be injured unless they have first practiced in a controlled setting with a certified trainer. A therapist should be available for a follow-up, too, because if a child has been subjected to any sort of past trauma or abuse, he may need help processing any disturbing memories that may be triggered.

ALERT!

Ideally, your child will discover that being physically and emotionally close to you is not dangerous but a comfort. It is a child's fundamental ability to trust her parents that enables her to defer to their authority; it is her ability to feel fundamentally loved by her parents that enables her to tolerate occasionally feeling angry at them.

The following description of this technique is meant for informational purposes only. Only training and practice in a controlled setting can adequately teach the technique and explain the risks and dangers.

1. The adult stands behind the child, reaches around her, and crosses the child's arms in front of her chest.
2. The adult loosely encircles the child's left wrist with the right thumb and forefinger, and encircles the child's right wrist with the left thumb and forefinger. The adult must not squeeze the child's wrists; this action will bruise her.
3. The adult holds the child's arms tightly enough to prevent her from getting enough leverage to hurl her upper body or head into the adult's chest. The adult does not pull the child's arms; this action can readily dislocate a small shoulder.
4. The adult tucks his chin down and to the side to protect it in the event that the child throws back her head.
5. The adult slides to the floor and places his legs over the child's legs to prevent kicking; he is careful not to crush them.

6. As the child rages and struggles (often spitting, cursing, and attempting to kick and bite, which is what causes some adults to lose their temper and respond with too much force), the adult speaks in soothing tones, saying things like, "It's okay. You're all right. I'll keep you safe until you can control yourself. I'll let go when you settle down."

7. The adult doesn't release the child when the crying and raging stops but continues the basket hold until the youngster is completely relaxed. Tantrums can last from one minute to one hour; often the child is exhausted to the point that she literally falls asleep.

When a parent says, "It looks like you're losing control. Do you want me to hold you?" to a child who has been placed in a basket hold several times, he may instantly cross his arms in front of his chest and sink to the floor in anticipation of being held.

It may be traumatic for such children to be released from a basket hold before they are calm, but tweens are big enough that some parents lack the physical strength to hold them for long. If they are released early, they may believe they have overpowered their parent or that the parent was going to hurt them, which can produce additional trauma. The point of the basket hold is for children to learn that it is safe for them to be vulnerable because parents can successfully contain them when they cannot contain themselves. On the other hand, parents *must* release a child if they are concerned about the youngster's safety or physical well-being.

Once the child is calm, parents should not discuss the events that led up to the basket hold or what the child said or did during the containment. Instead, they should let the experience speak for itself. Losing control scares tweens as much as adults. Once youngsters are familiar with this technique, they are often relieved to be contained when they cannot control themselves. Many make it clear by running to their parent and crossing their arms that they want to be placed in a basket hold so they can rage safely. At that point, the rages tend to be very brief or nonexistent, and it becomes clear that the child has at long last developed the internal controls that are sufficient for him to settle himself down.

Building Trust

Combining the basket hold with a technique to promote bonding has helped many youngsters become more securely attached to their parents. A physical technique involves altering your position after your child is spent and exhausted from a tantrum that ended in a basket hold. Slide her into your lap so you are holding her like a baby, or as close to that as possible given her size. Maintain eye contact if she is willing, rock her gently in your arms, but remain silent so she can focus on the comforting physical closeness and emotional warmth. Use your intuition to determine when your tween is ready to re-engage with the world, or help her to bed if she falls asleep. Do not discuss what transpired before, during, or after the tantrum unless your tween brings it up. The point is the experience itself.

Once your tween has experienced the comfort of being held and rocked when she is upset, ask if she wants you to hold her the next time her temper is heating up and she is losing control. Even many older tweens agree. Some seek solace in their parents' arms of their own accord when they are upset, wanting to be held and comforted until they feel better. When they are at the point when they can ask a parent to hold them, they usually feel better in a matter of moments.

ALERT! Like anything else, the basket hold and experience of being physically nurtured afterward is a miracle cure for some children, does nothing for others, and can be harmful to others if improperly used. Consult a mental health professional to formulate a specific treatment plan for your child.

It is difficult to live with a child who is angry and defiant or severely depressed, but it is important to understand that seeking professional treatment is rarely enough. You will remain your child's most important teacher, confidant, and guide. Accordingly, a little bit of your laughter and love will go a long way toward strengthening family bonds and restoring your tween's optimism. A lot of love and laughter goes even further! E

Chapter 20
Super Tweens

Super tweens have one thing in common: Their passionate intensity about a school subject, a sport, or a hobby drives them to dedicate the time and effort required to achieve at high levels. Some children discover whatever lights their fire on their own. Most need a parent to help them find it.

The Making of a Super Tween

Christine was a below-average student with an above-average number of problems. Her mother drank; she never knew her father; and she was ostracized by the other sixth-grade children because of her poor social skills. In addition, her plain looks, poor study skills, and unpleasant personality did nothing to endear her to her teachers. Her mother sought therapy for her at the school's insistence but was unwilling to become otherwise involved. Nevertheless, just six months and twenty-four therapy sessions later, Christine had transformed into a super tween.

The sessions began with Christine playing secretary and organizing the therapist's desk and drawers. She expressed a wish to have money like the other kids at her school, but she lacked any hobbies, interests, or other goals. When she learned about personal goal setting, she picked money as her goal and thought that baby-sitting would be a great way to earn it. That didn't sound reasonable for a troubled twelve-year-old, but the therapist nevertheless set about helping her figure out how to get started by suggesting that she interview some teen baby-sitters to learn more.

FACT

Super tweens pour themselves into an activity they dearly love. Goal setting can help turn your tween into a super tween by showing her how to take charge of her life.

A few weeks later, the therapist was surprised to find out that Christine had found and enrolled in baby-sitting and first-aid courses. She compiled a baby-sitting kit by filling a small suitcase with toys and a notepad for recording background and emergency information from parents. The therapist then suggested she make brochures to advertise her services in her neighborhood. Christine did, and then went door to door to drum up business; however, she always received the same response: She was too young.

Since money was Christine's goal and baby-sitting only a means to an end, and since she had demonstrated such determination and exceptional organizational skills, the therapist suggested she find older girls to baby-sit. Christine could handle the advertising, scheduling, and billing for a small percentage. A week later Christine had her first employee. A week after that, she had arranged the first job for her first employee. Six months later Christine had four teens working for her and was complaining about irresponsible workers.

Her take-charge attitude extended to school and her grades improved. Although friends continued to elude her, her skills as a businesswoman saved her from loneliness. The last time she saw the therapist, Christine mentioned that she was tired of her business but still wanted the money. When the therapist pointed out to her that she could hire and train someone else to run the business for her in exchange for a small percentage of the profits, her eyes lit up, and it was clear she intended to do just that.

Tween Capabilities

If tweens no longer have the physical energy they did as toddlers, perhaps it is because they expend some of it on mental pursuits. They remain incredibly active, even though they are not so constantly on the move. Tweens are young and inexperienced enough that they need adult guidance to help them direct their energy. Otherwise, they are likely to dribble it away during high-intensity computer games, run circles through the house, or dissipate it by watching TV.

Professionals typically see the rabble-rousing, pranks, and trouble some tweens concoct at home and in the classroom as signs of authority problems and misdirected anger. Often the cause is simply that a bright, energetic child is bored to tears, angry because there's nothing to do, and in conflict with those who inhibit him. Life can be a trial for children who aren't interested in academics and don't like to spend long hours sitting.

If your tween languishes in front of the TV and can't seem to generate interest in anything more substantial than *I Love Lucy* and *Mr. Ed* reruns, he either has an exceptionally low energy level, is very addicted to television, or doesn't know what else to do. Tweens are capable of the same intense involvements and passionate pursuits as any other age group. The problem is that very few have discovered what they care about, or they aren't being helped to pursue their passion.

Building Confidence

One thing that separates the movers and shakers of the world from those who stumble along is a sense of personal efficacy, which is the belief in one's personal power and personal ability to have a hand in shaping one's destiny. When children feel that nothing they do will make much difference because everything is controlled by factors over which they have no influence, they have little incentive to seize the reins and charge ahead. The youngster who believes he will never be able to read very well due to a learning disability won't feel there's much point to trying. However, a child *will* be motivated to put forth the time and energy needed to become a good reader if he is very motivated to explore the world of books, or if by reading he can achieve another goal he really cares about.

Children who have a sense of being in control of their lives are happier than those who feel helpless. Part of the rush to grow up is that many youngsters aspire to being able to take charge of their lives. Too many believe they are doomed to stay in a holding pattern of trying to survive until they are free of their parents and can begin to thrive.

ESSENTIAL

What separates super-achievers from the rest of the tween crowd is that they have found their passion and are actively pursuing it, and the benefits that accrue to them are enormous. The personal qualities children develop as they strive for stardom serve them in whatever field they end up in, even if they never do become a child star.

The Parent's Role

For tweens to accomplish the amazing feats that are sometimes described in magazines and newspapers requires passionate interest on the part of the tweens that lasts long enough for the youngsters to make some actual accomplishments. Parents' encouragement and cooperation are important as well.

Contrary to what many people think, tweens rarely achieve at high levels because they were pushed. Stage-door mothers might get their budding actress into an audition, but the girl must shine to get the part. You can't force a child to study day and night so he completes the winning science project that catapults him into college at age twelve. Child actors, Olympic gymnasts, ice-skating champions, and young musicians who perform with big-city symphonies have to be motivated from within to dedicate the sustained time and effort required for greatness. Moreover, a child must care passionately about whatever he is doing in order to maintain the zest and excitement that sweeps him to the top. Usually, it is the inspired tween who drags a reluctant parent in his wake, but his parent must be willing to go along.

You can help your child pursue his dreams without even understanding much of what he is up to. A youngster who develops a computer game and sells it to a national toy company may have parents who don't know computers well enough to send e-mail. A tween who wins a college scholarship for designing the farthest flying model rocket may have parents who don't know anything about physics, much less model rockets. Your role is to help your tween brainstorm solutions to the problems he encounters along the way. Otherwise, you must brainstorm ways to find help when he needs it. With the world at tweens' fingertips via the Internet, that can be very easy to do.

FACT

Assist your child in locating online help by telling her to "use a search engine to find the information you need or an online expert who can help you." Help her compose an e-mail, in which she explains what she is doing, describes the kind of help she needs, and asks for suggestions for finding assistance.

Being the parent of a super tween gives you bragging rights, but otherwise it's not a lot of fun. When a child becomes passionately involved in a project, your major tangible contribution will probably be serving as chauffeur. Parents inevitably foot the bill for children's expenses—they must find scholarships, locate corporate sponsors, and hold fundraisers if they can't afford them.

Steps to Stardom

Teaching your child personal goal setting can help him find his passion. Even if he doesn't, he will have begun exploring and defining possible areas of interest. At least, he will learn how to make things happen. He can use goal setting as a tool to change his life, improve himself, and recognize his own power to make his dreams come true. Even if he doesn't use the procedures now, they will be available to him in the future.

Children in Charge

Children are usually willing to devote time to goal setting once they realize that it can help them realize their own hopes, wishes, and aspirations, rather than a trick to get them to accomplish their parents' and teachers' aims. For your child to benefit, you may need to walk him through several examples so he can see how the process works. Many youngsters are very private about their goals (it is, after all, "personal" goal setting) and don't want anyone to know what they are, so it may be better to teach the process by making up a goal and walking your child through the steps instead of using one of his goals as an example. Consider sharing one of your goals with your child and having him help you figure out some steps you might take to try to accomplish it.

When teaching your child to set goals, you must honor his aspirations, even if his goal is to expand his collection of comic books and you want the goal to be doing dishes without having to be reminded. When teaching goal setting, you must honor your tween's aspirations *even though you personally dislike his goal.* Moreover, you must encourage him no matter how preposterous his goal seems to you. Instead of considering the problems, setbacks, defeats, and wasted money, time, and effort, you must do what you can to help and trust that he will come to terms with any setbacks and defeats that happen along the way.

In an effort to protect their children from disappointment, some parents encourage them not to get too excited or hope for too much. Super tweens must let their drive and determination carry them forward, and that is hard to do if their number-one supporters discourage them. When difficulties arise, a child may decide one of his goals isn't worth the struggle and give it up. However, if he finds his calling or something he loves enough to consider worth many sacrifices, he may accomplish amazing things. If your eleven-year-old turned his passion for comic books into a Web site that brought in thousands of dollars' worth of business from sponsors, advertisers, or contests, you might take a positive view of his venture. He would have gained the equivalent of a college degree in business, even though his original goal was just to buy a few more comic books so he could read them before tossing them into the trash. Even if his interest in comic books fizzles a week later and he decides that his new goal is to take swimming lessons, he will have learned an important lesson: how to set goals and brainstorm steps that can be taken to achieve them. Just being given permission to consider what he wants as opposed to what everyone else wants for him can empower your tween.

QUESTION?

My junior chess champ wants to quit. Should I let her?
See if she'll agree to one more month. Then, let it be her decision whether to continue. If you feel disappointed, perhaps you should be playing yourself. By all means, find a club for adults and join.

The Wish List

The first step is for your child to create a wish list of things that she would like to accomplish, do, or have. Each should be worded as a specific goal: "I will raise my grade in math by one letter" (not "I will make good grades") or "I will make three new friends" (rather than "I'll be popular"). Remember that a goal can be changed, revised, and edited as your child gets more clarity about exactly what she wants and what she will have to do to get it.

Next, your tween needs to decide when she hopes to accomplish each goal by establishing a specific target date. Like everything else about goal setting, emphasize that the dates are flexible and can be changed at any time.

Goals for Life

When teaching goal setting, suggest your youngster consider the following areas in developing goals:

- Academic/school (for example: make all *B*'s or above).
- Family/relatives (for example: get along with Mom).
- Financial/money (for example: save up for a bike).
- Hobby/recreational (for example: collect frog figurines).
- Personal/self-improvement (for example: stop biting my nails).
- Physical/health/nutrition (for example: give up sodas).
- Social/friends (for example: get Bobby to like me).
- Vocational/work (for example: get a job raking leaves).

Many successful adults formulated their lifelong goals in childhood. This is virtually required for people in especially demanding professions:

- Most medical doctors and professional athletes choose their professions before they are teenagers.
- Most professional musicians and dancers start taking lessons during early childhood.
- Many poets and authors began writing during primary school.
- Some artists know what they will do with their lives from the moment they make their first crayon scribbles.

Don't underestimate the power of a tween who is lost and drifting to begin shaping a life for himself! Don't underestimate the power of an average tween with a lofty goal.

Achieving Goals

After defining some goals comes the hard part: Your tween must list the specific steps she will take to achieve each one. Advise her that she will probably have to ask friends, parents, relatives, and teachers for suggestions. In fact, talking to other people, reading articles or books related to her goal, and searching the Internet for ideas count as important steps she can take toward fulfilling her goals. The number-one reason people don't fulfill their goals is that they can't figure out the right steps to take, so research counts as a critical step towards achieving any goal. Thinking and fantasizing about a goal count, too.

It helps if children make their goals specific rather than general, but to fulfill a goal they simply must make the steps very specific. As millions of children have proved, deciding they're going to raise their grades by "studying harder" doesn't get them anywhere. They need to have a brainstorming session for each goal and talk to other people about it to come up with a list of all the things they could possibly do. Then they need to decide what they want to do now, and keep notes about what they might consider doing later.

To raise their grades, the steps might include talking to other kids to see how they get good grades and asking the teacher for advice. They might end up with a list of other steps that include such things as taking notes in class, asking for help when they don't understand a lesson, doing the homework when it's assigned instead of putting it off, and reviewing for thirty minutes before each test. To get a new bike, the steps might include walking neighbors' dogs to raise money, opening a bank account to make it easier to save, going to bike stores to look at different brands, or following the classified ads in the newspaper to try to find a used one.

Instruct your child to keep her goal list in a place where she will come across it from time to time. Ideally, she should review her goals by reading through them every few months.

Subject to Change

The hardest part of teaching goal setting to tweens is helping them understand the importance of remaining flexible. They don't have to continue with a goal they've lost interest in; no goal is set in stone. Their interests will change, so it is fine for them to give up on one or all of the goals they wrote and create different ones. If your child doesn't do anything more than jot down some goals every six months or so, he will still benefit even if he never consciously tries to figure out steps to take in order to accomplish his goals. His unconscious will do some of the work for him.

Remind your tween that goal setting is a strictly personal business. No one is going to grade him on anything. When creating goal lists, spelling doesn't matter. Grammar doesn't matter. Handwriting doesn't matter. The only thing that matters is that he can make sense of what he's written.

The Sky Is the Limit

Tweens growing up in days gone by had paper routes, shined shoes, and worked in their parents' stores. They headed out alone into the forests to kill game for food. Modern tweens enter and win contests, start fan clubs, put on puppet shows, paint award-winning pictures, perform in professional and amateur plays, work as movie reviewers, publish magazines, raise prize chickens, breed champion dogs, bake award-winning cookies, and win hog-calling and yodeling contests. Your child can do something he considers equally exciting. All he needs is some help to start him on the road to being a super tween and an enthusiastic cheerleader to keep him going.

(E) **Resources for Parents**

Children don't need a village to raise them. Millions of single parents have proved that they can handle the job. However, parents definitely need a village to help, support, and advise them as they struggle to usher their youngsters through the turbulent tween years. The print and electronic village has produced many wonderful books and online resources.

Books

The Anti-Bullying Handbook by Keith Sullivan (New Zealand: Oxford University Press, 2000). Psychologists now know that the cost of bullying is untold misery for millions of children. Learn how to protect your child.

Best Friends, Worst Enemies: Understanding the Social Lives of Children by Michael Thompson and Catherine O'Neill Grace, with Lawrence J. Cohen (New York: Ballantine Books, 2001). This book provides a comprehensive, thoughtful tour of peer relationships from the toddler years through adolescence.

Beyond the Birds and the Bees: Fostering Your Child's Healthy Sexual Development by Beverly Engel (New York: Pocket Books, 1997). Learn how to help your child become comfortable as a sensual person and teach sexual values and responsibility while safeguarding against sexual abuse.

Books That Build Character: A Guide to Teaching Your Child Moral Values Through Stories by William Kirkpatrick (New York: Simon & Schuster, 1994). This annotated list of books and classic videos ensures your child is exposed to the best the media has to offer.

Bringing Up Boys by James Dobson (Wheaton, Ill.: Tyndale House Publishers, Inc., 2001). Boys have a unique set of needs that can be hard for mothers to understand. This book sheds light on typical boy behavior.

Child Safe: A Practical Guide for Preventing Childhood Injuries by Mark A. Brandenburg, M.D. (Three Rivers Press, 2000). Endorsed by the American Academy of Emergency Medicine, this must-have book is a comprehensive guide to keeping your child safe.

The Conspiracy Against Childhood by Eda J. LeShan (New York: Atheneum Books, 1980). Childhood began disappearing two decades ago. This book helps parents empathize with the pressures modern children face to grow up fast.

The Disappearance of Childhood by Neil Postman (New York: Vintage Books, 1994). This book traces the history of childhood and discusses the modern forces that are wiping this special time of life off the developmental map.

How to Help Your Child Say "No" to Sexual Pressure by Josh McDowell (Texas: Word Publishing, 1987). Learn what tweens will soon be up against so you can start preparing your child.

The Hurried Child: Growing Up Too Fast Too Soon by David Elkind (Addison-Wesley Publishing Company, Inc., 1988). Childhood, a modern invention, began disappearing in 1950 and is now all but gone. This cultural analysis describes how the media and technology have changed what it means to be a child.

Kids, Herbs, Health by Linda B. White and Sunny Mavor (Loveland, Colo.: Interweave Press, 1998). This book gives lots of natural remedies for common ailments and tells when it is important to have your child seen by an M.D.

Miss Manners' Guide to Rearing Perfect Children: A Primer for Everyone Worried about the Future of Civilization by Judith Martin (New York: Atheneum Books, 1984). Written in a tongue-and-cheek style, this book gives solid parenting advice and is not an Emily Post guide as its title may suggest.

Raising Boys: Why Boys Are Different and How to Help Them Become Happy and Well-Balanced Men by Steve Biddulph (Berkeley, Calif.: Celestial Arts, 1997). Boys with insufficient fathering are at risk for having problems with hyperactivity and learning disabilities. This book explains what boys need in a father.

Raising Cain: Protecting the Emotional Life of Boys by Dan Kindlon and Michael Thompson, with Teresa Barker (New York: Ballantine Books, 1999). Boys need special help to identify and express their feelings. This book is filled with important suggestions about helping your boy develop into a loving human being.

Reviving Ophelia: Saving the Selves of Adolescent Girls by Mary Pipher, Ph.D. (New York: G. P. Putnam's Sons, 1994). The women's movement notwithstanding, too many girls continue to define themselves based on their looks and popularity. This classic is essential reading for parents of female preteens.

Sex and Sensibility: The Thinking Parent's Guide to Talking Sense about Sex by Deborah M. Roffman (Cambridge, Mass.: Perseus Publishing, 2001). This exceptionally intelligent book gives parents a whole new way to think about the sexual pressures children confront. It will strengthen your determination to have the important conversations needed to keep your child safe and will show you how.

Siblings Without Rivalry: How to Help Your Children Live Together So You Can Live Too by Adele Faber and Elaine Mazlish (New York: Avon Books, 1987). A bestselling book that gives parents suggestions for minimizing this perennial problem.

Teaching Your Children Values by Linda and Richard Eyre (New York: Simon & Schuster, 1993). Learn how to inculcate a strong set of character-building values through compassionate means that will serve your tween throughout life.

Understanding Your Child's Temperament by William B. Carey (New York: Simon & Schuster, 1997). Different children pose different parenting challenges. Learn how to take inborn temperamental factors into account to better meet your child's emotional needs.

Your Child's Self-Esteem: Step-by-Step Guidelines for Raising Responsible, Productive, Happy Children by Dorothy Corkille Briggs (Doubleday & Company, Inc., 1975). This book teaches parents how to instill self-confidence and boost self-esteem by helping children appreciate their unique strengths.

Web Sites

✍ *http://family.go.com.* From hygiene struggles to middle-school life, this site has lots of articles on topics of interest to parents of tweens.

✍ *www.DrSonna.org.* Get personalized answers to your parenting questions from the author.

✍ *www.parentsoup.com.* A place for parents to get expert advice, read articles, and chat with other parents online.

Appendix B

Resources for Tweens

E ducating while entertaining child-ren isn't the challenge that it used to be. Point your youngster to a tween-friendly Web site you can trust, such as *www.pbskids.org*. Be sure to keep a new activity book tucked away to bestow as a surprise "happy unbirthday" present to add fun to a boring day. And every child needs a good book on sex education.

Books

Asking about Sex and Growing-Up: A Question-and-Answer Book for Boys and Girls by Joanna Cole (New York: Morrow Junior Books, 1988). With lots of illustrations and language an eight-year-old can understand, this is a good book for younger tweens.

Changing Bodies, Changing Lives: A Book for Teens on Sex and Relationships by Ruth Bell (New York: Random House, 1998). While your child learns the basics, parents learn the material they forgot or were never taught in the first place. When a question about inverted nipples or testicular self-exams crops up, you'll have the answer.

It's Perfectly Normal: Changing Bodies, Growing Up, Sex, and Sexual Health by Robie H. Harris, Michael Emberley (illustrator) (Cambridge, Mass.: Candlewick Press, 1996). Middle and older tweens (ages ten to fourteen) will gladly devote themselves to studying this engaging, comprehensive book written in a lighthearted manner and filled with cartoons and illustrations.

Kid Concoctions & Contraptions by John and Danita Thomas (Cleveland, Ohio: Kid Concoctions Company, 2001). Whether or not your child is interested in science, these intriguing activities will undoubtedly whip up some enthusiasm.

Kidstravel: A Backseat Survival Guide by the editors of Klutz Press (Palo Alto, Calif.: Klutz Press, 1994). Zap travel boredom for good. This book and kit has everything your tween needs to wrap hair, play hand games, make bracelets, spot license plates, read palms, and do tons of other activities. Designed for ages nine to twelve; older children may enjoy this book, too.

What's Happening to My Body? Book for Boys: A Growing-Up Guide for Parents and Sons by Lynda and Area Madaras. (New York: Newmarket Press, 2000). Designed for ages eight to fifteen and endorsed by the National PTA, this book does a good job of giving the information and addressing a tween's concerns, but check the chapter on romantic and sexual feelings first to decide if it is appropriate for your child.

What's Happening to My Body? Book for Girls: A Growing-Up Guide for Parents and Daughters, 3rd edition, by Lynda Madaras, Area Madaras (contributor), Simon Sullivan (illustrator), Jackie Aher, Marcia Herman-Middens (New York: Newmarket Press, 2002). This book, intended for ages eight to fifteen, is endorsed by the National PTA and was selected as a "Best Book for Young Adults" by the American Library Association.

What Your Sixth Grader Needs to Know: Fundamentals of a Good Fourth-Grade Education (Core Knowledge Series) by E. D. Hirsch (editor) (Delta Books, no date available). The Core Knowledge Series has a different volume detailing what kids in kindergarten and first, second, third, fourth, fifth, and sixth grades need to know. These books are designed for students, but parents can learn from them as well.

Where Did I Come From? by Peter Mayle, Paul Walter (illustrator), and Arthur Robbins (illustrator) (Secaucus, N.J.: Lyle Stewart, 2002). If you can't figure out how to begin the birds-and-bees conversation, this children's picture book could be a good way to provide basic sex information to a young tween (for ages four to eight).

Hotline

Girls and Boys Town National Hotline. Parents or tweens can call ✆ (800) 448-3000, a twenty-four-hours-a-day service, to talk about kid problems.

Magazines

American Girl. A wholesome magazine filled with fun activities and articles tween girls will actually read. To subscribe, call ✆ (800) 845-0005 or visit ✍ *www.americangirl.com.*

New Moon Magazine. A magazine for thinking girls with a multicultural focus. Order from ✍ *www.newmoon.org* or pick it up at a newsstand.

Web Sites

✍ *www.pbskids.org/itsmylife.* Activities, fun, games, and self-help articles that teach kids how to deal with friend, school, and family problems.

✍ *www.plannedparenthood.org.* Kids can read the online information about puberty and get answers to common tween questions.

✍ *www.puberty101.com.* Tweens can ask personal questions on the forum. Parents need to check first to determine its suitability for their child.

Workbooks

Activity books from Williamson Publishing Company, which has produced dozens of award-winning children's activity books on every subject imaginable. From multicultural cooking to knitting to science experiments to making scrapbooks and eco-art projects, your tween will have enough rainy-day fun to last through a monsoon. All of the titles are high quality, but be sure to check the targeted ages—some are for younger children. To order, call ✆ (800) 234-8791.

Klutz Press Books. These activity kits are guaranteed hits with kids. Different books teach tweens what they most want to know: how to tie dozens of knots, play dozens of card or swimming pool games, make dozens of paper airplanes, do dozens of magic tricks, etc. If you need to buy a birthday present for a tween, look no further.

School Zone Publishing Company workbooks. These graded workbooks provide excellent remedial and enrichment activities in all academic areas for students in grades prekindergarten to sixth. Available at department stores or online at ✍ *www.schoolzone.com.*

E Index

The EVERYTHING Series!

BUSINESS & PERSONAL FINANCE

Everything® Accounting Book
Everything® Budgeting Book, 2nd Ed.
Everything® Business Planning Book
Everything® Coaching and Mentoring Book, 2nd Ed.
Everything® Fundraising Book
Everything® Get Out of Debt Book
Everything® Grant Writing Book, 2nd Ed.
Everything® Guide to Buying Foreclosures
Everything® Guide to Fundraising, $15.95
Everything® Guide to Mortgages
Everything® Guide to Personal Finance for Single Mothers
Everything® Home-Based Business Book, 2nd Ed.
Everything® Homebuying Book, 3rd Ed., $15.95
Everything® Homeselling Book, 2nd Ed.
Everything® Human Resource Management Book
Everything® Improve Your Credit Book
Everything® Investing Book, 2nd Ed.
Everything® Landlording Book
Everything® Leadership Book, 2nd Ed.
Everything® Managing People Book, 2nd Ed.
Everything® Negotiating Book
Everything® Online Auctions Book
Everything® Online Business Book
Everything® Personal Finance Book
Everything® Personal Finance in Your 20s & 30s Book, 2nd Ed.
Everything® Personal Finance in Your 40s & 50s Book, $15.95
Everything® Project Management Book, 2nd Ed.
Everything® Real Estate Investing Book
Everything® Retirement Planning Book
Everything® Robert's Rules Book, $7.95
Everything® Selling Book
Everything® Start Your Own Business Book, 2nd Ed.
Everything® Wills & Estate Planning Book

COOKING

Everything® Barbecue Cookbook
Everything® Bartender's Book, 2nd Ed., $9.95
Everything® Calorie Counting Cookbook
Everything® Cheese Book
Everything® Chinese Cookbook
Everything® Classic Recipes Book
Everything® Cocktail Parties & Drinks Book
Everything® College Cookbook
Everything® Cooking for Baby and Toddler Book
Everything® Diabetes Cookbook
Everything® Easy Gourmet Cookbook
Everything® Fondue Cookbook
Everything® Food Allergy Cookbook, $15.95
Everything® Fondue Party Book
Everything® Gluten-Free Cookbook
Everything® Glycemic Index Cookbook
Everything® Grilling Cookbook
Everything® Healthy Cooking for Parties Book, $15.95
Everything® Holiday Cookbook
Everything® Indian Cookbook
Everything® Lactose-Free Cookbook
Everything® Low-Cholesterol Cookbook

Everything® Low-Fat High-Flavor Cookbook, 2nd Ed., $15.95
Everything® Low-Salt Cookbook
Everything® Meals for a Month Cookbook
Everything® Meals on a Budget Cookbook
Everything® Mediterranean Cookbook
Everything® Mexican Cookbook
Everything® No Trans Fat Cookbook
Everything® One-Pot Cookbook, 2nd Ed., $15.95
Everything® Organic Cooking for Baby & Toddler Book, $15.95
Everything® Pizza Cookbook
Everything® Quick Meals Cookbook, 2nd Ed., $15.95
Everything® Slow Cooker Cookbook
Everything® Slow Cooking for a Crowd Cookbook
Everything® Soup Cookbook
Everything® Stir-Fry Cookbook
Everything® Sugar-Free Cookbook
Everything® Tapas and Small Plates Cookbook
Everything® Tex-Mex Cookbook
Everything® Thai Cookbook
Everything® Vegetarian Cookbook
Everything® Whole-Grain, High-Fiber Cookbook
Everything® Wild Game Cookbook
Everything® Wine Book, 2nd Ed.

GAMES

Everything® 15-Minute Sudoku Book, $9.95
Everything® 30-Minute Sudoku Book, $9.95
Everything® Bible Crosswords Book, $9.95
Everything® Blackjack Strategy Book
Everything® Brain Strain Book, $9.95
Everything® Bridge Book
Everything® Card Games Book
Everything® Card Tricks Book, $9.95
Everything® Casino Gambling Book, 2nd Ed.
Everything® Chess Basics Book
Everything® Christmas Crosswords Book, $9.95
Everything® Craps Strategy Book
Everything® Crossword and Puzzle Book
Everything® Crosswords and Puzzles for Quote Lovers Book, $9.95
Everything® Crossword Challenge Book
Everything® Crosswords for the Beach Book, $9.95
Everything® Cryptic Crosswords Book, $9.95
Everything® Cryptograms Book, $9.95
Everything® Easy Crosswords Book
Everything® Easy Kakuro Book, $9.95
Everything® Easy Large-Print Crosswords Book
Everything® Games Book, 2nd Ed.
Everything® Giant Book of Crosswords
Everything® Giant Sudoku Book, $9.95
Everything® Giant Word Search Book
Everything® Kakuro Challenge Book, $9.95
Everything® Large-Print Crossword Challenge Book
Everything® Large-Print Crosswords Book
Everything® Large-Print Travel Crosswords Book
Everything® Lateral Thinking Puzzles Book, $9.95
Everything® Literary Crosswords Book, $9.95
Everything® Mazes Book
Everything® Memory Booster Puzzles Book, $9.95

Everything® Movie Crosswords Book, $9.95
Everything® Music Crosswords Book, $9.95
Everything® Online Poker Book
Everything® Pencil Puzzles Book, $9.95
Everything® Poker Strategy Book
Everything® Pool & Billiards Book
Everything® Puzzles for Commuters Book, $9.95
Everything® Puzzles for Dog Lovers Book, $9.95
Everything® Sports Crosswords Book, $9.95
Everything® Test Your IQ Book, $9.95
Everything® Texas Hold 'Em Book, $9.95
Everything® Travel Crosswords Book, $9.95
Everything® Travel Mazes Book, $9.95
Everything® Travel Word Search Book, $9.95
Everything® TV Crosswords Book, $9.95
Everything® Word Games Challenge Book
Everything® Word Scramble Book
Everything® Word Search Book

HEALTH

Everything® Alzheimer's Book
Everything® Diabetes Book
Everything® First Aid Book, $9.95
Everything® Green Living Book
Everything® Health Guide to Addiction and Recovery
Everything® Health Guide to Adult Bipolar Disorder
Everything® Health Guide to Arthritis
Everything® Health Guide to Controlling Anxiety
Everything® Health Guide to Depression
Everything® Health Guide to Diabetes, 2nd Ed.
Everything® Health Guide to Fibromyalgia
Everything® Health Guide to Menopause, 2nd Ed.
Everything® Health Guide to Migraines
Everything® Health Guide to Multiple Sclerosis
Everything® Health Guide to OCD
Everything® Health Guide to PMS
Everything® Health Guide to Postpartum Care
Everything® Health Guide to Thyroid Disease
Everything® Hypnosis Book
Everything® Low Cholesterol Book
Everything® Menopause Book
Everything® Nutrition Book
Everything® Reflexology Book
Everything® Stress Management Book
Everything® Superfoods Book, $15.95

HISTORY

Everything® American Government Book
Everything® American History Book, 2nd Ed.
Everything® American Revolution Book, $15.95
Everything® Civil War Book
Everything® Freemasons Book
Everything® Irish History & Heritage Book
Everything® World War II Book, 2nd Ed.

HOBBIES

Everything® Candlemaking Book
Everything® Cartooning Book
Everything® Coin Collecting Book
Everything® Digital Photography Book, 2nd Ed.

Everything® Drawing Book
Everything® Family Tree Book, 2nd Ed.
Everything® Guide to Online Genealogy, $15.95
Everything® Knitting Book
Everything® Knots Book
Everything® Photography Book
Everything® Quilting Book
Everything® Sewing Book
Everything® Soapmaking Book, 2nd Ed.
Everything® Woodworking Book

HOME IMPROVEMENT

Everything® Feng Shui Book
Everything® Feng Shui Decluttering Book, $9.95
Everything® Fix-It Book
Everything® Green Living Book
Everything® Home Decorating Book
Everything® Home Storage Solutions Book
Everything® Homebuilding Book
Everything® Organize Your Home Book, 2nd Ed.

KIDS' BOOKS

All titles are $7.95
Everything® Fairy Tales Book, $14.95
Everything® Kids' Animal Puzzle & Activity Book
Everything® Kids' Astronomy Book
Everything® Kids' Baseball Book, 5th Ed.
Everything® Kids' Bible Trivia Book
Everything® Kids' Bugs Book
Everything® Kids' Cars and Trucks Puzzle and Activity Book
Everything® Kids' Christmas Puzzle & Activity Book
Everything® Kids' Connect the Dots
    Puzzle and Activity Book
Everything® Kids' Cookbook, 2nd Ed.
Everything® Kids' Crazy Puzzles Book
Everything® Kids' Dinosaurs Book
Everything® Kids' Dragons Puzzle and Activity Book
Everything® Kids' Environment Book $7.95
Everything® Kids' Fairies Puzzle and Activity Book
Everything® Kids' First Spanish Puzzle and Activity Book
Everything® Kids' Football Book
Everything® Kids' Geography Book
Everything® Kids' Gross Cookbook
Everything® Kids' Gross Hidden Pictures Book
Everything® Kids' Gross Jokes Book
Everything® Kids' Gross Mazes Book
Everything® Kids' Gross Puzzle & Activity Book
Everything® Kids' Halloween Puzzle & Activity Book
Everything® Kids' Hanukkah Puzzle and Activity Book
Everything® Kids' Hidden Pictures Book
Everything® Kids' Horses Book
Everything® Kids' Joke Book
Everything® Kids' Knock Knock Book
Everything® Kids' Learning French Book
Everything® Kids' Learning Spanish Book
Everything® Kids' Magical Science Experiments Book
Everything® Kids' Math Puzzles Book
Everything® Kids' Mazes Book
Everything® Kids' Money Book, 2nd Ed.
Everything® Kids' Mummies, Pharaoh's, and Pyramids
    Puzzle and Activity Book
Everything® Kids' Nature Book
Everything® Kids' Pirates Puzzle and Activity Book
Everything® Kids' Presidents Book
Everything® Kids' Princess Puzzle and Activity Book
Everything® Kids' Puzzle Book

Everything® Kids' Racecars Puzzle and Activity Book
Everything® Kids' Riddles & Brain Teasers Book
Everything® Kids' Science Experiments Book
Everything® Kids' Sharks Book
Everything® Kids' Soccer Book
Everything® Kids' Spelling Book
Everything® Kids' Spies Puzzle and Activity Book
Everything® Kids' States Book
Everything® Kids' Travel Activity Book
Everything® Kids' Word Search Puzzle and Activity Book

LANGUAGE

Everything® Conversational Japanese Book with CD, $19.95
Everything® French Grammar Book
Everything® French Phrase Book, $9.95
Everything® French Verb Book, $9.95
Everything® German Phrase Book, $9.95
Everything® German Practice Book with CD, $19.95
Everything® Inglés Book
Everything® Intermediate Spanish Book with CD, $19.95
Everything® Italian Phrase Book, $9.95
Everything® Italian Practice Book with CD, $19.95
Everything® Learning Brazilian Portuguese Book with CD, $19.95
Everything® Learning French Book with CD, 2nd Ed., $19.95
Everything® Learning German Book
Everything® Learning Italian Book
Everything® Learning Latin Book
Everything® Learning Russian Book with CD, $19.95
Everything® Learning Spanish Book
Everything® Learning Spanish Book with CD, 2nd Ed., $19.95
Everything® Russian Practice Book with CD, $19.95
Everything® Sign Language Book, $15.95
Everything® Spanish Grammar Book
Everything® Spanish Phrase Book, $9.95
Everything® Spanish Practice Book with CD, $19.95
Everything® Spanish Verb Book, $9.95
Everything® Speaking Mandarin Chinese Book with CD, $19.95

MUSIC

Everything® Bass Guitar Book with CD, $19.95
Everything® Drums Book with CD, $19.95
Everything® Guitar Book with CD, 2nd Ed., $19.95
Everything® Guitar Chords Book with CD, $19.95
Everything® Guitar Scales Book with CD, $19.95
Everything® Harmonica Book with CD, $15.95
Everything® Home Recording Book
Everything® Music Theory Book with CD, $19.95
Everything® Reading Music Book with CD, $19.95
Everything® Rock & Blues Guitar Book with CD, $19.95
Everything® Rock & Blues Piano Book with CD, $19.95
Everything® Rock Drums Book with CD, $19.95
Everything® Singing Book with CD, $19.95
Everything® Songwriting Book

NEW AGE

Everything® Astrology Book, 2nd Ed.
Everything® Birthday Personology Book
Everything® Celtic Wisdom Book, $15.95
Everything® Dreams Book, 2nd Ed.
Everything® Law of Attraction Book, $15.95
Everything® Love Signs Book, $9.95
Everything® Love Spells Book, $9.95
Everything® Palmistry Book
Everything® Psychic Book
Everything® Reiki Book

Everything® Sex Signs Book, $9.95
Everything® Spells & Charms Book, 2nd Ed.
Everything® Tarot Book, 2nd Ed.
Everything® Toltec Wisdom Book
Everything® Wicca & Witchcraft Book, 2nd Ed.

PARENTING

Everything® Baby Names Book, 2nd Ed.
Everything® Baby Shower Book, 2nd Ed.
Everything® Baby Sign Language Book with DVD
Everything® Baby's First Year Book
Everything® Birthing Book
Everything® Breastfeeding Book
Everything® Father-to-Be Book
Everything® Father's First Year Book
Everything® Get Ready for Baby Book, 2nd Ed.
Everything® Get Your Baby to Sleep Book, $9.95
Everything® Getting Pregnant Book
Everything® Guide to Pregnancy Over 35
Everything® Guide to Raising a One-Year-Old
Everything® Guide to Raising a Two-Year-Old
Everything® Guide to Raising Adolescent Boys
Everything® Guide to Raising Adolescent Girls
Everything® Mother's First Year Book
Everything® Parent's Guide to Childhood Illnesses
Everything® Parent's Guide to Children and Divorce
Everything® Parent's Guide to Children with ADD/ADHD
Everything® Parent's Guide to Children with Asperger's
    Syndrome
Everything® Parent's Guide to Children with Anxiety
Everything® Parent's Guide to Children with Asthma
Everything® Parent's Guide to Children with Autism
Everything® Parent's Guide to Children with Bipolar Disorder
Everything® Parent's Guide to Children with Depression
Everything® Parent's Guide to Children with Dyslexia
Everything® Parent's Guide to Children with Juvenile Diabetes
Everything® Parent's Guide to Children with OCD
Everything® Parent's Guide to Positive Discipline
Everything® Parent's Guide to Raising Boys
Everything® Parent's Guide to Raising Girls
Everything® Parent's Guide to Raising Siblings
Everything® Parent's Guide to Raising Your
    Adopted Child
Everything® Parent's Guide to Sensory Integration Disorder
Everything® Parent's Guide to Tantrums
Everything® Parent's Guide to the Strong-Willed Child
Everything® Parenting a Teenager Book
Everything® Potty Training Book, $9.95
Everything® Pregnancy Book, 3rd Ed.
Everything® Pregnancy Fitness Book
Everything® Pregnancy Nutrition Book
Everything® Pregnancy Organizer, 2nd Ed., $16.95
Everything® Toddler Activities Book
Everything® Toddler Book
Everything® Tween Book
Everything® Twins, Triplets, and More Book

PETS

Everything® Aquarium Book
Everything® Boxer Book
Everything® Cat Book, 2nd Ed.
Everything® Chihuahua Book
Everything® Cooking for Dogs Book
Everything® Dachshund Book
Everything® Dog Book, 2nd Ed.
Everything® Dog Grooming Book

Everything® Dog Obedience Book
Everything® Dog Owner's Organizer, $16.95
Everything® Dog Training and Tricks Book
Everything® German Shepherd Book
Everything® Golden Retriever Book
Everything® Horse Book, 2nd Ed., $15.95
Everything® Horse Care Book
Everything® Horseback Riding Book
Everything® Labrador Retriever Book
Everything® Poodle Book
Everything® Pug Book
Everything® Puppy Book
Everything® Small Dogs Book
Everything® Tropical Fish Book
Everything® Yorkshire Terrier Book

REFERENCE

Everything® American Presidents Book
Everything® Blogging Book
Everything® Build Your Vocabulary Book, $9.95
Everything® Car Care Book
Everything® Classical Mythology Book
Everything® Da Vinci Book
Everything® Einstein Book
Everything® Enneagram Book
Everything® Etiquette Book, 2nd Ed.
Everything® Family Christmas Book, $15.95
Everything® Guide to C. S. Lewis & Narnia
Everything® Guide to Divorce, 2nd Ed., $15.95
Everything® Guide to Edgar Allan Poe
Everything® Guide to Understanding Philosophy
Everything® Inventions and Patents Book
Everything® Jacqueline Kennedy Onassis Book
Everything® John F. Kennedy Book
Everything® Mafia Book
Everything® Martin Luther King Jr. Book
Everything® Pirates Book
Everything® Private Investigation Book
Everything® Psychology Book
Everything® Public Speaking Book, $9.95
Everything® Shakespeare Book, 2nd Ed.

RELIGION

Everything® Angels Book
Everything® Bible Book
Everything® Bible Study Book with CD, $19.95
Everything® Buddhism Book
Everything® Catholicism Book
Everything® Christianity Book
Everything® Gnostic Gospels Book
Everything® Hinduism Book, $15.95
Everything® History of the Bible Book
Everything® Jesus Book
Everything® Jewish History & Heritage Book
Everything® Judaism Book
Everything® Kabbalah Book
Everything® Koran Book
Everything® Mary Book
Everything® Mary Magdalene Book
Everything® Prayer Book

Everything® Saints Book, 2nd Ed.
Everything® Torah Book
Everything® Understanding Islam Book
Everything® Women of the Bible Book
Everything® World's Religions Book

SCHOOL & CAREERS

Everything® Career Tests Book
Everything® College Major Test Book
Everything® College Survival Book, 2nd Ed.
Everything® Cover Letter Book, 2nd Ed.
Everything® Filmmaking Book
Everything® Get-a-Job Book, 2nd Ed.
Everything® Guide to Being a Paralegal
Everything® Guide to Being a Personal Trainer
Everything® Guide to Being a Real Estate Agent
Everything® Guide to Being a Sales Rep
Everything® Guide to Being an Event Planner
Everything® Guide to Careers in Health Care
Everything® Guide to Careers in Law Enforcement
Everything® Guide to Government Jobs
Everything® Guide to Starting and Running a Catering
   Business
Everything® Guide to Starting and Running a Restaurant
**Everything® Guide to Starting and Running
   a Retail Store**
Everything® Job Interview Book, 2nd Ed.
Everything® New Nurse Book
Everything® New Teacher Book
Everything® Paying for College Book
Everything® Practice Interview Book
Everything® Resume Book, 3rd Ed.
Everything® Study Book

SELF-HELP

Everything® Body Language Book
Everything® Dating Book, 2nd Ed.
Everything® Great Sex Book
**Everything® Guide to Caring for Aging Parents,
   $15.95**
Everything® Self-Esteem Book
Everything® Self-Hypnosis Book, $9.95
Everything® Tantric Sex Book

SPORTS & FITNESS

Everything® Easy Fitness Book
Everything® Fishing Book
Everything® Guide to Weight Training, $15.95
Everything® Krav Maga for Fitness Book
Everything® Running Book, 2nd Ed.
Everything® Triathlon Training Book, $15.95

TRAVEL

Everything® Family Guide to Coastal Florida
Everything® Family Guide to Cruise Vacations
Everything® Family Guide to Hawaii
Everything® Family Guide to Las Vegas, 2nd Ed.
Everything® Family Guide to Mexico
Everything® Family Guide to New England, 2nd Ed.

Everything® Family Guide to New York City, 3rd Ed.
**Everything® Family Guide to Northern California
   and Lake Tahoe**
Everything® Family Guide to RV Travel & Campgrounds
Everything® Family Guide to the Caribbean
Everything® Family Guide to the Disneyland® Resort, California
   Adventure®, Universal Studios®, and the Anaheim
   Area, 2nd Ed.
Everything® Family Guide to the Walt Disney World Resort®,
   Universal Studios®, and Greater Orlando, 5th Ed.
Everything® Family Guide to Timeshares
Everything® Family Guide to Washington D.C., 2nd Ed.

WEDDINGS

Everything® Bachelorette Party Book, $9.95
Everything® Bridesmaid Book, $9.95
Everything® Destination Wedding Book
Everything® Father of the Bride Book, $9.95
Everything® Green Wedding Book, $15.95
Everything® Groom Book, $9.95
Everything® Jewish Wedding Book, 2nd Ed., $15.95
Everything® Mother of the Bride Book, $9.95
Everything® Outdoor Wedding Book
Everything® Wedding Book, 3rd Ed.
Everything® Wedding Checklist, $9.95
Everything® Wedding Etiquette Book, $9.95
Everything® Wedding Organizer, 2nd Ed., $16.95
Everything® Wedding Shower Book, $9.95
Everything® Wedding Vows Book, 3rd Ed., $9.95
Everything® Wedding Workout Book
Everything® Weddings on a Budget Book, 2nd Ed., $9.95

WRITING

Everything® Creative Writing Book
Everything® Get Published Book, 2nd Ed.
Everything® Grammar and Style Book, 2nd Ed.
Everything® Guide to Magazine Writing
Everything® Guide to Writing a Book Proposal
Everything® Guide to Writing a Novel
Everything® Guide to Writing Children's Books
Everything® Guide to Writing Copy
Everything® Guide to Writing Graphic Novels
Everything® Guide to Writing Research Papers
Everything® Guide to Writing a Romance Novel, $15.95
Everything® Improve Your Writing Book, 2nd Ed.
Everything® Writing Poetry Book